Haynes *for* **HOME DIY**

Haynes
THE BOOK ®

REPAIR AND RENOVATION

The complete guide to structural
refurbishment and improvement

John Wickersham

To David.
The technical knowledge you so generously share is invaluable:
so, too, is your brotherly encouragement.

First published in 1995

Published by:
Haynes Publishing
Sparkford, Nr Yeovil, Somerset BA22 7JJ

British Library Cataloguing-in-Publication Data:

A catalogue record for this book is available from the British Library.

ISBN 1 85960 101 4

Printed in Great Britain by J H Haynes & Co Ltd.

REPAIR AND RENOVATION

Contents

Chapter 3   90

Interior Work

Essential information   156

Introduction

This book focuses on structural repairs, replacements and improvements, which many self-building amateurs have shown to be within their scope. Some sections deal with quite ambitious undertakings, and you may not want to tackle all the jobs they describe. Indeed, the essence of DIY success is *not* to try to do it all yourself.

Recognise your strengths

We all have different skills, and we would be ill-advised to tackle jobs that tradesmen have trained for long periods to master. In major projects, it is necessary to accept your limitations, recognise your strengths, and to bring in professional help for tasks beyond your personal ability. However, knowing how a job should be carried out will allow you to check that a tradesman is adopting good practice and not taking short-cuts.

An associated difficulty is the fact that building practices have changed significantly over the last few decades. So, too, have the Building Regulations, which have become increasingly stringent. Keeping up with new materials, new building techniques and technological improvements is a problem that faces professionals and amateurs alike, so it is essential to check the current position before starting on any building project.

Practical advice

The sheer diversity of house designs and structures makes it impossible to explain how every job should be tackled, so this book includes explanations of the way elements are built. It gives practical advice on the way to go about the work, with cautionary advice where necessary. However, it does not describe how to design your own home extension or house building project. Building a roof, or a suspended floor, or an underground drainage system is one thing; designing it is quite different. This work should be entrusted to an architect or qualified building surveyor. The advice given here is based on the assumption that you have discussed the project with such a professional, whose plans have gained the approval of the local authority's building control department.

The topics covered will be of equal interest to anyone who wants to embark on new work or refurbish an older property. In a renovation project, some of the work may not need Building Regulations approval. Despite this, it makes sense to follow the regulations applicable to new work, since their purpose is to secure the safety and comfort of the building's occupants.

And don't forget that any structural change made to an existing property – like improving the outside drainage arrangements – is governed by the Building Regulations. Similarly, if you plan to alter a surface in a building – by installing a pine-clad ceiling, for example – it changes its fire characteristics, so this may also need Building Regulations approval. If in any doubt, seek information at your local building control office.

This manual is written in the hope that the pages will be turned, and the margins left dirty. Many DIY books offer inspirational illustrations that portray beautiful homes, but little more. The aim of this book is to help you make such images of splendour become more than personal pipe dreams.

Chapter 1

Before You Begin

Gaining approval

Before embarking on structural repairs, alterations, or major home improvements, you must establish whether the work will need local authority approval. If you proceed without formal consent, you may be required to dismantle your work.

Two entirely separate applications may be needed: for planning permission and Building Regulations approval. Some types of work need no formal consent, but you must establish the position first.

General guidance

In the last few years, considerable efforts have been made to help householders understand how formal approvals can be gained. For example, the Central Office of Information has prepared booklets for the Department of the Environment that explain the planning system. Material has also been published as a result of the Citizen's Charter initiative. Local councils also provide information about planning and building control applications.

Most of the literature available on these subjects is written in plain English with an absence of technical jargon. This, plus the method of presentation often adopted, is aimed at removing the impression that planning legislation is confusing or enshrouded in red tape.

Planning permission

Planning regulations exist to protect our countryside, villages, towns and cities. Indeed, it is within the context of environmental protection and the control of visual amenity that sections of the planning system apply to our homes. The planning system ensures that the appearance of a building is appropriate for its location.

Planning laws are made by Parliament, but the main responsibility for ensuring that planning requirements are put into practice rests with the local authorities. Accordingly, you need to approach the planning department of your district, city or borough council for guidance and formal approvals to proceed with a development. All authorities are required to have development plans for the next 10-15 years, which set out how land in the area will be used, and all planning applications must fit in with these proposals.

In 1993, local authorities were given a charter guide to act as a model on which they could draw up their own planning guidance literature. Naturally, these guides are all different, but they are usually very helpful and the guidance is very clear. However, if you need further information, more literature is available from the Department of the Environment and the Welsh Office.

With this information so freely available, the points covered here are intentionally brief, and while everything is purposely made to seem simple, there will be occasions when applications to make alterations to a building are far from straightforward. For instance, if you live in a listed building, proposals to alter the structure will be subjected to special scrutiny. Similarly, in conservation areas, you may even need permission to take down certain types of fences or railings. Even modern buildings on open-plan estates may be subject to special restrictions that could affect your proposals. So it is essential that you seek advice from your local authority before starting any work.

Development control

The key point is that if you intend to make a large extension to your home – or build a new one – the work will be subject to development control. This means that you must submit plans to the local authority's planning department, and the details of your intentions will be made known to other people. Neighbours may be informed of your plans, so it is prudent to discuss your ideas with them first.

Before reaching this stage, however, you must confirm that your proposals really do need planning consent. Small extensions are sometimes exempt and are referred to as 'permitted development'. At the time of writing, a porch, for example, is unlikely to need planning permission if:

● The external ground area is less than 3m² (32ft²)
● The height is no more than 3m (10ft)
● It is more than 2m (6ft) from a road.

However, some projects allowable as permitted development may not be acceptable in the case of a listed building.

You may also be allowed to construct some types of small building on the land around your house without applying for planning permission, such as garages, sheds and greenhouses. Even so, you must still check with the local authority, because there are certain provisos. For example, the proximity of the new building to a highway may make it necessary to gain planning permission. Similarly, if your proposed outbuilding meant that more than half the land around the house would be covered by additions, planning permission would be needed.

Home extensions may also not need planning permission. Exemption is governed by the size of the extension, its proximity to the road, and the amount of free space available. Approval will be needed if it will be within 2m (6ft) of the boundary of your property, and is over 4m (13ft) high.

In special locations, like national parks, you can add a home extension up to 50m³ (1765ft³), measured externally, or up to 10 per cent (whichever is greater) of the original house without planning permission – but this does not apply to loft extensions. The same proportions apply to a terraced

Where an extension raises the height of the original building, planning permission will be needed.

property, irrespective of location. With other types of house, planning permission is not normally needed for an extension of up 70m³ (2470ft³), or a maximum of 15 per cent, whichever is greater.

Permission is needed if the construction will exceed the highest point of the original roof. Moreover, it is also needed for the addition of a dormer window on a roof that faces a road.

In general, planning permission isn't needed to re-roof a property or to add skylights. Wall cladding is different, and you may need permission before adding stone facing tiles, or timber or plastic cladding. Note that the concern of planning laws is with external features. With the exception of buildings of special architectural merit or historical significance, you do not normally need planning permission for internal alterations.

Application forms

If the planning department advises you that planning permission is needed for a project, you will need to obtain the necessary application forms. They will also advise on the application fee, and the amount of detail needed on the drawings you submit.

The planning application will be held for inspection by members of the public, and neighbours may be notified of your intentions. Sometimes the proposals are reported in a local newspaper.

As a rule, a council should decide the outcome of your application within eight weeks, but they may require longer. You must be prepared for this delay, and should always make your applications as early as possible before the intended start date.

Building control

If planning laws are concerned with the appearance of a building, the Building Regulations are concerned with how it is built. Even if you have a home improvement project that is exempt from planning permission – such as a small extension – it is almost certain to need Building Regulations approval. Many matters will be taken into account, including whether the structure is weathertight, protected from fire, drained satisfactorily, and thermally insulated to conserve fuel and power.

Until the mid-1960s, building bye-laws were made by individual local authorities. However, in 1965 the Building Regulations were introduced to take their place. Metrication and revisions were made in 1972, and the Regulations were made applicable to England and Wales. Separate arrangements were made for Inner London Boroughs, the London Building Acts being the statutory instruments that governed developments in the capital. Similarly, there were separate regulations for Northern Ireland and Scotland.

Readable documents

There have been many developments since 1972, and concern for the environment has led to detailed sections in the Regulations on matters such as the conservation of fuel and power. The documents today are also more readable, but regrettably they are very expensive.

Differences still exist in the statutory instruments, so that building in Scotland is covered by the Building Standards (Scotland) Regulations. However, both in spirit and major matters of content, areas of concern are the same as those contained in the regulations for England and Wales.

In the past few years, several books have been written to explain the implications of particular regulations in practical terms. These are extremely helpful guides once you want to put theory into practice and start building. It is also interesting to note, however, that more recent Regulations have been accompanied by similar publications of guidance. The guidelines are contained in Department of the Environment and The Welsh Office Approved Documents. These extremely readable and helpfully illustrated publications deal with specific parts of the Regulations. This means that the self builder does not need to purchase sections that are more applicable to factories or public buildings.

Whereas these are important detailed publications, a broad overview of the Building Regulations is available from your local authority. This takes the form of booklets available to assist in planning matters. These are usually most helpful in explaining procedures to the home owner. However, it is important to check that the information they contain is up to date and takes into account any recent amendments to the Building Regulations.

Matters of concern

Several matters are included in the Building Regulations, but the issues most likely to concern work on a 'habitable dwelling' fall into the following categories:

- Structure
- Fire Safety
- Site preparation and resistance to moisture
- Toxic substances (this refers to cavity insulants)
- Resistance to the passage of sound
- Ventilation and condensation
- Hygiene
- Drainage and waste disposal
- Heat producing appliances
- Stairs, ramps and guards
- Conservation of fuel and power
- Glazing – materials and protection.

It will be appreciated that these elements are especially wide in their scope, and while several of the projects contained in this manual may be exempt from planning approval, a large proportion will require Building Regulations approval. For example, you need that approval to carry out the following work:

- Re-roofing (but not repair work)
- Erection of new chimneys or flues
- Installing windows in the walls or in the roof
- Installing any new heating appliance, apart from electrical appliances

The addition of a window in a wall or in a roof must be approved by the building control department of your local authority.

Because of the structural alteration, this loft conversion with a dormer window would certainly need Building Regulations approval.

- Installation of bathrooms, showers and WCs
- Installation of new drains
- Internal alterations to structure, including the of loadbearing walls
- Addition of extension, like conservatories, utility rooms, kitchens
- Any work involving demolitions.

At the same time, some buildings do not need Building Regulations approval, including:

- Small sheds
- Greenhouses
- Aviaries, hen houses
- Some designs of carport.

Nevertheless, it is essential to know whether your project is likely to need approval, and the building control staff are available to help and give advice.

Formal application

The building control service will also explain the procedures for making a formal application to undertake building work. Although three approaches are currently available, many building schemes involve a 'full plans application'. This requires the completion of an application form, the depositing of full plans and specifications, and payment of a fee.

The plans will be scrutinised, and if elements of the project do not comply with the Regulations, you will be given an opportunity to amend them. It is often best for the submission process and the fulfilment of any amendments to be carried out by an architect or

building surveyor, acting on your behalf.

When approvals have been given, inspections will be carried out by a building control surveyor at several important stages. A second fee is also payable after the first inspection. The work will be checked at the following stages:

- When foundations have been excavated
- After concreting of foundations
- Before any drains are covered up
- At damp-proof course
- When hardcore has been laid over the site
- During major structural work
- Before occupation
- On completion.

When the work has been completed, a final inspection will be carried out, and a completion certificate will be issued on request. This incurs a small extra charge, but it can be useful in the future – for example, if the house is offered for sale.

Other sources of information

Planning permission and Building Regulations are the key elements involved in gaining approval to undertake home improvement or repair work. However, it is also useful to be aware of the work of the Building Research Establishment. Their publications can be most helpful, and sometimes take the form of 'Practical Guides'. These are intended to support the Building Regulations, and deal with good design and construction practice.

Safety

The safety of everyone involved in building projects is crucial; injuries in the construction industry are not unusual, and the amateur builder must observe all precautionary measures taken by the professional.

This may be self evident when working above ground, but rather less obvious are the risks when working below ground – trench collapse has led to many fatalities.

Dangers are also present when using power tools, plant and machinery. In the last few decades, awareness of industrial injuries has grown considerably, but the amateur must not presume that a brief excursion into DIY building will make protective clothing unnecessary. On the contrary, an accident may be more likely when the 'weekend worker' is wielding unfamiliar items of equipments.

Personal protective gear

Most builders' merchants and major DIY stores sell protective clothing. Make sure that the products sold carry the British Standard kite mark, and don't be tempted to regard normal clothing as a suitable substitute for purpose-designed work wear. The following protective gear is important:

● A safety helmet is essential for many tasks, and not merely as protection from falling objects. It will be needed anywhere you might bump your head.

● Gloves come in several types and for different

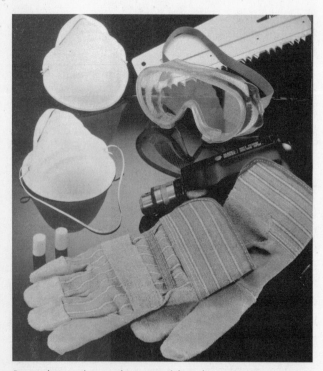

Personal protective gear is an essential purchase.

purposes. When shifting or unloading masonry thick leather gloves will protect your hands from abrasion. Similarly, industrial-grade PVC or rubber gloves are essential when working with chemicals. Your hands may even need protection from mortar.

● Steel-capped footwear is necessary for many building and demolition operations. There is a range of styles to choose from.

● Eye protection is essential when working with any power tool, and can take the form of goggles, industrial spectacles or shields for ordinary glasses.

● Ear protection is necessary when using noisy machinery, especially in an enclosed space. Don't dismiss ear muffs; the cumulative effect of noise on the aural system can cause long-term damage.

● Nasal protection is commonly required in building work. Even something as simple as sawdust can act as an irritant. Similar hazards occur during stone cutting and when chasing out plaster with power tools. A dust mask is cheap, although some products have a short life. For long-term use, a mask that accepts replaceable filters is better.

● Overall body protection may not always seem appropriate on a hot summer day, but there is no place for beachwear in building work. Suitable overalls do more than keep the wearer warm.

● Take care when choosing clothes to work in. When using equipment that has rotating parts, loose clothing can easily become caught in the mechanisms. On a similar note, long hair, jewellery, anorak toggles and draw strings are equally likely to fall foul of moving parts on machines.

Access equipment

Many repair and renovation jobs will involve some form of access equipment. A variety is available, depending on the job in hand:

Trestles Materials will often need raising above ground level. Equally, you may need to stand on a raised platform to reach inaccessible parts of the work. Purpose-designed trestles are useful in this respect and have a number of other uses.

Step ladders Look carefully at the design when purchasing a set of steps. Some are notoriously unstable, and they are more suited for occasional use around the home than for serious building work.

Ladders Lightness and weather resistance are two advantages of an aluminium ladder. There are several points to remember when choosing a ladder: there should always be at least three rungs above the highest point on which you'll put your feet; in the case of an extending ladder, there must always be a good overlap between the sections; and finally, when it is set up against a wall, the foot should stand away from the wall by a quarter of its height.

Ladder accessories Never rest a ladder against guttering. If there is a substantial eaves overhang, a ladder 'stand-off' should be used. These are readily available and easily fitted. The foot of a ladder must be stable and level; if necessary, it should be fitted with a ladder leveller. Another useful fitting is a platform that increases the area of any rung on which you need to stand for a prolonged period.

A ridge hook will convert a normal ladder for roofing work.

For long term use, the top of a ladder should be tied to a large screw eye set in the fascia board, while the foot can be tied to a stake driven into the ground.

Roof ladders Gaining a footing on a pitched roof is very difficult – and dangerous; moreover, the tiles may not bear your weight. A roof ladder is the answer to these problems. Purpose-designed roof ladders can be hired, but it is also possible to adapt an ordinary ladder by adding a wheeled ridge hook.

Installing a roof ladder is quite difficult, and it is best manoeuvred into place from a tower or scaffold platform. Don't attempt it from a ladder.

Access towers Most tool hire companies offer access towers. All require a sound base and, in all but low structures, the tower should be constructed with outriggers to provide good stability. It should also be tied to the structure at suitable points. Handrails at the top, and a sound platform with kick boards at the sides are essential features.

Scaffolding For major projects, a contractor should be employed to erect scaffolding. Although the contractor will be responsible for erecting a safe structure, maintenance of safety falls squarely on the builder. Access ladders should be removed when not required, and warning notices displayed where appropriate. Never allow children to climb on scaffolding or access towers.

Chimney staging Repairs are often needed to chimney stacks, and purpose-made staging may be hired to provide a sound working base. These structures are usually made from pre-assembled sections, and many are made of lightweight tubing for easy transport.

A ladder leveller will provide a firm footing on uneven ground.

Portable power tools

Instruction leaflets supplied with portable tools are very detailed, and many manufacturers include comprehensive safety guidance. It remains for the purchaser to act on that advice.

However, if a machine is borrowed from a friend, or hired, the important documentation may be missing. Tool hire companies normally display free leaflets containing general guidance about particular products they may have available. The provision of this information is an obligation to the customer, and if it is not on display, you should ask for it.

Information concerning a particular product can often be obtained by contacting the manufacturer's technical services or customer advice department. As a rule, manufacturers are most helpful, since it is in their interest to ensure that their products do not cause injury – even if this may be the fault of the user rather than the equipment itself.

Electrical safety

The danger of electrocution is ever present when using power tools, so an understanding of electrical safety is essential. The following will be of use:

Double insulation The majority of mains-powered tools are 'double insulated', which means that they do not need an earth connection via a three-core lead. To achieve this, the casing is usually made of plastic, and the electrical components are contained within a separate insulated housing. However, the appliance must still be fitted with a 13 amp fused plug containing a fuse of the appropriate amperage.

Extension leads Where an extension lead is required, it should be capable of carrying the load demanded by the appliance. As a general rule, an extension cable should be unwound from its drum to avoid overheating. This is particularly important when using high-wattage appliances.

Residual current device An essential precaution when operating mains tools outdoors is to connect them via a residual current device (RCD). This safety cut-out may also be referred to as an 'earth leakage circuit breaker' (ELCB). There are many ways of operating through an RCD, and some modern properties may have one linked to the main consumer unit serving the house. If working in a house with an older electrical system, it is easy to fit a special RCD socket to the point from which power tools will be supplied. RCD adaptors are also manufactured for plugging into any 13 amp socket that you want to use. Alternatively, portable RCD units are available combined with a pre-wired extension lead. In the event of a fault developing in a power tool, or if the user should inadvertently touch a live wire in the supply cable, the RCD instantly cuts off the supply, affording complete protection from electrocution.

Cordless tools Despite these safety measures, it is inadvisable to work outdoors with mains-powered equipment when it is raining. This has led to the popularity of rechargeable cordless power tools. In particular, drills are effective because they work at a low wattage. Some cordless jig saws are equally successful for light work. However, portable circular saws need more powerful motors, and cordless versions are seldom available.

While the electrical safety of cordless tools is one of their merits, the absence of a trailing lead makes them particularly suitable for high-level work. For instance, when repairing guttering, a cordless drill is much safer than a conventional mains-powered tool that has to trail a lead from the top of a ladder.

A portable RCD will provide protection against electrocution.

Cutting tools

You are more likely to have an accident with a blunt saw than a sharp one. If progress is slow, and you force a blunt hand saw through material, the risk of the saw jumping becomes more probable. The same applies when working with a blunt chisel. Thus, keeping all cutting tools sharp is a pre-requisite for safety, not to mention the quality of finish achieved.

Another traditional tip is to ensure that you keep your hands behind any cutting edge. You are asking for trouble if you try to hold down a workpiece by hand in front of an advancing chisel or saw blade. The same applies when working on a saw bench. Experienced craftsmen claim that most accidents occur from behind the blade rather than in front of it. Typically, the operator finds that a small workpiece is lifted by the blade, and the temptation is to hold it down at the back of the table while the remaining material passes the blade. However, if the material catches again, the hand can be thrown into the blade.

Such accidents should not happen if: the equipment is properly guarded; there is a riving knife behind the blade to keep the saw cut open; and a push stick is used to move the workpiece across the table.

It is essential to buy good-quality equipment and obtain correct instruction before using a machine of this kind. With this in mind, consult text books on technique and safety, or attend woodwork classes. Like many other power tools, a saw bench is a great asset, provided you understand how to use it properly and safely.

Abrasive disc machines

When fitted with a disc for cutting masonry, a portable grinder can fashion bricks or paving slabs into intricate shapes. It can also be used for chasing out a mortar course before adding lead flashing.

Unfortunately, these machines are potentially very dangerous, and safety clothing must be worn. The most serious problem is the ever-present risk that a disc working under load may disintegrate and fly in all directions. In practice, this seldom happens, as abrasive discs are made with binding materials that keep them intact. However, goggles – or even a full face shield – will be necessary in case particles fly away from the disc, or it breaks up unexpectedly.

For the same reason, suitable clothing is needed to protect the arms, and reinforced leather gloves are equally important, as is a dust mask. Enormous amounts of dust are generated when cutting through masonry. If the work is carried out indoors, every effort should be made to protect yourself, and to contain the dust to the immediate area.

Despite these disadvantages, an abrasive disc machine can be very useful. For instance, if you need to chase out a groove in a floor screed to insert a section of narrow ducting, few tools will complete the work as quickly, efficiently and neatly. Similarly, it will make far cleaner cuts in paving slabs than with a club hammer and bolster chisel.

Full protection is essential when using an abrasive disc machine.

Tools and materials

Before embarking on home repair or improvement work, you must have suitable tools and equipment, and know how to use them correctly. Some items will be used for all manner of jobs and should be purchased, whereas others will be very specialised and used only for specific jobs. In this case, hiring is a better option. For example, the special wooden mallet needed for shaping lead sheet (a task referred to as 'dressing') is not likely to be used very often. Therefore, hiring one, rather than buying, would be more sensible if you only need to dress a lead apron on a chimney stack.

Hand tools

Any work involving timber will require a selection of carpentry tools. Basic items like a hammer, a jack plane, a hand saw and a measuring tape can be found in most DIY tool boxes, but a few G-cramps will be useful for temporarily holding timber in place. A punch is essential for burying the heads of nails in timber. Screwdrivers for slotted screws are obvious, but the industry is increasingly using cross-headed screws, so appropriate screwdrivers are needed. Space precludes listing all the important tools you may need. Quite often, the best policy is to make sure you have a selection of basic tools, but delay purchasing any others until a need arises.

Compromise is essential, because there are many special products within each tool category. For instance, hand saws come as rip saws, cross-cut saws and panel saws. Each has a specific use, with variations in length of blade, tooth shape and the number of teeth. In practice, many carpenters compromise by purchasing a saw that performs a variety of functions: a cross-cut saw with a coarse cut of five or six teeth per 25mm (1in) can be used for rip cutting – provided it's not pushed too hard – and fulfils a wide variety of needs.

The situation is much the same with planes. For general use, a jack plane is often chosen, whereas its shorter partner is better for smoothing work, and a try plane (called a jointer) has a long sole for achieving straight, true surfaces on boards.

Sharp blades

With use, all cutting tools will become blunt, so you will need a means of sharpening them. An oil stone will be required for sharpening chisels and plane irons, together with a certain amount of skill to do the job correctly. However, a sharpening guide will simplify the job of achieving the correct cutting and honing angles (25 and 30 degrees respectively). A coarse oil stone is needed for the former, and a finer stone for making the honing angle.

High-speed twist drills also need a special guide, and various products are available. Flat bits (also called spade bits) must be sharpened by hand, but careful work with a fine file can revive a dull edge.

Saws are a different matter and should be taken to a saw doctor, who will carry out the skilled job of sharpening for a modest charge. In the last few years, hand saws have become available with specially hardened teeth that cannot be sharpened, but which stay sharp for much longer than those of a conventional saw. These saws are so inexpensive that they can be used until blunt, then thrown away. However, it is worth keeping an old saw for cutting plasterboard and similar teeth-blunting work.

An oil stone will be needed for sharpening chisels and plane irons.

General tools and equipment

As regards general items of equipment, a steel builders' barrow with a pneumatic tyre is virtually essential. Don't waste time trying to use a small wheelbarrow designed for garden waste – it will lack the necessary strength. Similarly, a good shovel is worth purchasing, but keep it clean. Concrete has a remarkable facility for sticking to shovels and the bowls of mixers. Therefore, meticulous cleaning of tools used for concreting work is an essential discipline, as indeed is keeping all your tools clean. If you look after your tools properly, they will reward you with many years of use.

Checking levels

Tools for measuring and checking levels are particularly important in building work. When measuring and marking out a new structure, a steel rule is usually more accurate than a fabric or coated glassfibre flexible tape.

A spirit level is also an essential tool, being used for bricklaying, carpentry, joinery, checking drain falls, screeding floors, fitting rainwater guttering, erecting fitted furniture, and a host of other tasks. A 1m (3ft) spirit level will be useful in many situations, although in restricted spaces a small level may be needed, too. Some spirit levels incorporate features that allow them to measure angles, too, which can be a very useful facility.

This unusual small spirit level offers the facility of measuring 30 and 45 degree angles. Tools like this can often prove very useful.

Other small hand tools needed on site include a bolster chisel, a club hammer, a pick-axe and trowels of various sizes. A string line is also important for setting-out operations, and a sledge hammer will occasionally prove useful.

Trestles and a portable work bench will be invaluable for a variety of jobs. You can make a trestle with the aid of a pair of special folding brackets. Each has two sockets that accept lengths of timber for the legs; these can be secured with nails or screws. The top of the bracket takes the form of serrated jaws, which simply bite into the cross-piece to secure it when the legs are opened.

In building work, a pair of trestles and some G-cramps will be invaluable for supporting a wide range of workpieces.

String line, trowels, a club hammer, a bolster chisel, a measuring tape and a long spirit level are needed for bricklaying work.

Power tools

Electric power tools have a major role to play in repair and renovation work. However, sustained use is far more likely to damage a portable power tool than a weekend DIY repair. In recent years, the manufacturers have recognised that some home owners are willing to tackle serious projects, and have developed more robust tools.

Regrettably, it isn't always easy to differentiate between product types. For instance, some DIY drills look large and purposeful, but the bearings and motor are of a lower specification to suit occasional DIY use. The problem is aggravated by the inclusion of tools in a DIY range that, hitherto, have been regarded as being for professionals.

Before buying a power tool, you should establish whether its specification is suitable for the kind of work you intend to do. A tool specialist is more likely to help you in this respect; staff at DIY supermarkets seldom have the necessary technical knowledge, and if you buy from this source, you must be sure that you know exactly what you want.

Generators

On some sites, the lack of a mains electricity supply may make it necessary to obtain a generator.

Robust power tools, such as this Black & Decker Pro-line drill, are being offered to cope with ambitious projects tackled by amateurs.

Industrial models can be obtained from tool hire companies, but the advent of smaller 'leisure' generators has added an alternative source for the amateur user. These machines are normally powerful enough to operate electric drills, jig saws and planers. However, a circular saw, with its larger motor, may require a larger generator, as will electrically-operated machines like cement mixers and site pumps. A tool hire company will be able to advise you on the correct model.

Special equipment

There are many other items that may be needed in structural improvement work, and most can be hired. For instance, a punner will be useful for simple consolidation work when preparing a base for a concrete slab. Vibrating plates and rollers are more elaborate machines for carrying out consolidation work on a grander scale.

Concrete mixers can also be hired, as can miniature excavators that will operate in the smallest of spaces. Many amateur builders use these machines successfully, and there is much advantage to be gained from using mechanical assistance in preference to digging by hand.

A saw bench is invaluable for many woodworking tasks; a site saw is usually equipped with a large blade to provide a good depth of cut, although its accuracy for jointing work may not be very

A vibrating roller may be necessary when laying concrete. A tool hire company can supply one and will deliver it to the site.

impressive. Site saws with pressed-steel table tops seldom provide accurate adjustment, and the side or cross-cutting fences are less reliable in joinery work. For accuracy, a cast-iron top is much better, although cast-aluminium tops used on portable models are equally accurate and much lighter. With one of these machines, you can make mitre cuts for door architrave, grooves in a fascia board for a soffit , and various cross- or rip-cutting operations.

Whatever equipment you need to hire, it's important to know how to use it. Large companies publish operating guides for their tools; their staff will also be able to demonstrate the equipment.

Safety is critical; if used without care, some power tools can cause serious injuries. Make sure that you obtain the appropriate protective clothing.

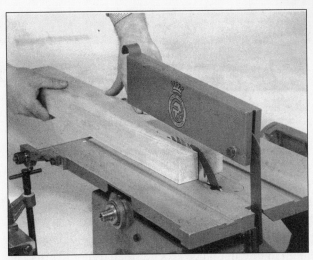

A portable aluminium table saw provides accurate cutting and is excellent for many home improvement projects.

Selecting materials

Choosing the correct materials is an essential part of any repair or renovation project. In fact, the Building Regulations require you to use materials that are fit for their purpose. The wisdom of this is beyond dispute, but if you are not closely associated with the building industry, you may find it difficult to determine whether a material is sound for a particular job. Tracking down suppliers and verifying the claims made about the performance of their products may also seem daunting. Fortunately, there are several sources of useful information:

The Building Centre One of the best ways to find out about manufactured products is to visit The Building Centre in London. Its facilities include a bookshop, an information service and a permanent exhibition of products.

Trade Associations Information on products is sometimes available through specialist Trade Associations, several of whom are listed on page 158. However, there are many more, and details are available from The Building Centre.

British Board of Agrément (BBA) This is an important national – but totally independent – body that assesses and tests construction products. If the product passes the BBA tests, it is given an Agrément Certificate, which acknowledges its 'fitness for purpose'. BBA Certificates refer directly

to the Building Regulations. In essence, this is an important reassurance to any builder that a product is fit for the purpose claimed by its manufacturer.

The BBA is an important contact organisation for the builder and home improver. It works in close relationship with regulatory authorities, including the British Standards Institution, the Building Research Establishment, the National House-Building Council, and several other organisations.

Building Regulations Not surprisingly, the Building Regulations take into account the suitability of materials. This includes structural performance, characteristics in the event of fire, dangers associated with fumes and so on.

Text books Another way to learn about materials and their suitability is to consult text books. However, technical building books may not be kept in a local library, although they can be borrowed via inter-library loan services. Alternatively, if you have access to a college of further or higher education that runs building courses, you may be able to gain the use of its library.

Manufacturers Most manufacturers operate advice services, although in some instances you may need to contact the technical service department rather than the customer service department. As a rule, manufacturers are very helpful, and are usually willing to supply informative technical data sheets.

Chapter 2

Exterior Work
Damp-proofing

Damage to the fabric of our homes is often caused by damp. Its sources are various, and like many problems in building, preventing the development of damp in the first place is better than trying to effect a cure later on. In most cases, the occurrence of damp is due to the following causes:

● Plumbing faults inside the property
● Faulty guttering, tiles, flashing, etc.
● Condensation
● Release from masonry
● Weather penetration
● Rising damp.

Faulty rainwater systems and plumbing failures are self evident, and the remedies are usually straightforward. The focus in this section is on the last four sources listed above.

Detection

A problem with identifying damp is the fact that on many materials dampness may not be visible. Moreover, the damage to materials like structural timbers might be taking effect long before dampness is apparent to the touch.

For this reason, identification of damp conditions sometimes needs a moisture meter. Inexpensive versions are available in DIY stores, whereas more professional test equipment can often be hired. However, hiring a meter is one thing; knowing how to use it properly is another, and any good tool hire company should provide full instructions on its use.

The problem for an inexperienced user is to understand the percentage moisture content of different materials, recognising that an acceptable level in one material might be unacceptable in another. Equally, the source of a problem can be difficult to identify, and it is important to be able to differentiate between dampness arising from condensation as opposed to, say, rising damp.

In many instances, it's better to seek the help of an experienced surveyor. For example, the presence of salts in masonry, left as a result of water penetration from a redundant flue, or from an earlier problem of rising damp, can cause a meter to register a high level of moisture. A surveyor would recognise this and adapt the test procedures accordingly.

Condensation

In recent years, the need to conserve energy has led to improved thermal insulation of our homes coupled with effective means of draughtproofing. At the same time, there has been a tendency for householders to use more facilities that create water vapour: hot showers, washing machines, tumble driers, dishwashers, etc. As a result, we live in sealed buildings that contain a number of vapour producing elements.

The air in our homes is also able to hold more moisture because of higher room temperatures brought about by the widespread use of central heating. When that warm, moisture-laden air comes into contact with a cold surface – such as cold water pipes, lavatory cisterns, metal window frames or mirrors – it cools and the vapour it contains converts into condensation.

This is often very inconvenient, and can lead to damage. Even more serious, however, is interstitial condensation. Vapour is able to penetrate many materials used in buildings, and if condensation occurs within the interstices of components like the roof timbers, severe damage can be caused.

Trapped moisture

It is not uncommon for fireplaces in older properties to be sealed off; the installation of central heating renders open fires unnecessary, the opening often being bricked up and the chimney capped. However, this means that any moisture in the flue may become sealed in. With no flow of air through the flue to disperse any dampness held in the masonry, moisture often starts to come through chimney breasts and is seen inside the rooms. The application of barrier materials on the inside, like polystyrene lining or a thin veneer of metal foil, is a common treatment, but it is not always successful in the long term because the damp remains in the structure. Fitting ventilators in bricked-up fireplaces and in chimney stacks is a much better strategy.

Rising damp

Another serious threat to buildings is posed by rising damp. A course of slate laid just above ground level was an early preventative measure, but many buildings constructed during the last century have no provision at all. Occasionally, two courses of blue engineering bricks were laid to prevent rising damp, and this can work satisfactorily. The common practice today is to lay a damp-proof course (DPC), using strips of bituminous or plastic material. This is built into the inner and outer skins of a cavity wall, and should be at least 150mm (6in) above the surrounding surface. This prevents heavy rain from splashing up to hit the wall above the DPC. Damp may start to penetrate masonry if soil from a border is allowed to touch an external wall above the DPC.

Weather problems

Driving rain and melting snow pose a threat to the structure of a building. A broken tile or a failed flat roof covering are obvious sources of trouble that can be seen and dealt with, but difficulties occur where there is no specific fault in the structure – other than the fact that it was built when construction methods were less efficient than they are today.

The external walls of post-war properties have two skins of masonry with a cavity between them. Most pre-war houses have solid walls, comprising two layers of brick. Unfortunately, bricks are porous and driving rain may eventually penetrate such a wall.

Even with a double-skin wall, it is not unusual for dampness to develop within the cavity. To ensure

that this doesn't lead to further problems, modern practice is to install plastic weep holes in some of the brick joints. Within the cavity, a damp proof membrane will be installed above window lintels and angled so that if water runs down the cavity, it will be dispersed via the weep holes.

A cavity tray may be installed within an area of exposed brickwork, particularly where an extension abuts the house wall. The tray collects water running down the cavity and directs it to the outside.

Rainwater driving against a chimney stack may also penetrate the masonry. For this reason, a damp proof course should be incorporated to prevent water from percolating downwards.

After installation of a damp proof membrane over a lintel, weep hole units are built into vertical joints in the outer layer of brickwork. (Illustration courtesy Rytons Building Products Ltd)

Some cavity trays built into a cavity to collect moisture are made with attached sections of lead flashing.

Tackling condensation

There are three lines of approach when it comes to dealing with condensation:

● Eliminating the creation of vapour at source
● Eliminating cold surfaces
● Introducing effective ventilation.

Eliminating condensation at source is the best strategy, although this is not always practical. However, confining it to the area where it is produced will help. So, too, will venting it to the outside air, by means of extractor fans.

Reducing the number of cold surfaces where condensation may form is another precautionary measure. For example, where a single pane of glass is fitted in a window, its outside surface may be cold, and since glass conducts heat fairly well, coldness is conducted to the inner surface. One of the reasons for fitting double-glazed units is that the cold outer pane is separate from the inner pane.

A similar situation occurs in older metal-framed windows, because the cold surface of the outer part of the frame leads to a lowering of temperature on the inner face of the frame. To overcome this, metal frames are now made with a layer of insulating material between the outer and inner parts.

Another way of preventing the formation of condensation is to introduce a system of controlled ventilation, such as cross ventilation in roof structures and suspended floors. Unlike extraction systems that use fans, cross ventilation is induced naturally, airways having to be created and kept clear. The position of ventilators in such a system is critical, as is the size of openings, so expert guidance

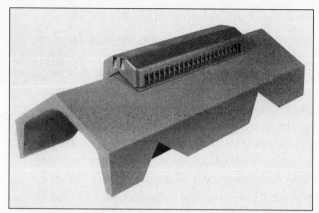

Ventilation at the ridge of a roof can be achieved in various ways, including the use of special ventilating ridge tiles. (Photograph courtesy Redland Roof Tiles Ltd)

is essential. Ventilation in modern houses also makes use of trickle ventilators built into the frames of windows.

The fact that vapour can pass through many of the materials used in building is important to recognise. For example, problems of condensation in roof voids is due to its ability to pass through normal plasterboard. A better answer is to install specially-made foil-backed plasterboard. However, continuity of the foil barrier is essential if it is to be successful, and all joints must be sealed.

An alternative is to install a vapour control layer above the ceiling. This should be sealed where wires or pipes pass through it. The material used is 0.12mm (500 gauge) polyethylene, and if more than one sheet is needed, all joints and edges must be taped or covered with a sealant ribbon.

Cladding walls

On an exposed site facing the prevailing wind, the walls of a property come under a particular threat. In some circumstances, the only satisfactory solution to damp penetration is to clad the wall with a protective layer. This may require planning permission; additionally, you should seek advice from the local authority building control office, because the addition may have structural implications. For example, facing brickwork with modern concrete tiles would provide a notable barrier. It would also

have the advantage of allowing any damp already in the wall to disperse, since the tiles wouldn't seal in the residual moisture.

A similar strategy would be to fit a cladding material such as weather-boarding. The disadvantage of adding timber cladding, however, is that it will need regular maintenance. In some circumstances, uPVC cladding might be better.

A cement-based render could also be used to protect the wall. However, like the other precautionary measures, this would not be a cheap option, and the costs would need careful consideration.

Water-repellent treatments

Walls can be protected from penetrating damp by applying a silicone-based waterproofing agent. It involves cleaning the masonry, removing any algae or surface vegetation with a stiff brush and scraper. This should be followed by an application of a fungicide. The liquid itself should be applied in good weather, when the surface is completely dry. Use a large brush on a smooth surface, or a deep-pile roller on a heavily-textured one.

This method can be very successful, although the treatment will need repeating periodically. There may be undesirable side effects, however, and you need to understand the potential problems.

To begin with, this treatment must not be regarded as a curative measure if a wall has even fine cracks in it. Equally, there's a risk that a surface treatment may seal in any moisture, which could lead to frost damage. Some products are said to allow brickwork to 'breathe'. Nevertheless, it's fairly certain that the outward passage of vapour will be reduced.

Also, you should not apply a surface treatment to the outer leaf of a cavity wall if there is a complete fill of cavity insulant. Moisture can be trapped between the silicone and foam, leading to frost damage.

A further difficulty arises if only part of a wall is treated. The fast run-off of rain from the treated area will place the adjacent untreated area under a greater amount of wetting than normal.

Damp-proof courses

The addition of a DPC to an older building can be achieved in a number of ways, including introducing damp-proof material brick-by-brick, or removing a line of mortar with an abrasive disc machine and inserting the DPC with a dry mortar bedding. A more common approach, however, is to inject a moisture-repellent fluid into the masonry.

A completely different approach involves passing an electrical charge through a wire embedded in the wall, known as the electro-osmotic process. The operating principle is based on the fact that capillary action is influenced by an applied voltage, and that moisture will move from a positive anode to a negative cathode whenever an electrical current flows through a special conductor.

Installation involves cutting a horizontal groove in the walls of the property, and burying a titanium wire in the groove. Subsequently, the groove is made good with mortar. When completed, the system is connected to a mains supply.

Other measures

Damp-proof membranes are used for larger areas in contact with the ground, such as concrete floor slabs. These are described on pages 94-95. Where a plastic sheet is used, this must be overlapped with the damp-proof course in the walls to achieve complete continuity. Further provisions are needed at door and

Strips of bituminous or purpose-made plastic material are used in most buildings nowadays to create a damp-proof course.

window openings, where the outer skin of a cavity wall joins with the inner skin. Traditionally, a length of damp-proofing strip was embedded vertically in the masonry that formed the reveal, thus providing a break in the continuity of permeable materials. More recently, an insert has been developed for placing in the cavity. This not only breaks the continuity between the two skins of brickwork, but also provides thermal insulation.

▶ SEE PAGE 24 FOR STEP-BY-STEP INSTRUCTIONS ON INSTALLING A CHEMICAL DPC

Installing a chemical DPC

Although you can employ a contractor to inject a chemical DPC in the walls of your house, the work is not difficult and kits are available allowing DIY treatment. Moreover, injection equipment can often be obtained from tool hire companies. However, the work can be quite messy, so it is essential to remove any items from the vicinity that could be damaged by the chemical. Essentially, a section of brickwork, running around the house, is soaked in the water-repellent chemical, preventing moisture from rising through the masonry.

A typical DIY injection kit comprises a container of DPC chemical (usually 25 litres/6gallons), a pressure pump, injector nozzles and hoses, and tapered wall plugs. The procedure for installing the DPC is as follows:

● Indoors all skirting boards should be removed from the walls being treated. All plaster affected by rising damp should be hacked off to a distance of 450mm (18in) above the visibly affected area.
● Holes are drilled in two adjacent courses of brickwork then fitted with tapered plugs to receive the nozzles of the pump unit.
● The chemical is pumped into the hole until the surface of the masonry is seen to be saturated; then the nozzles are moved to the next set of holes and the process repeated.
● When treatment has been completed, holes outside are left as long as possible before plugging with mortar containing a special waterproofing agent.
● Indoors, the walls should be left to dry out for a month for each 25mm (1in) of thickness. If this is not possible, a waterproofing render or waterproofing additives can be used when replastering the walls. Before replacing skirting boards, treat the back with preservative.

Drilling the holes

Drill the holes for the fluid with a 13mm (½in) masonry bit fitted to an electric drill with a hammer action. As a rule, the holes for the fluid should be spaced about 112mm (4½in) apart. If the bricks are particularly dense, space the holes about 75mm (3in) apart.

When treating a single-leaf wall, no thicker than 112mm (4½in), drill the holes from one side only to a depth of 75mm (3in). A cavity wall with two single leaves will need drilling from both sides to the same depth. A 225mm (9in) thick solid wall of two leaves of bricks will need drilling in the same way. Alternatively, drill from one side only to a depth of 75mm (3in), inject the fluid, then drill the same holes to a depth of 190mm (7½in) and inject again.

HOW MUCH?

☐ The thickness of the wall being treated, together with the porosity of the bricks will determine the amount of fluid you require. It is normally sold in 25 litre (6 gallon) drums.
☐ For a single-leaf, 112mm (4½in) thick wall, you will need approximately 3 litres (⅔ gallon) per 1m (3ft) of wall length. For a cavity wall, or 225mm (9in) thick solid wall, the amount required should be doubled.

1 Indoors, carefully lever off the skirting boards. Then use a bolster chisel and club hammer to hack off all plaster damaged by rising damp. Cut back 450mm (18in) into sound plaster.

2 Drill the holes for the injection nozzles, 150mm (6in) below floor level, making them 75mm (3in) deep. Use a depth stop or wind masking tape around the bit. Angle the holes downwards.

3 Having drilled all the holes (on both sides of the wall if necessary), prepare the equipment for injecting the fluid. Insert the pick-up hose into a drum of the DPC fluid.

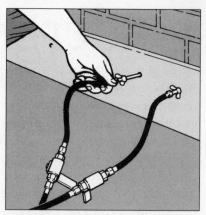

4 Sufficient nozzles and hoses will be supplied to allow several holes to be treated at a time. Insert the nozzles into the first set of holes, making sure that the control valves are closed.

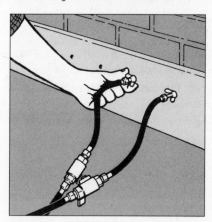

5 Leave one nozzle free, then tighten the tapered plugs of the others to ensure a liquid-proof seal. Take care not to over-tighten the fittings, as you may damage them.

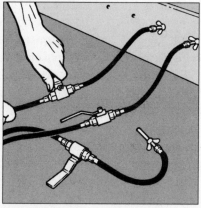

6 Open the valves in the hoses feeding the nozzles fitted in the holes. Then switch on the electric injection pump so that the DPC fluid begins to flow through the hoses.

7 Take the free nozzle, hold it over a can and open the valve so that fluid is able to flow freely from it. This will bleed off any air in the system. Then close the valve and fit the nozzle in its hole.

8 The surface of the brickwork will darken as it becomes saturated with the liquid. When the surface appears wet, close the valves and move the nozzles to the next set of holes.

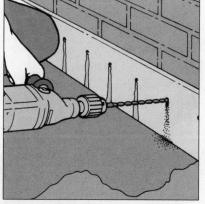

9 If you are treating a 225mm (9in) solid brick wall by drilling from one side only, after the initial injection of fluid, return to each hole and drill it to a depth of 190mm (7½in).

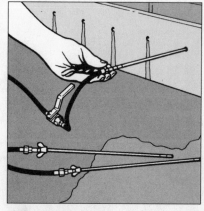

10 Longer nozzles must be fitted to the hoses to treat the deeper holes. Secure them in the holes as before, and repeat the injection process until you have treated the entire wall.

Underground drainage

An efficient drainage system is essential, and its correct design and construction are rigorously governed by statutory acts. The requirements are explained in the Building Regulations.

No work on new or existing systems should commence until you have gained formal approval from your local authority's building control department. Even if the existing system is inefficient, you must draw up any improvement plans and submit them for approval. The work will be inspected by a building control officer at various stages of construction.

In practice, work on underground drainage is not particularly difficult, as long as the principles of design and site practice are understood. You should also be familiar with the following terms:

Effluent Waterborne waste, usually discharged from toilets.

Stormwater The result of rain or melting snow. It is usually kept completely separate from effluent and the waste water from baths and sinks.

Plumbing The system for dealing with waste water and effluent inside the building is regarded as part of the plumbing. However, the system outside the building ceases to be the concern of the plumber, and is usually constructed by a general builder.

Drains When waste water and solids leave a building, but remain within the building plot, service pipes are referred to as 'drains'. Their maintenance is the responsibility of the owner.

Sewer When a drain passes beyond the boundary of a building plot and links with the system serving other properties, it is referred to as a 'sewer'. It is maintained by the water authority.

Private sewer Sometimes drains pass from plot to plot before entering the water authority sewer. Upkeep of each section is the responsibility of the individual on whose plot the run falls. This calls for neighbourly co-operation, because a blockage at the end of a run will affect all households on the upstream side of the problem.

Separate systems Two separate drainage systems are considered necessary: one carries stormwater to a nearby watercourse; the other removes effluent, which flows via the sewer to a water treatment works. Where it is not possible to run pipes to a watercourse, soakaways must be provided for rainwater. A more severe problem occurs if there's no sewer system. In this case, a septic tank will be installed. This has to be emptied periodically by a contractor.

Combined system Many older properties have a combined system. This is less expensive to construct, and in periods of heavy rain, the drains receive a helpful flush of water, although the deluge may overload the water treatment works. An

A wash basin waste pipe enters the underground drain via a sealed cap, marking the end of the plumbing and the start of the drains.

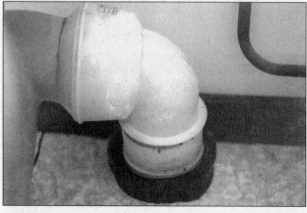

A MultiKwik adaptor on a toilet pan provides a connection with the underground drainage system.

Septic tanks are installed in rural areas where there's no main drainage system. They are emptied periodically by a contractor.

A back inlet gulley taking water from a sink links with a deep water trap; water from a path will also drain into this gulley.

indicator of a combined system is a hopper head situated on a rainwater downpipe. This provides a junction for a waste pipe from a bath or washbasin.

Partially separate In some cases, a small quantity of rainwater from a path may be allowed to discharge into the drain that deals with effluent. This is achieved with a back inlet gulley placed outside the building and close to the outlet from a sink. It has a deep water trap to prevent drain smells from escaping.

Fall All sections of pipework must have a gentle slope or 'fall' to ensure that waterborne waste is transported effectively to the sewer.

Inspection chamber Allows access to the drainage system for maintenance and clearing blockages.

Pipe sizes

The design of a domestic drainage system should be entrusted to an architect, who will calculate the maximum flow rates, and specify pipes of the appropriate diameter. A pipe should never work to full capacity, since this can cause siphonage, emptying deep water traps and allowing odours to escape from the system. In practice, a pipe's internal diameter must be at least 100mm (4in), but a larger pipe is seldom needed for domestic premises.

Calculating falls

When constructing a new system, the builder has to ascertain the height difference between the base of a soil stack and the point where the drain will enter the public sewer. Useful data is often given on the architect's drawing, figures marked on a manhole cover showing its height above the bottom of the gulley in the chamber. A builder will verify this with surveying equipment such as a Cowley level, which may be hired.

Once the height difference is confirmed, the length of the pipe run needs measuring. If this information shows that the height difference between the exit point from the house and the entry point at the sewer is 1m (3ft), and the pipe run is 40m (120ft) long, the fall is expressed as 1:40. As a rule, the fall should remain constant throughout the system, although a

height change may be permissible between the final inspection chamber on the plot boundary, and in the final pipe run to the sewer. This, together with the final connection into the sewer, must be constructed by an approved contractor. It is worth having plenty of height available at the final inspection chamber in case the pipe crossing the highway has to pass above or below other service pipes. This must be taken into account when making the fall calculation.

Where the available fall is minimal, a larger-diameter pipe will be used because water is able to flow at more gentle gradients. Where possible, however, 100mm (4in) pipe is used, for which the ideal fall is 1:40. It is important to remember that settlement can occur at a later date; on an unstable site, extremely gentle falls should be avoided.

Soil stack

Another important element in the overall design of a drainage system is the soil stack – sometimes called a soil and vent pipe. A soil stack constitutes the starting point in the system. Older properties will have a cast-iron stack running down an outside wall. In modern houses, it is made of uPVC and must be installed internally, a practice that helps to eliminate problems arising from severe frosts.

The soil stack is the only part of a modern system that is vented, the opening being high up on the roof. Venting is essential to prevent siphonage.

The base of a soil stack must have a gentle bend to prevent the accumulation of solid waste and foaming caused by detergents. Above this point, the stack will be fitted with collars at various points to accept waste pipes from toilets, baths, sinks and basins.

Passing through walls

From the foot of an internal stack, the pipe will pass through the wall of the house, below the surface. To allow for differential settlement in the building and the drainage system, the two should be independent of each other. One way of achieving this is to fit a large-diameter duct in the foundation structure. The pipe will run through the duct, but there should be a clearance of at least 50mm (2in) all around. Another method is to build an opening in both skins of the wall, supporting them with a lintel. In each case, rigid sheet material must be placed around the pipe to keep out vermin.

An external soil stack on an inter-war house. In this case, the original cast-iron stack has been replaced with a uPVC version.

A uPVC duct for building into a wall so that a pipe can pass through without differential settlement causing problems.

An opening in brickwork, below the DPC, allows a pipe to pass without touching the foundations. Note the lintel (arrowed).

Inspection chambers

Provision must be made for clearing blockages, and can include manholes, inspection chambers, rodding eyes and access fittings. All parts of the system should be accessible with rods, and at the high and low points, an inspection chamber is normally fitted. In some cases, a rodding eye is acceptable. This is a special branch pipe, with an airtight cover, through which drain rods can be inserted.

Pipe runs must be laid in straight lines, inspection chambers being constructed where they change direction. Because an inspection chamber is heavy and may be subject to settlement, flexible joints are fitted to pipes where they enter or leave the chamber.

Drains can be unblocked using rods inserted at an inspection chamber, or into a modern uPVC inspection unit, such as this.

Pipe vents

In an older property, you may come across a small vent pipe, adjacent to the last inspection chamber in a system. This is to prevent siphonage, because in old systems a deep water trap was sometimes fitted immediately after the final inspection chamber, at the start of the final pipe section leading to the sewer. Its purpose is to prevent odours from the sewer passing into the property's drain system. However, the practice is no longer followed because solids passing out of the drains can block the trap.

Testing the system

All parts of a drainage system must be airtight and watertight. If not, water from the surrounding soil will enter the system if the water table is high, and the pipes will act as a land drain. On the other hand, in an area with a low water table, effluent may leak out of the system, contaminating the ground.

When an inspection is carried out by a building control officer, a test of the system's integrity may be carried out. This usually involves checking that it is airtight, and the procedure necessitates sealing off sections of the system with expanding bungs. Air is blown into the system via a nozzle in one of the bungs, which is then connected to a U-tube filled with water. Air released from the section under test will force the water up one side of the tube, and the level will be sustained if the drain is airtight. If air escapes from the section under test, the level of water will fall.

A test of this kind is easy to carry out, and a preliminary check should be done before a building control officer is called in. The equipment can often be obtained from tool hire companies.

Clearing blockages

To find a blockage in a drainage system, it is necessary to lift the inspection chamber lids. Chambers downstream of the obstruction will be empty, while the one directly upstream will fill up. If the blockage isn't cleared at once, other inspection chambers may become affected.

Drain rods can usually be obtained from a tool hire company. The important point to remember is that the rods must constantly be turned clockwise while pushing them into the drain, so that they are tightened. If you turn them anti-clockwise, they may come undone and be left in the drain.

Where possible, it is always better to rod the blockage from the empty inspection chamber. However, you must be prepared for a sudden gush of effluent when the blocked material is shifted.

Another approach is to hire a high-pressure water cleaner with a drain cleaning attachment. Various types are available, some with retrojets so that a cleaning unit will advance along the pipe unaided. The pressure created by one of these machines is usually sufficient to clear most blockages.

Pipe materials

There is much variety in the materials used for drainage systems. For instance, in older properties it's not unusual to find pipes in glazed stoneware, concrete, asbestos cement, pitch fibre and cast or spun iron; more recently, unplasticised polyvinylchloride (uPVC) has become very popular. Each product has advantages and disadvantages. For example, in areas where the ground is unstable, perhaps because of subsidence, iron is favoured because of its strength. However, this is not suitable if the soil is acidic or where there are sulphates in subsoil water, as these lead to pipe corrosion.

Inspection chambers

Changes have also occurred in the materials used for inspection chambers. The traditional practice of constructing an inspection chamber with a double skin of engineering bricks has given way to the use of prefabricated units. These include pre-formed concrete sections, which are built up to the required height and encased in concrete. Also popular are moulded uPVC inspection chambers, which are manufactured with a variety of coupling points to suit different pipe layouts.

A small pre-formed uPVC inspection chamber will be far quicker to install than a traditional brick-built structure.

Nowadays, most residential properties are served by either glazed stoneware or uPVC pipework. The comparative merits of these materials are set out in the accompanying table.

Glazed stoneware	uPVC (plastic)
Advantages ● High resistance to chemical attack. ● Easily connected using a flexible coupling. ● Bonds to concrete or mortar; at ICs, for instance. ● Less subject to expansion/contraction, and therefore suitable for encasing in concrete if laid in close proximity to foundations. **Disadvantages** ● User needs to hire a pipe cutter. ● Not available in long lengths. ● Internally smooth, but not as shiny as uPVC, and therefore less efficient when laid with a very gentle fall. ● Heavy to handle. ● More joints per run than with uPVC, so a greater risk of leakage; more labour intensive; and more breaks in the smooth internal surface.	**Advantages** ● Available as long pipes – typically 3 and 6m (10 and 20ft). ● Very light to handle. ● Fewer joints to construct in long sections. ● Easily cut to length with a saw. ● Very smooth internal surface; 100mm (4in) pipe can often be laid to a fall as gentle as 1:80. ● Special adaptors available for connection to other pipe materials. **Disadvantages** ● Inclined to flex and distort in uneven ground. ● Tends to become brittle in cold weather. ● More easily damaged when rodding. ● Subject to expansion/contraction, so only suitable for bedding in a gravel trench fill. ● Unsuitable near loadbearing foundations.

Joining pipes

Changes have also occurred in the methods used for joining lengths of pipe together. Originally, glazed stoneware pipes were made with a plain end (called a spigot) and a socket end, allowing the pipes to be fitted together to make a run. Mortar was used to seal each joint, but this could crack if there was any subsequent settlement. Modern pipes, whether stoneware or uPVC, are connected using flexible collar couplings, which include watertight rubber seals. Provided the pipe ends are smooth, these are easy to install. Moreover, they have the advantage of permitting a small degree of movement during settlement without failing.

Modern pipes are connected together by collar couplings, which incorporate watertight rubber sealing rings.

Adaptors

When building an extension, it is often necessary to extend the original drainage system. In some cases, this means laying new pipe runs in metric sizes that have to be connected to the existing pipes, which may have been made to imperial dimensions. It may also mean connecting a modern pipe, using collar couplings, into a system that was originally constructed using spigot-and-socket connections.

Fortunately, the manufacturers of modern drainage systems take account of this and include a variety of adaptor couplings in their product ranges. These usually include fittings that permit modern uPVC pipes to be connected to glazed stoneware products. There are also adaptors that permit metric-sized pipes to be coupled with older pipes made to imperial sizes.

An adaptor union enables modern 100mm metric uPVC pipe to be coupled to a 4in imperial cast-iron soil stack.

Construction techniques

When laying drainage pipes, the trenches should be at least 300mm (1ft) wider than the pipe diameter. If a deep trench is needed, it is essential to shore up the sides with timber to prevent collapse.

Normally, construction of a pipe run begins at the highest point, i.e. the section nearest the house. A joint collar should be fitted to the downstream end of the first pipe, which should be prevented from moving by driving in a peg at its upstream end.

Before fitting the joint, the end of the pipe should be smeared with a special collar lubricant. It is essential that the end of the pipe is smooth so that the rubber seal in the collar won't be damaged or displaced. The connectors fit tightly, and the easiest way to slide one onto a section of pipe is to lay the collar on a flat board and push the pipe down into it.

When a new section of pipe is ready to offer up, its end should be smeared with lubricant and pushed into the collar of the pipe in the trench. The run is laid in this manner until reaching a junction or an inspection chamber.

Achieving the correct fall

The best way of laying pipes is on a bed of gravel. Each should be laid temporarily at a steeper slope than needed. A spirit level and gauge board are rested on top of the pipe, which is lifted at the lower end until the correct fall is achieved. Then the gravel is packed in to maintain the angle.

It is essential to keep the gravel out of the collars. If one of the rubber seals becomes displaced, the joint will not be watertight.

In a large-scale project, the fall is checked by

A wooden block (arrowed), attached to the end of this spirit level, is cut to the correct size to produce a 1:40 fall on the pipe.

taking measurements from horizontal sight rails erected over the trench. These are all set at the same height, and measurements are taken between them and the pipes with a stick called a boning rod. On a smaller scale, the fall can be monitored by preparing a gauge board, which is wider at one end than the other to reflect the slope needed. Alternatively, a small block of wood can be fixed to one end of a spirit level.

Inspection chambers

An inspection chamber (IC) must be waterproof, and robust enough to withstand loads such as a car passing over it in a driveway. A deep IC may need a larger chamber at low level and step irons to allow safe entry.

An IC will incorporate a half-round gulley, or gulleys, the sides of which are shaped to contain the effluent; these sides are referred to as 'benching'.

If a uPVC unit with pre-moulded gulleys in the required layout is available, a considerable amount of time can be saved in construction. However, it must sit on a concrete base, and be surrounded with concrete for added strength.

The construction of brick ICs is labour intensive, but chambers made from pre-formed concrete sections are much quicker to build. Work starts by laying a 150mm (6in) concrete base on which half-round gulleys are laid. Any branch joins are formed, making certain that they are at an oblique angle in line with the flow, and that the fall is preserved.

Entry and exit pipes must be cut so that they just appear within a concrete section, and collars must be fitted outside the structure to allow for differential settlement between the pipe network and the IC.

Next, dry-mix concrete is heaped around the structure, and the first concrete section placed on top, carefully levelled, then left for the concrete to set. Benching is formed in concrete, rising vertically until level with the top of the entry/exit pipes, then being sloped outwards at a gradient of about 1:12. The surface of the benching should be topped with a 1:1 cement mortar mix and carefully trowelled to form a smooth, impervious surface. Thereafter, the remaining sections are bedded on mortar to the required height.

Inlet pipes are cut to terminate just inside the walls of this custom-built sectional inspection chamber.

Each of the pipes entering this sectional unit is fitted with a flexible coupling to allow for differential movement.

The top of a concrete inspection chamber is capped with a section that's moulded to accept the frame for the lid.

The finished structure should be surrounded with 150mm (6in) of concrete. A concrete capping can be fitted at the top, any small height adjustments being made with engineering bricks. Finally, an airtight frame is added and coated liberally with grease. The grease ensures an airtight seal with the lid and facilitates its removal at a later date. If an IC is on a patio or in a building, a pressed-steel self-fill lid can be added to match the surrounding surface.

Back inlet gulleys

Waste water from a sink or ground floor washbasin may pass into the drainage network via a back inlet gulley (BIG). Situated outside the house, this will be covered with a grid that provides a drainage point for rainwater from the surrounding surface.

The opening in a BIG would allow drain odours to escape were it not for the inclusion of a deep water trap. Moulded uPVC versions have an integral bottle trap, whereas clayware units usually need connecting to a separate P-trap.

Inserting new pipes

Occasionally, underground pipes may become damaged – through ground movement or having something like a fence spike driven into them. If blockages are common, this may be the cause.

Obviously, the damaged pipe must be replaced, but in an old system, a complete run may need replacing if matching units are unavailable. In a modern system with push-fit joints, the task is possible.

A collar is normally moulded with an integral pipe stop, which makes it difficult to insert a pipe into an existing run. The solution is to cut the stops from two collars with a sharp knife, and slide the collars onto the new pipe, flush with its ends. Then the pipe can be offered up to the run and the collars slid outwards to connect with the existing pipework. Make sure the collars are centralised over each joint.

Backfilling

A trench must not be backfilled until a building inspector has approved the work. Where pipes are laid on concrete, a partial concrete backfill may be needed. Normally, they are covered with 100mm (4in) of gravel. This is followed by 300mm (12in) of soft soil, which must be free of rubble and large lumps. The remaining top-up is less critical, but remember that settlement will occur, and it may be many months before the ground regains its stability.

Initially, the trench is backfilled with pea gravel before the addition of soft soil that is free of rocks and bricks.

Rainwater systems

Significant amounts of water are discharged from a roof in wet weather. This could be extremely inconvenient, so a system of collection, transport and dispersal is a fundamental requirement of any property. Since faulty guttering or downpipes can cause severe damage to a building, it is not surprising that the adequacy of the system is a requirement of the Building Regulations.

On older buildings, rainwater systems are often in need of repair or improvement. Curiously, on thatched buildings it is unusual to find any form of collection system, rainwater simply being allowed to fall from the eaves. Only in a few isolated instances will you find guttering on a thatched roof.

Important considerations

A rainwater drainage system should take into account the pitch of the roof, its overall size and the type of covering materials. This will have implications for the dimensions of eaves guttering and the number of downpipes required, together with their positions. For instance, if a single downpipe is placed centrally, the guttering can drain a roof area twice as great as it would if the downpipe was situated at one end of the run. This is because no section of guttering will ever hold more than half of the total discharge from the roof.

Other aspects of a system that determine efficiency include the slope, or fall, of the guttering. Whereas it's considered acceptable to construct eaves guttering completely level, it will be around 20 per cent more efficient if it is laid with a fall of 1:600, which equates to 25mm (1in) in 15m (50ft). Some gutter brackets used on older buildings even have a height adjustment facility to allow the fall to be set; these are normally bedded into a mortar joint, which will be more or less level.

Useful information

Information about design requirements is often given in the technical data sheets that accompany catalogues of rainwater goods. This information is very useful for anyone constructing a shed, porch or small extension. Alternatively, guidance is given in two other sources: a British Standard (BS 6367) and the Building Regulations.

The procedure involves calculating the 'effective design area' of the roof surface to be drained. On a flat roof, this is the same as the plan area shown on the drawings. On a pitched roof, the plan area has to be increased by a factor that is determined by the pitch of the roof:
● On a roof with a pitch of 45 degrees, the plan area must be multiplied by 1.4 to give the effective design area.

A single downpipe, placed centrally, will be able to drain a roof area that is twice as great as one where the downpipe is placed at the end of a guttering run.

Some support brackets can be adjusted to alter the height of the guttering and to adjust the fall. They are usually designed to be secured in a mortar joint and are used where no fascia board is fitted.

● On a roof with a pitch of 30 degrees, the factor to use is 1.15.

● On a roof with a pitch of 60 degrees, the factor to use is 2.00.

A full table of these factors is provided in the Building Regulations.

Deciding on the size

Knowledge of the effective roof area allows you to determine the size of guttering needed, together with the minimum diameter of the outlets. For example, a roof with an effective area not exceeding 18m² (200ft²) can be adequately served by 75mm (3in) gutter with a 50mm (2in) diameter outlet. A roof with an effective area up to 37m² (400ft²) can be effectively drained by 100mm (4in) gutter and a 63mm (2½in) outlet. However, there are other considerations to be taken into account.

These examples apply to guttering that is laid level; in practice, however, a fall is often preferred to ensure a more efficient rate of discharge. Sharp bends in a run of guttering also have an influence on performance. These have a detrimental effect because they slow down flow rates, leading to a greater likelihood in the build-up of water.

Downpipe positions

The number of downpipes and their positions are further factors that will influence the rate at which water is removed from the guttering. Moreover, the position of a downpipe also has implications for the design of the underground drainage system.

The design of a system isn't particularly complicated to work out if you are draining a simple roof. However, on larger projects, where greater quantities of storm water need to be dealt with, or on roofs of complex design, it is advisable to seek expert assistance. Rainwater goods can be surprisingly expensive, and if the system overflows due to bad design, remedial work may add even more to the total cost.

Sharp bends in a run of guttering will reduce the rate at which rainwater is discharged quite significantly.

Materials and maintenance

Although most modern rainwater systems are made of plastic, over the years, a variety of other materials has been used. Their merits vary, and some may need periodic maintenance. If repairs are necessary, the method used will depend on the material.

Wood

On some older properties, eaves guttering is made from moulded timber sections, referred to as 'spouting'. This is quite common on terraced housing built at the turn of the century. In good condition, the material is robust and seldom becomes damaged if a ladder is rested against the guttering. It needs periodic attention, and in dry weather, generous coats of a bitumen-based mastic or paint should be applied to the internal surfaces to provide protection. If the wood starts to rot, however, the only answer is to replace it completely.

Cast-iron

Bitumen coatings are also suitable for preserving cast-iron guttering. If a joint leaks, this can often be cured by applying bitumen mastic inside the joint. If this fails, the old connecting bolt should be sawn off, and the joint remade with a new bolt, sandwiching a fresh layer of mastic between the two sections.

Asbestos cement

Although popular a number of years ago, asbestos

Wooden guttering is fitted on may be found on some terraced properties; it needs periodic treatment with bitumen.

cement is a brittle material that is easily damaged. In addition, concerns over the effects of asbestos on health would commend its replacement. Before undertaking this yourself, it would be advisable to contact your local authority to discuss its removal and disposal.

Lead

Lead rainwater systems are comparatively rare on ordinary domestic buildings, but lead may be used to line box-section gutters and valley gutters, which are constructed where two adjacent roof slopes intersect.

Replacing a lining isn't difficult, but repair work to moulded lead components requires specialised skills. However, some of the more ornate components can be purchased in glass fibre replica form.

Aluminium

In recent times, rainwater systems cast in aluminium have become popular. These can be manufactured in traditional profiles, but without the attendant problems of maintenance. In some instances, the materials can be coloured during manufacture to produce attractive, as well as long lasting, components. This material has much to commend it, but unfortunately it's quite costly.

Another approach to aluminium systems is to have guttering specially fabricated on site. Contractors have machines that convert sheet aluminium into continuous runs of guttering in the required profile. At junctions, the unions are caulked with mastic, and a mechanical joint may be used as well. Along the gutter itself, the lack of joints is a particular advantage. This system is almost maintenance-free.

Plastic

Advantages of uPVC rainwater goods include the fact that any profile can be easily moulded, and the material isn't subject to corrosion or problems due to pollution. In addition, the products can be pre-coloured and need minimal maintenance.

However, over a long period, colours can fade, some plastics become brittle and shatter easily, while joints on eaves guttering sometimes develop leaks. Joint failure is partly caused by the problem of thermal movement. Plastic expands considerably in hot weather, and it's not unusual to hear rainwater systems creaking in the sun as pressure is put on the brackets and joints. Extremes of seasonal temperature aggravate this problem, and stresses occur in the joints between drain outlets and at all connectors linking sections of gutter. In time, the rubber seals cease to give a water-tight union, and the gutter may drip quite badly.

Any attempt to remedy this will require a sealant that is very flexible. In practice, a long-term cure may not be found, and the only satisfactory answer is to replace each of the faulty unions.

On downpipes, a more common problem is impact damage. A patch-up operation can be accomplished using bitumen-backed foil, which is used as an inexpensive alternative to lead flashing. The bitumen has impressive powers of adhesion, provided the plastic surface is completely dry, and products of this type may successfully cure a leak in a downpipe for ten or more years. Unfortunately, it lacks the flexibility needed to cover over a join in a gutter union.

This plastic downpipe was damaged as a result of receiving an accidental knock from a ladder.

A successful repair can be effected by wrapping the pipe with a piece of bitumen-backed foil used for flashing.

▶ **SEE PAGE 40 FOR STEP-BY-STEP INSTRUCTIONS ON FITTING PLASTIC GUTTERING**

Matching new with old

In some improvement work, the rainwater system of a new extension may have to be linked to the system of the parent building. Fortunately, several manufacturers of modern rainwater goods offer adaptors for this purpose. These are also useful if a new run of guttering is fitted to a terraced property and needs to be connected to the systems on each side. In many cases, the link will be between an older cast-iron system and a modern product made from uPVC.

In a few situations, a suitable connector may not be available, but it may be possible to fabricate a connection in situ, using the type of glass fibre repair kit sold in car accessory shops. However, this is not an easy task, and differential expansion between plastic and another material may cause leakage later. In this case, the only effective solution is to replace the entire system.

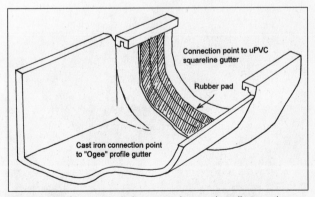

Connection point to uPVC squareline gutter

Rubber pad

Cast iron connection point to "Ogee" profile gutter

Several manufacturers include gutter adaptors that allow modern plastic guttering to be connected to an old cast-iron system.

Problems may also occur in matching new guttering with old downpipe, although quite often the gutter outlet will fit inside the downpipe to give a satisfactory join.

Preventing blockages

Rainwater systems of properties that have been built near trees can suffer from persistent blockages, particularly during the autumn. Dead leaves not only settle in the guttering, but they also accumulate at the heads of downpipes, preventing rainwater from flowing away. The resulting overflow can, at the very least, be annoying, but more seriously, it may cause damp problems by running down the walls of the property.

To prevent a blockage in a downpipe, the normal precaution is to fit 'balloons' in all the gutter outlet points. These are made from galvanised wire, and look very similar to a balloon in shape. Moulded plastic versions are also available, but look rather different. The installation of a balloon undoubtedly prevents leaves from entering a downpipe, but they tend to collect around it and, together with other waterborne debris, will eventually block it completely, causing an overflow. In consequence, this build-up will need clearing, and regular inspections are often necessary – especially during the autumn. However, this periodic chore is better than dismantling a downpipe in an attempt to

remedy an unreachable blockage. A few systems include an inspection point that can be fitted into downpipes. This features a screw cap that allows access to the interior of the pipe. Regrettably, this is only a feature of a few ranges.

Gutter mesh

Another way to keep leaves out of the system is to install strips of a mesh material along the guttering. Several versions are available and can be purchased from builders' merchants and major DIY stores. Made from moulded plastic, the grid is either held flat on top of the guttering with special clips, or is simply bent so that the edges fit inside the gutter. In the latter case, the spring in the material is sufficient to hold it in place.

Water drains through the holes in the mesh, whereas leaves remain on the top, dry out and blow away. Like the balloon, however, periodic cleaning is advisable, as the holes in the mesh may become clogged with silt from the roof.

It is easy to clear blockages where a shoe is fitted at the bottom of a downpipe, directly above an open drain.

In a closed downpipe system, some manufacturers provide an access point to help when clearing blockages in downpipes.

Underground dispersal and soakaways

The final removal of rainwater from the guttering and downpipes is through an underground network of pipes, similar to the soil pipe systems described on pages 28-33. The same type of uPVC or clay pipes are normally used, having a diameter of either 75mm (3in) or 100mm (4in), and are laid with a fall of not less than 1:100. Occasionally, 150mm (6in) pipe is used to cope with larger quantities, or where it is necessary for the fall to be less than 1:100. These are connected to a stormwater drainage arrangement that generally discharges into a nearby watercourse. Further information on the requirements for rainwater drainage is given in the Building Regulations.

Combined system

Only in older properties is rainwater discharged into the same system that takes sewage. Nowadays, there must be two completely distinct drainage systems. One of the clues that a property has what is referred to as a 'combined system' is the inclusion of a hopper head in a downpipe. If this is inspected carefully, it can often be seen to act as a collecting point for both a rainwater pipe and waste water pipes running from a bath and washbasin.

Constructing a soakaway

In some areas, stormwater drains are not provided, and a combined system is not permitted because it would lead to unacceptable surges at the local water treatment works whenever there's a storm. In this situation, the only solution is to construct a soakaway and lay the pipes to it.

The success of a soakaway is dependent, in part, on the nature of the soil and the height of the water table. In clay areas, soakaways are nowhere near as successful as in areas with sandy soils. Moreover, in an area with a high water table, water from the surrounding soil may drain into a deep soakaway when the intention is for the reverse to take place.

Although it is possible to install purpose-made concrete chambers with drain holes in the walls, many builders construct a rubble-filled soakaway.

Whichever method is chosen, the construction must be situated some distance from the foundations of a building; this will be specified by your local building control office and checked during building operations by a building control surveyor.

The method for constructing a rubble-filled soakaway is as follows:

● A hole of the appropriate size for the roof area and the volume of discharge is dug at some distance from the foundations of the house. This is linked to the foot of the downpipe by a trench, and the necessary underground pipes laid. Remember that the pipes must have a fall towards the soakaway for the water to drain away efficiently.

● The hole for the soakaway should be filled up to the level of the trench with large pieces of masonry, brickbats or rock to prevent the sides of the hole from caving in. However, the gaps between the pieces should be as large as possible, since these will become filled with water, prior to its final dispersal into the surrounding ground through natural seepage. Therefore, the individual pieces of rubble should be quite large.

● The final pipe should be laid so that it will discharge roughly into the centre of the soakaway. Then more rubble is added to cover the pipe. Take care when placing this around the end of the pipe, arranging it so that any debris carried along by the water will fall down into the pit, rather than accumulate around the point of discharge. Failing to do this may mean that the end of the pipe will eventually become blocked, preventing the water from draining away effectively.

● The pipe trench should be backfilled, surrounding the pipe with a layer of gravel before adding the soil.

● Finally, cover the top of the soakaway with about 100mm (4in) of gravel, which should be followed by a sheet of heavy-gauge polythene prior to the placement of at least 100mm (4in) of concrete. Once the concrete has been allowed to cure, you can add an appropriate depth of topsoil for plants or a grassed area to cover the construction and hide it from view.

Fitting guttering and downpipes

Given safe access, installing a rainwater system is a relatively simple task. However, some roofs are quite intricate in design, and linking the guttering and downpipe may not always be straightforward. Fortunately, most rainwater systems include a range of fittings that make this possible.

The methods of connecting sections of guttering and downpipe vary slightly from one manufacturer to another, but the basic principles of installing a system are the same:

● Assuming that the guttering is to be attached to a fascia board, check that the board is level so that its lower edge can be used as a reference point for setting the fall to the outlet.

● At the high point of the run, offer up a section of guttering, with a support clip attached, to see how close it can be positioned to the tiles or slates. Mark the clip's position on the fascia and measure this distance from the lower edge of the board.

● Measure the distance to the outlet point, and make another pencil mark to give a fall of 25mm (1in) in 15m (50ft), using the measurement at the high point of the run as a guide. Also bear in mind that the roof drip shouldn't be greater than 50mm (2in).

● Run a string line between the two pencil marks. This will indicate the required height of the clips along the run. Their recommended spacing will be given in the product data sheets; a maximum 1m (3ft) spacing is normal.

● Screw the clips to the fascia. Where there is no fascia board, special brackets are needed for fixing into a mortar course; these include a gutter height adjuster. Another type screws onto the rafters.

● Finally, assemble the sections of guttering and fit them to the clips and outlet. If you are installing uPVC rainwater goods in cold weather, you may find it takes a surprising amount of thumb pressure to make the connections in gutter unions and outlets.

● On a modern roof with sarking felt laid below the tiles to form a secondary barrier, 50mm (2in) of the felt should protrude so that it can be dressed down into the guttering.

Eaves overhang

Downpipes in uPVC slot together without the need for adhesive. If there's an eaves overhang, a swan neck (sometimes called an offset) needs to be prepared. Manufacturer's leaflets sometimes give advice on how to calculate the length of pipe needed for the offset, but you can usually work this out by offering-up a short length of pipe together with angle connectors and assessing the dimensions in situ.

On a house with a tile-hung upper storey, a smaller offset is needed at the bottom of the tiled area so that the downpipe can be attached to the wall. This can usually be constructed using a pair of angle connectors.

SAFE ACCESS

☐ When installing a rainwater system, safe access is essential, and working from a ladder is dangerous. A tower or scaffolding provides a much better work platform if the building is of two storeys or more. However, on a bungalow, a platform made of boards and trestles may be adequate.

3 The distance between the bottom of the bracket and the lower edge of the fascia board is checked. Then a string line is stretched along the run to show the required fall.

7 Lengths of guttering should be joined with gutter unions. Moulded-in stop marks (arrowed) show the limit of gutter insertion, allowing room for expansion movement.

TOOLS AND MATERIALS

☐ Spirit level
☐ Tape measure
☐ Pencil
☐ Hammer
☐ Stringline and nails
☐ Bradawl
☐ Screwdriver
☐ Hacksaw
☐ Electric drill and masonry bit
☐ Rustproof screws
☐ Wall plugs
☐ Guttering, downpipe and fittings

1 First, the lower edge of the fascia board is checked with the aid of a spirit level. It must be level to act as a good reference point from which to take measurements for fitting the brackets.

2 With a bracket temporarily clipped to a piece of guttering, the high point of the run is marked on the fascia board. Hold the guttering so that it is just beneath the edge of the tiles.

4 At the other end of the fascia board, a temporary gutter clip is offered up alongside the outlet section so that their positions can be checked against the string line.

5 With its position established, the outlet section should be screwed firmly to the fascia board. Use rustproof screws, starting them by pushing a bradawl into the wood.

6 Screw intermediate brackets to the fascia board at the recommended intervals, setting the bottom of each against the string line. In this way, there will be a steady fall to the outlet.

8 With all the brackets, unions and outlet fixed to the fascia board, the guttering itself can be offered up. Slip the back edge under the clip, pull down and snap the front of the clip over the top.

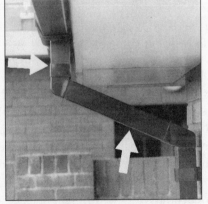

9 The final job is to attach the downpipe to the wall and connect it to the guttering. Short lengths of pipe (arrowed) and angle sections are used to form a swan neck offset.

10 When installing a downpipe on the side of a tile-hung house, the necessary offset can usually be formed using a pair of angle connectors (arrowed).

Brickwork and render

An external wall must be able to withstand the weather. In many instances, however, the appearance of a wall is important, too. The visual impact of brickwork, stonework or render can be notable, and flaws are not easy to hide. Moreover, when repair work is carried out, it is important to retain the character of a building, especially if it has particular architectural merit or historic significance.

Sources of help

The information contained in this section covers the more common tasks that need to be carried out. However, if problems arise, help can come from a variety of sources:

● The Brick Development Association (BDA) is a most important point of contact and publishes a valuable range of leaflets and technical booklets.

● Information booklets are often available from manufacturers' technical departments, as well.

● If a repair job requires replacing bricks, and a match is required, a visit should be made to a brick library. These collections of bricks can sometimes be found at brickyards and good builders' merchants, but one of the most impressive displays is at The Building Centre in London.

● If the bricks required are no longer made, there are companies that will make replicas, but this can be expensive. A less costly solution is to look for a company that specialises in selling reclaimed building materials, as they may have similar bricks taken from a demolished property of the same age.

● When working with natural stone, finding matching material is often difficult, particularly when local quarries have been worked out. However, there are good examples of reconstituted stone that provide a useful alternative.

● Guidance on rendering materials is available from the British Cement Association (BCA). The manufacturers of specialised products may also be worth contacting.

Types of brick

In broad terms, there are five types of brick, most of which are made from clay:

Engineering These have a dense, semi-vitreous character to withstand the heavy compressive loading when supporting machinery. Their level of water absorption is negligible. This type of brick is seldom used in domestic building, except to provide a decorative course in a contrasting colour. In some buildings, they may have been used as a DPC.

Common A general-purpose brick with no particular quality of strength, density or weather resistance. These bricks have no decorative qualities either, although they were used as facing bricks for inexpensive Victorian housing.

Fair faced common To add to their decorative quality, some common bricks are manufactured with a special facing on one long side (stretcher) and one short side (header). These may have a textured sand finish; others have an additional colour added to the facing. This type of brick can look attractive as long as the decorative facing isn't chipped by accident.

Facing These bricks are manufactured from a clay of distinctive colour to maintain their appearance throughout the unit. A variety of textured finishes is also available.

Hand-made The traditional method of manufacture involved pressing clay into a mould by hand. Although this is a slow process, the surface of the brick is notable for its creases and textured finish. Hand-made bricks are expensive, but are justifiably popular for internal feature walls.

A more detailed classification could include bricks with a ceramic facing, stock bricks and bricks of different density and durability. In addition, some bricks are made with a recess known as a 'frog', some have perforations, while others are solid. It should be stressed that the term 'brick' refers to the size of the unit, rather than its constituents.

Weather damage

Good building practice ensures that brickwork is spared the persistent passage of rainwater by the construction of overhangs. These include projecting roof structures, sills on window and door frames, and copings that act as cappings on garden walls. However, these features will not keep driving rain from the face of a wall, and on particularly exposed sites, a good builder would select bricks that provided the best resistance to frost damage.

In addition, in cavity wall construction, butterfly ties should always be placed with the wire twist facing downwards to shed water, rather than allow it to percolate into the brickwork. It's not unusual for moisture to develop in a cavity, which is why modern practice ensures the inclusion of weep holes in perpendicular joints as drainage outlets.

It should be emphasised that some bricks will absorb more rain than others, and in winter this can lead to damage. When freezing water expands, some bricks will begin to crumble, whereas with other types, the face will start to fall away in layers. This process is known as 'spalling'.

The problem of spalling seldom occurs with harder masonry, such as engineering bricks; softer bricks, on the other hand, are much more prone to attack. For instance, facing bricks with a wire-cut rustic finish are more likely to hold droplets of water. This is aggravated if they are not laid with the feathered cut on the face pointing downwards. Some hand-made decorative bricks also have deep fissures created when the clay is pushed into the moulds; these act as water traps. In some cases, hand-made bricks are best reserved for interior feature walls only.

Curing the problem

Where a brick has crumbled badly, one answer is to cut it away and replace it. Use a sharp cold chisel, as this is less likely to shake the surrounding structure than a bolster, and its tip will remove small fragments at a time. Greedy 'bites' invariably lead to wider damage; patience is preferable to brute force. The replacement should be laid on a bed of fresh mortar and surrounded with more mortar by pressing it into the joints with an offcut of wood.

If, on the other hand, only the face of a brick is damaged, an approved remedy is to cut away a shallow recess, about 30mm (1¼in) deep. This can be filled with a small section of brick called a 'slip'. You can buy ready-made slips from major DIY stores; sometimes they are used to clad plaster internal walls to give the impression of an exposed brick finish. Alternatively, you can cut them yourself, using a special brick saw. Once prepared, the slip can be affixed using mortar.

The twist on a butterfly wall tie should always point downwards to shed any water that may accumulate on it.

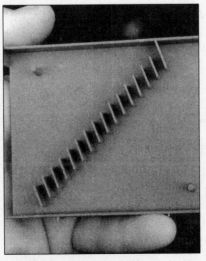
Ready-made weep holes, built into perpendicular joints in brickwork, will help to shed water from the cavity.

A remarkable case of failing brickwork, where frost and rainwater has caused bricks to spall and crumble.

Mortar

The appearance and sound structure of brickwork is dependent on the mortar. This can take many forms depending on its constituents, the main one being sand. For brickwork, the sand should have graded particles, and it is often referred to as builders' sand, as opposed to sharp sand, which is coarser and more suitable for concrete. In new building, soft sand should not be used for mortar because its fine silt content leads to shrinking when it sets. However, for repointing existing brickwork, a soft washed sand is more suitable.

Variable colour

Since sand is a natural product, its colour can vary considerably depending on the region from which it comes. Where consistency in new work is important, this has to be taken into account. In properties built in the early part of this century, or before, lime was added to sand to make a mortar mix. Today, lime is not considered suitable because it is weak and sets slowly. However, it can be purchased in small quantities for renovation work on old buildings.

The modern binding constituent is ordinary Portland cement (OPC), and a typical mix for new work using clay bricks is 1 part cement and 3 parts sand (by volume). This produces a strong, durable mix with good frost resistance when set. However, it is also brittle, and in some circumstance a small amount of lime is added to produce a less rigid mortar that is less likely to develop cracks due to thermal movement. A typical mortar mix for clay

bricks is 1 part OPC, ½ part lime and 4 parts sand.

A considerably less durable mix, is 1 part cement to 6 parts sand. This would be suitable for brickwork that is sheltered from the weather. A weak mix of 1 part cement to 7-8 parts sand is recommended when working with calcium silicate bricks, but these are less common than the clay type.

Plasticiser

When using ordinary Portland cement with sand, many bricklayers add a mortar plasticiser, which adds tiny air bubbles to the mix. This is known as air-entrainment, and the resulting mortar has a creamy constituency, making it easier to use. Plasticiser also gives a degree of frost resistance during the setting period, which is helpful when building in winter.

Mineral filler

Masonry cement can also be used for mortar. It is specially manufactured using ordinary Portland cement with a 25 per cent addition of a mineral filler. The filler introduces air into the mortar to improve its workability, in much the same manner as air-entrainment is achieved using a plasticiser.

When selecting a mix for new work, consideration should be given to the type of brick, the likelihood of thermal movement, and the degree of exposure to the weather. A selection of suitable mixes is shown in the table below.

Mortar mixes

Information supplied by the British Cement Association.

Mortar type and suitability	Non air-entrained mortar cement:lime:sand	Air-entrained mortar masonry cement:sand	Air-entrained mortar cement:sand with plasticiser
Strongest and most durable	1:¼:4 or 1:¼:4½	1:2½ or 1:3½	1:3 or 1:4
Reasonably durable	1:1:5 or 1:1:6	1:4 or 1:5	1:5 or 1:6
Weak mix suitable for calcium silicate bricks	1:2:8 or 1:2:9	1:5½ or 1:6½	1:7 or 1:8

Repointing

In time, mortar joints may deteriorate due to frost, water damage and structural movement. The solution is to repoint them.

● Only mix small batches of mortar at a time. If a batch starts to dry, throw it away; don't be tempted to add more water.

● Select a mortar mix to suit the bricks:

Normal exposure 1:1:6 (Cement:lime:sand)

Soft facing bricks 1:2:9 (Cement:lime:sand)

Hard dense bricks in exposed sites 1:¼:3 (Cement:lime:sand)

● Soft, washed sand is best for pointing; avoid sharp sand.

● Using mortar pigments can lead to problems in maintaining colour consistency, especially with the need to mix many small batches. It is better to use a pre-coloured sand.

TOOLS AND MATERIALS

- ☐ Plugging chisel
- ☐ Club hammer
- ☐ Old paint brush
- ☐ Bucket
- ☐ Hawk
- ☐ Pointing trowel
- ☐ Metal tube
- ☐ Stiff-bristled brush
- ☐ Cement, lime and sand

1 Remove all moss and other vegetative matter, then rake out the vertical joints (perpends) to a depth of 10-20mm (⅜-¾in). Use a plugging chisel and a club hammer, or even a mini grinder.

2 Remove the old mortar from the horizontal (bedding) joints in the same manner. Brush any dust and debris from the joints and faces of the bricks with an old paint brush.

3 Wet the joints with clean water. In dry weather, the bricks can be slightly dampened, too, but don't soak them. This prevents them from absorbing water from the mortar too quickly.

4 Mix a small quantity of mortar on a board or hawk. Flatten it and slice off a small strip with a pointing trowel. Scoop it up on the underside of the trowel's blade.

5 Press the strip of mortar firmly into a perpend, filling it completely. Treat several perpends in this way, then fill some of the horizontal bedding joints in the same manner.

6 When several joints have been filled, give them a rounded finish by drawing a metal tube along them. Allow the mortar to harden slightly, then brush any splashes from the bricks.

Cracks in brickwork

Structural damage to brickwork usually occurs for two reasons. A failed foundation will cause settlement, and cracks will appear in the mortar joints, or even the bricks. Similar damage may occur through thermal movement. In the latter case, however, the structure is not at risk – although the cracks must be monitored.

In the case of a failed foundation, a surveyor should be consulted. There are various reasons for failed foundations, but one of the most common is a clay subsoil, which can shrink and expand quite considerably depending on its moisture content. This will have a destructive effect on inadequate foundations, which are common in buildings built in the last century. However, even modern properties fail: concrete cannot flex with soil movements, so if it lacks sufficient depth, it will crack.

A failed foundation is a serious matter, but a building can often be given a new, deeper foundation by underpinning. However, this is a costly and complex task that requires expertise.

Curing cracks

Shrinkage cracks can be dealt with in a variety of ways, some being cosmetic repairs rather than long-

Applying thixotropic resin grout to an area of substantial cracking. (Photograph courtesy Sealocrete PLA Limited)

term cures. One answer is to cut away the cracked bricks and replace them with new ones. Problems occur, however, if no matching bricks are available. In this case, a remedy is to drill a series of holes along the crack, and inject them with a special resin grout. The face of the brick is then repaired with colour-matched mortar.

Damaged mortar courses can be repaired in a similar fashion. This produces a permanent, structural repair, which is difficult to detect once the joint has been finished with colour-matched mortar.

Removing stains

A variety of brick cleaners is available for removing mortar and paint stains. These contain significant amounts of acid, so it is essential to follow the maker's instructions. You must wear appropriate clothing and eye protection. When using a product of this type, try it on a small test area first, before moving on to a larger area.

In some cases, a stained area will need treating with a stiff bristle brush, given that dried stains can be exceptionally stubborn. However, the use of wire brushes or other abrasive tools should be avoided, as they will damage the surface of the bricks.

Chemical treatments must not be used to remove efflorescence – the white salts that often appear on new brickwork – and it is often best to allow it to weather away naturally. Since the deposit appears after the bricks and mortar have dried out, excessive

water should not be used, since this merely allows the salts to be re-absorbed. At the very most, only a damp sponge should be used, rinsing it often. The best advice is to remove the salts with a stiff brush.

Lime stains on brickwork are usually an indication that mortar, or nearby concrete, is repeatedly getting wet. The discolouration can often be removed with a bristle brush, but over a longer period, it must be treated with a proprietary acid cleaner.

When it comes to removing grime from the face of a building, high-pressure hosing is preferable to sandblasting. The former is less likely to damage the surface, although the absorption of large amounts of water may produce efflorescence. High-pressure cleaners are available from most tool hire companies. Take care, however, since a powerful water jet can smash glass and cause injuries.

Repairing rendered walls

Render is a thin layer of mortar applied to an exterior wall to provide protection and a form of decoration. Various finishes are used, including textured or painted surfaces and pebbledash.

Problems occur, however, if a crack allows rainwater to penetrate the render; subsequent frost action will soon pull sections away from the masonry below.

Rendering a large area is a skilled job, but patching is less difficult if you follow these steps:

● Use a bolster and club hammer to break away loose render, wearing eye protection to guard against flying fragments. Cut back to a sound base and, if the surface is smooth, add score marks to improve the bond. Brush away all dust and debris.

● Coat the surface with a 1:6 solution of PVA bonding agent and clean water.

● Prepare a 1:1:6 mortar of Portland cement, hydrated lime and sharp sand. Alternatively, you can buy bagged pre-mixed render in small quantities from DIY stores. Add water to produce a stiff mortar mix, which can be shaped on the board with a trowel. If it slumps, it is too wet.

● In dry conditions, flick water onto the wall with a paint brush. Then apply the mortar with a rectangular steel trowel. The correct technique is to

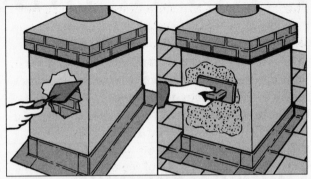

If the area is quite small, the render can be applied with a normal bricklayer's trowel. On larger repairs, use a rectangular steel trowel.

place the mortar on a hawk, tip it towards you and push up with the trowel at the same time to scoop the mortar off. Press the mortar into the wall before smoothing it off and levelling it with the surrounding render, using a straight wooden batten.

● Various finishes can be added when the render has begun to harden. A metal trowel will produce a smooth finish suitable for painting, whereas a wooden float produces a rougher texture. In some cases, the area might be treated with a plastic foam to create texture, or it can be scored with a broom. The addition of pebbles pressed into the mortar is another popular finish.

Repairing stonework

Compared with repairing bricks, repairing stonework is less straightforward. Some stones have notoriously poor weather resistance, and may also be attacked by airborne industrial chemicals.

One method of remedying a crumbling stone is to replace it, but this presumes that quarries still produce material that matches. In other instances, material can be brought to the surface when foundations are dug for new buildings. A belt of stone just below the surface can yield useful material for renovation work.

Some builders' merchants sell stone, too, and if the colour is not an accurate match, it is better to distribute pieces randomly across the exterior of a building, rather than to focus on one area in particular. Another possibility is to use manufactured reconstituted stone. The better quality products of

this type are made to match the natural stone found in particular regions of the country and can be quite effective.

Whatever repair strategy is used, it is inevitable that on an older property, an area of repair will stand inappropriately proud of the original masonry. Equally inevitable is the fact that it takes time for repaired areas to weather and to gain the colourful addition of lichens. However, a useful technique for hastening the growth of vegetative matter on fresh stone is to coat the surfaces with a dilute solution of water and cow dung. This should be brushed onto the surface when rain is not expected and left to dry. The liquid manure will encourage the growth of various moulds, thus speeding the ageing process of the stonework. This method can also be used to tone down new areas of roof tiles.

Exterior timber

Wood is used on the exterior of most houses. On some properties, the material may only be used to finish off the edges of the roof, whereas other houses can have sizeable areas of cladding or other decorative features. Wood is also commonly used for doors and the frames of windows. However, wood is vulnerable to weather damage, and in all cases, it's essential to ensure that it is carefully and regularly maintained, using appropriate paint, varnish or preservative treatments.

Timber treatments

Traditionally, oil-based paint has been used for the preservation of cladding and fascia boards. However, in the last 20 years, wood stain preservative has become a popular alternative. Not only does this finish look attractive, but also subsequent coats can be added without the elaborate preparation normally needed if conventional paint has been used.

Sometimes marine varnishes are used on cladding to emphasise the grain of the wood. However, the choice of varnish needs careful consideration, because some products create a film on the surface that prevents the wood from breathing. Where nails puncture its surface, rainwater finds a way through, but it becomes trapped below the skin, leading to discolouration of the timber.

Paint and preservative stains are undoubtedly successful, provided the surface is re-treated at regular intervals. However, if rot starts to develop, replacing sections of timber can sometimes be deferred by using chemical injection products. These include:

● A brush-applied wood hardening chemical that reinforces decayed wood and adds a seal against further moisture penetration.
● A filler paste that's applied to a damaged area with a palette knife. This dries to provide a surface that can be planed, sanded and shaped.
● Preservative tablets which, when placed into pre-drilled holes, dissolve and release a powerful preservative that spreads through the wood fibres.

These treatments can be used on fascia boards, particularly at corners or joins in a run of boarding where deterioration often appears first.

Preservative wood stains are easy to apply, and subsequent coats can be added without too much preparation of the surfaces.

Replacing fascias, soffits and barge-boards

Any substantial damage in exterior timber may need cutting out and replacing with a new piece. If this isn't feasible, the whole board may need renewing.

In either case, it is important to identify the way in which the original structure was built:

● Fascias are horizontal boards that run along the eaves; they may be attached directly to the face brickwork, or in the case of a boxed eaves construction, nailed to the trimmed ends of the rafters. With the aid of a wrecking bar, a bolster and a cold chisel, the boards can be prised away.

● A soffit fits between the lower edge of the fascia and the wall in a boxed eaves construction. It may be of tongued-and-grooved board or exterior-grade plywood. If the soffit is made from asbestos panels, take great care when removing them. Also, discuss its disposal with your local authority.

Where a sheet material has been used, the fascia is often grooved to support the outer edge of the soffit. In this case, replacement fascias need to be similarly prepared. A groove can be formed by passing the board across a circular saw blade several times, progressively altering the side fence until the groove is of the correct width. Alternatively, use a grooving plane. If you don't have the tools for this, the timber supplier may be able to do it for you.

If you decide to replace a large amount of timber, it's wise to upgrade the roof by adding ventilation at the same time. Strip ventilators are available that have a housing groove for the soffit board, removing

The barge-board (arrowed) finishes the verges of a gable-ended roof. An additional support board is often fitted behind.

the need to cut one along the fascia boards.

● Barge-boards are the angled timber facings that run along the verges of a gable-ended roof. They may be nailed directly to the brickwork, or fixed to noggings that form the roof overhang. A length of timber, approximately 100 x 35mm (4 x 1½in), may be fixed to the noggings first to provide a sturdier fixing for the barge-board.

A barge-board is seldom grooved to accept the soffit. Normally, the soffit will be cut accurately to width and nailed to the underside of the noggings.

Adequate support

If you decide that a repair only calls for a short section of board to be replaced, instead of a complete run, you must ensure that it will be supported by the structure behind. The new piece should also be fixed using an exterior-grade wood adhesive and nails. You may need to add a wooden bearer behind the joints in the old and new board.

If you are replacing a complete board, it should be mated to any adjacent board with a scarf joint. This involves mitring the end of each board so that they overlap when joined. If shrinkage occurs later, it will not open up a visible gap.

Whether you replace a short section or an entire length, the board should be attached using lost-head round wire nails. These are easy to punch below the surface; when the holes are filled, and fresh paint applied, the fixings will be invisible.

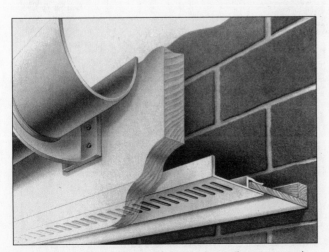

If you have to replace soffits and fascias, strip ventilators are worth fitting. (Illustration courtesy Rytons Building Products Ltd)

Timber cladding

Some houses have their external walls clad with timber boards mounted on a sub-frame. Occasionally, oak or cedar shingles may be used instead of boards. Both types of finish can improve the weather protection of the building and add charm to its appearance, but if you are considering such an addition to your home, you should discuss it first with your local building control officer.

The Building Regulations require that the external construction of the building resists the spread of fire over the walls, and from one building to another. By adding timber cladding to an external brick wall, you will alter its fire characteristics. In some circumstances, this alteration might constitute an unacceptable hazard.

A suitable material

If the building control officer accepts your plans for timber cladding, you need to decide on a suitable material. A good timber merchant should be able to supply boards with a variety of profiles, such as feather-edged boards or shiplap rebated boards. These need to be fixed to a timber sub-frame. Furthermore, it is normal to lay the boarding on a base of bitumen felt to give greater weather protection. Annular shanked nails are recommended for securing the boards, because they grip the wood more effectively. Moreover, if these are of the lost-head type, they can be punched below the surface and concealed with filler.

All the wood used for the job should be treated well with preservative; you may be able to have the supplier do this for you before delivery, using a pressure impregnation system, which is preferable. If this is not possible, you should brush a liberal coat of preservative onto each piece, making sure that it is worked into all endgrain and treating each piece before it is installed.

Once the cladding is in place, you can either paint it or treat it with a wood stain. Bear in mind that once you have decided on a finish, it will be almost impossible to alter it at a later date.

A timber merchant or building merchant may also be able to supply cedar shingles, which need nailing to horizontal battens over a layer of felt, much like tiling a roof.

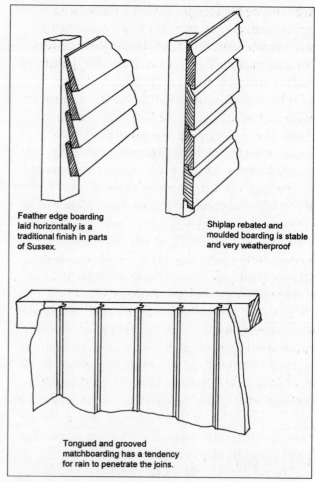

Feather edge boarding laid horizontally is a traditional finish in parts of Sussex.

Shiplap rebated and moulded boarding is stable and very weatherproof

Tongued and grooved matchboarding has a tendency for rain to penetrate the joins.

Different types of boarding are available for cladding, and a good timber merchant should be able to supply a variety to choose from.

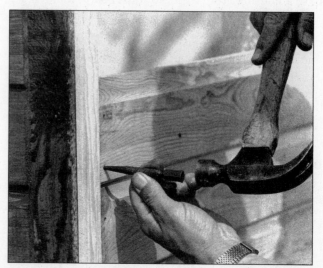

Nails holding wooden boards in place should be driven below the surface with a punch. Then the holes can be filled to conceal them.

Plastic fascia and barge-board systems

Recognising the fact that exterior timber needs regular maintenance to preserve its appearance, many builders fit uPVC and similar plastic-based products instead. These are available for finishing timbers around roofs, as well as for cladding.

Light, pre-coloured, maintenance-free boards are manufactured in various profiles for installation as fascia boards, barge-boards and soffits. Special fixings are used, including stainless steel nails, some of which have a coloured cap to match the board.

White is one the most popular colours for this type of material, but manufacturers usually offer a choice of colours.

Installation is straightforward, provided the manufacturer's instructions are followed. Good support is needed, and allowance must be made to accommodate thermal movement. Expansion gaps are generally required in long runs of fascia board, and a special capping is fitted to cover the spaces between adjacent sections.

One of the useful features of these products is the availability of a moulded soffit that incorporates a ventilation grille. This enables a roof void to be

A range of impressive soffit and fascia finishes in uPVC is available for use instead of wooden boards. (Photograph courtesy Swish Home Improvements)

ventilated when this is required by Building Regulations, but eliminates the need to add separate ventilation components.

These specially-moulded materials can be cut and drilled using normal woodworking tools. Once fitted, they only need occasional washing to keep an attractive appearance.

Plastic wall cladding

Interlocking moulded cladding boards are also popular because of their maintenance-free qualities. In addition, uPVC offers good insulation and can improve the thermal efficiency of an external wall.

Installation involves constructing a sub-frame of preservative-treated battens that are screwed to the wall. During installation, the battens need to be checked with a straight-edge and carefully adjusted to provide a flat base on which to mount the uPVC boards. This is important, because any irregularity in the framework of battens will be reflected in the surface of the cladding.

Product ranges invariably include trims to provide a neat finish around door and window openings. External sill covers are also available.

Like plastic soffits and fascia boards, uPVC cladding needs no maintenance other than occasional sponging down. This is a great asset, and it is little wonder that this system has become so popular.

Feather-edge boarding made in plastic, and available from major DIY stores, provides a neat, low-maintenance exterior finish.

Flat roofs

The construction of a flat roof involves two elements. Firstly, there's a supporting structure, referred to as the decking. Secondly, there's a protective covering on top of the decking, and in most housing developments this comprises layers of bitumen felt. Industrial buildings often have flat roofs of reinforced concrete with a covering of asphalt; but this is seldom seen on dwellings.

Advisory services

It is no secret that there is considerable rivalry between the pitched and flat roofing industries.

Anxious to ensure that flat roofs are correctly designed, skillfully constructed and properly specified, several manufacturers of roofing products offer free advisory services. These are not exclusively for building contractors; the leading companies operate free technical advice and recommendation services that the home owner can take advantage of. If the problem warrants it, this may include a site visit from a technical representative. Anyone with a particular roofing problem would be strongly commended to seek advice from these specialists.

Faulty coverings

If built correctly, a flat roof will have a gentle fall so that rainwater discharges into drainage outlets or a run of guttering. If there is a tendency for water to accumulate, the life of the covering material will be relatively short, particularly during frosty weather. To solve this problem, known as 'ponding', the decking structure will need altering.

On domestic premises, the covering material normally comprises three layers of roofing felt that have been bonded with hot bitumen to form a composite sandwich. More recently, high-performance roofing felts have been developed, allowing an effective cover to be achieved by using only two layers. Most houses, however, are likely to have the older system, using felt manufactured from a bitumen compound reinforced with a hessian core. This is often referred to as a 'rag felt', and its disadvantage is the tendency for the hessian to rot. Around the perimeter of the roofed area, a mineralised felt will normally have been used to reinforce the edges.

Longer life

In the last few years, considerable improvements have been made in the manufacturing process, and the life expectancy of high-performance felt is much greater. This has a core of rot-proof polyester, and because of its strength, modern roofs made with this felt may only have two layers of the material. Some manufacturers anticipate that its life may be as long as 50 years.

In contrast, an expected lifespan of around 12 years is typical for a traditional built-up felt roof, although in some locations the material will last much longer. South-facing roofs are more likely to fail early because of damage caused by the sun. Irrespective of location, however, problems will occur at some stage in the life of the covering, and the first strategy is to patch any areas of damage. Only when leaks become persistent is it time to strip and replace the material completely.

Several problems are associated with this type of roof, and the slow discharge of rainwater is one of the main disadvantages. In addition, the dark colour of a non-reflective cover material absorbs the heat of the sun. Extremes in temperature cause the felt to expand and contract quite considerably, which eventually causes the bond between the layers to fail. As soon as gaps develop between layers of bitumen felt, the roof is unlikely to provide a weatherproof cover for much longer.

▶ SEE PAGE 55 FOR STEP-BY-STEP INSTRUCTIONS ON REPAIRING BLISTERED FELT COVERINGS

New decking and coverings

Building a timber deck is well within the ability of a competent carpenter. However, the design of the structure, and the specification of the materials, must be prepared by a qualified person.

Installing the bitumen felt is a different matter. On a small outbuilding like a shed, this is easy to tackle, because the roof of this type of building can be covered using cold bitumen. On your home, however, a built-up felt roof must be constructed by using hot bitumen to bond the materials; this is potentially dangerous. Preparing molten bitumen in a boiler, and carrying it up a ladder in buckets is not a task for the inexperienced. This is usually referred to as the 'pour and roll' technique.

Admittedly, some DIY enthusiasts have achieved success with the torching technique. In this process, a special felt is used that has a bitumen adhesive applied to one surface. This compound is heated on the roof itself, using a gas-fuelled torch. Then, it is simply unrolled from the special applicator. However, torch-on roofing needs special equipment, and like the 'pour and roll' technique, the work is best entrusted to a roofing contractor.

Small outbuildings

On small sheds, you can use cold bitumen. A three-layer covering is recommended, particularly if a

Installing bitumen felt is a straightforward job on a small outbuilding.

conventional Type 1 hessian felt is used. If you use a modern high-performance, tear-resistant material, containing a polyester core rather than hessian, two layers are considered sufficient.

Around the edges of the roof, a mineralised felt should be used to form the drip sections that discharge rainwater – usually into a run of guttering. These are formed by nailing strips of felt to the side timbers, coating them with mastic, and folding them back to form a double layer of material.

In the 'pour and roll' technique, molten bitumen is poured onto the decking from a bucket.

Working with a wide bladed scraper, the bitumen is distributed across the decking as the felt is unrolled. Subsequent layers are built up in the same manner.

Inspection and maintenance

Periodic inspection of a flat roof is essential, and several aspects need attention:

● Check any drain outlets and make sure that there is no debris on the roof to prevent the free discharge of rainwater.

● Remove moss and leaves. If the chippings are in poor condition, add more. If a solar reflective coating has been used instead of chippings, repaint this if it has lost its bright appearance.

● Check flashing materials on upstands – where the roof abuts a wall, for example. Check the condition of perimeter flashing around rooflights.

● Check for wrinkling in the felt, blisters, cracks, and any evidence of separation.

Typical problems

Even the smallest amount of water penetrating a layer of the covering can hasten its demise. In hot sun, trapped moisture often vapourises and forms a blister. In cold weather, ingress of water may be followed by freezing, and the expansion of the ice will cause more layers of felt to break apart.

Once delamination begins, any water entering the outer cover will track between the separate layers. If there is a break in the base layer, it will enter the decking structure and damage the ceiling below.

This problem can be exceedingly difficult to trace and cure, because a leak through the ceiling may occur some distance from where the water originally penetrated the outer cover.

In addition to weather damage, the covering may be punctured when a ladder is carelessly erected on the roof to gain access for window cleaning or other maintenance work. Once a break has occurred in the outer layer of felt, wrinkling may develop. This is a sign that delamination is reaching an advanced state. You may also notice that the surface has a mottled look, which is a sign that the bitumen is degenerating as a result of oxidation.

Testing for leaks

The best way to locate a leak in built-up flat roofing is to use an electronic test meter. This is a battery-operated device that has two settings, allowing it to be used on either a smooth surface or one covered with a layer of chippings. Two rubber electrodes on the base of the meter transmit low-frequency signals. When these come into contact with a zone of moisture, an audible and visual signal is transmitted. As soon as the moisture is located, you follow the strongest signal across the roof until its point of origin is revealed.

Making repairs

A range of roofing repair compounds is available from builders' merchants and major DIY stores. Cold bitumen roofing compound can be purchased for sealing gaps, and it also acts as an adhesive for patch repairs. All you need to do is cut out a patching piece from a spare roll of felt and fix it in place with the roofing compound.

If a blister develops, it will have been caused by a pressure build-up from trapped water vapour. This is more likely to occur if the protective cover of solar chippings is poor – or absent altogether. The technique for making a repair is shown opposite.

Repair compounds

Another method of waterproofing a leaking flat roof

is to apply an elastomeric treatment. This is often advertised as liquid rubber. If the roof is in poor condition, the chippings, together with all vegetative matter, are scraped off first. When the roof covering has been cleared of all loose matter, the repair liquid can be liberally applied with the aid of a large brush or a soft broom.

When the chemical sets, it forms a continuous skin on top of the felt, providing a very effective waterproof barrier. However, the disadvantage with this system is the fact that any damp that may be present in the structure becomes sealed in. There is also the possibility that the addition of a 'non-breathing' membrane of this type may cause the structural timbers of the roof to deteriorate over a period of time.

Other treatments include products that employ a bitumen-based coating. This can be strengthened by the addition of a flexible reinforcing fabric. The coating has the advantage of being compatible with the bitumen material used to produce the original roof covering.

Complete replacement

Needless to say, whatever approach is followed, making patch repairs or recoating the roof will not provide a long-term solution to a covering that is in poor condition. Eventually, the time will come when the whole cover needs to be stripped off and replaced completely. Compared to roofs built with slates or tiles, built-up felt roofs deteriorate much more rapidly, and need their covering materials replaced at more frequent intervals.

PATCHING BLISTERS

1 Blistering is caused by a build-up of vapour beneath the surface where rain has penetrated the layers or felt. This is aggravated if the solar reflective chippings are absent or in poor condition.

2 Scrape chippings clear of the blister and make star cuts across it with a knife. Try not to cut through more layers than is necessary.

3 Prise the cut sections upwards, warming the felt with a hot-air gun if it is brittle.

4 Dry the underside of the folds and the exposed section of underfelt. A hot-air gun is ideal for the job, but make sure you don't overheat the area.

5 Coat the exposed felt with cold bitumen roofing compound.

6 Press the raised pieces back into place, using a decorator's roller to bed them into the compound.

7 Cut a felt patch and coat it with cold bitumen. Place this over the damaged area, using the roller again to bed it down. Spread a final layer of bitumen compound over the repair to provide bedding for fresh solar reflective chippings.

Decking structures

A great deal of research has been carried out to identify flat roof failures, and the conclusions suggest that faults can often be attributed to design errors. This applies as much to the deck structure as to the cover material. For instance, a designer needs to know if anyone is likely to walk on the structure; the structural specification will be less stringent if the decking will only be used for occasional access, such as repair work. It will be completely different if the roof will be used as a balcony.

A further issue concerns insulation. To comply with the Building Regulations, a flat roof over a habitable room must include thermal insulation, but this won't be necessary for an unheated outbuilding. Depending on the placement of the insulant, the structure will either be referred to as a 'cold roof' or a 'warm roof'. If it is a cold roof, a system of ventilation is essential.

Cold roofs

A cold roof refers to a structure in which the insulant is placed directly over the ceiling boards, preventing warmth from the room below from escaping into the void between the joists. Any space above the insulant will remain cold. The problem with this arrangement is that water vapour can escape through the insulating material, and once it reaches the unheated void, condensation will form on cold surfaces. Over a period of time, this leads to rot in the timbers, and early structural failure is inevitable.

The problem is less likely to arise, however, if a vapour control layer has been installed above the ceiling boards, and ventilators have been built into the roof. This arrangement still has its weaknesses, as the wiring for a light fitting will puncture the vapour control material, forming a weak spot. Moreover, if you are upgrading an older structure, the addition of a vapour control material and the installation of ventilators can involve major alterations. A better strategy might be to extract the ceiling-level insulation from the voids by removing an exterior fascia board, and convert the entire structure into a warm roof.

Warm roofs

In a warm roof, heat from rooms below is permitted to enter the void above the ceiling. The insulation may be installed in one of two ways. A warm deck sandwich may be constructed by placing block foam insulant above the decking on a vapour control layer, followed by the weatherproofing felt. Alternatively, an inverted warm deck may be created. In this case, the weatherproofing felt is laid on the decking, followed by the insulating boards. These are topped by a layer of ballast or a permeable sheet material.

A warm roof can be created in refurbishment work, but a specialist needs to verify that the structure is adequate to accept the additional loading. In some instances, you may find that the original decking board has begun to deteriorate, but

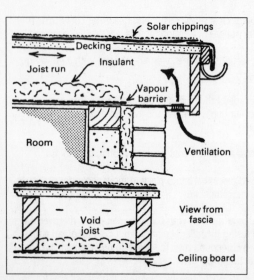

Left *A cold roof has insulant at ceiling level. It must also have a vapour control layer, together with some means of ventilating the void.*

Right *A warm roof has a vapour control layer, followed by purpose-made insulation material placed above the decking.*

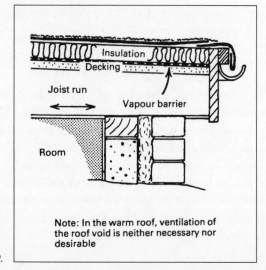

Note: In the warm roof, ventilation of the roof void is neither necessary nor desirable

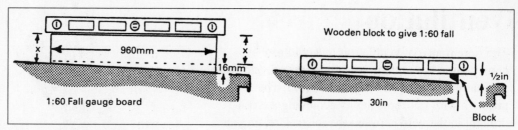

When constructing the decking, a gauge board can be made and used with a spirit level to check the fall (left). Alternatively, a block can be attached to one end of the spirit level (right).

as long as the joists are sound, you can replace it with a composite board that combines both deck material and insulant. Some products comprise a triple sandwich of plywood, insulant and felt, all bonded into one.

In many cases, you can lay insulant directly on top of an original layer of felt. However, it doesn't take long to strip off the remnants of deteriorating felt, scooping them up with a shovel. Then you can lay the insulant on a flat base.

It will be appreciated that warm roof construction eliminates the need for ventilation. Vapour may still percolate into the roof void, but since the timbers are warmed by heat escaping from below, there are no cold surfaces on which condensate may develop.

Arranging a fall

Another important aspect of flat roof construction is the fall of the roof. The slow rate at which rainwater discharges from the surface poses a greater threat to this type of roof than a pitched one. Therefore, a flat roof must have a fall, and the steeper, the better. Many older roofs will have been built with a very modest slope, and subsequent settlement will have caused depressions in the surface so that 'ponding' occurs during wet weather. This can be serious.

Some roofing felt manufacturers suggest that the fall should be no less than 1:60; recommendations in the Building Regulations, however, encourage a minimum of 1:40. There is no doubt that the steeper the slope, the greater the self-cleansing effect as rainwater passes over its surface.

When building a flat roof structure, the joists are normally set in a level plane so that the ceiling boards attached to the underside will also be level. To create a fall for the decking, tapered strips of timber, called 'firrings', are nailed to the tops of the joists. A timber merchant should be able to machine firrings to the fall you require.

On an existing roof, a steeper fall can be produced by fixing tapered boards to the decking. Usually, these are made from an insulant. They provide a distinct slope, as well as a new layer of insulation.

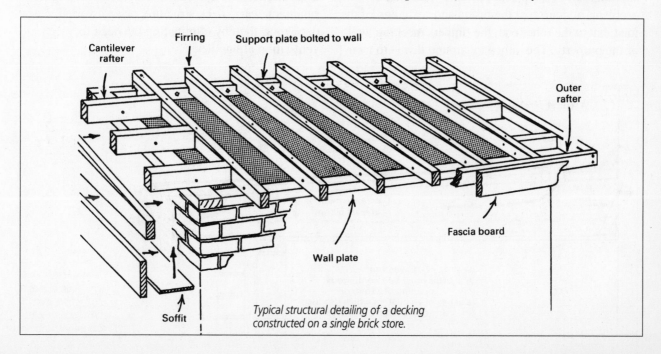

Typical structural detailing of a decking constructed on a single brick store.

Ventilation

The importance of ventilation in a cold roof construction has already been emphasised, and there are many suitable vents to choose from. The problem with flat roofs lies in achieving a cross-draught in the void between the joists. Creating an opening at a fascia board or soffit is usually quite easy to arrange, and grilles made with a mesh to keep out insects are readily available. Under the current Building Regulations, a continuous opening should be at least 25mm (1in) wide. Alternatively, if panel vents are used instead of a continuous strip, these must afford the same amount of open area and be positioned so that there's an opening between every joist. In addition, the draught gap between the top of the insulant and the underside of the decking must be at least 50mm (2in).

Research into this subject, however, suggests that for buildings with a span of 5-10m (16-32ft), eaves ventilation requires a gap of at least 30mm (1⅛in), while the throughway in the void must be at least 60mm (2⅜in).

A difficult task

Unfortunately, it is difficult to install a complete cross-ventilation system in lean-to extensions, because the joists usually run at right angles to the support wall of the parent building. There's no problem, of course, at the fascia and soffit end of the joist, but at the other end, the timbers meet the wall of the property. The only way around this is to form

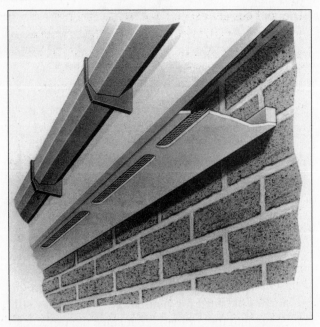

Soffit ventilators permit the void to be ventilated in a cold roof construction. (Illustration courtesy Rytons Building Products Ltd)

openings in the decking itself, near the abutment with the wall, and to fit purpose-designed mushroom ventilators. However, these must be fitted very carefully so that the roof covering remains completely waterproof. Without doubt, this situation is much more easily dealt with by constructing a sandwich warm deck structure, or an inverted warm deck roof, thereby eliminating the need for ventilation altogether.

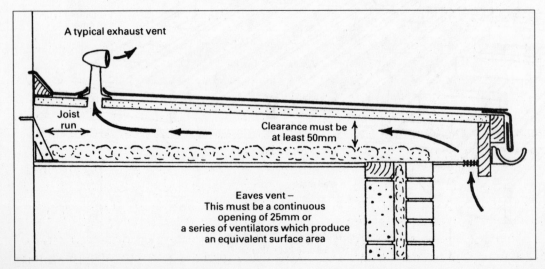

A typical exhaust vent

Joist run

Clearance must be at least 50mm

Eaves vent –
This must be a continuous opening of 25mm or a series of ventilators which produce an equivalent surface area

Detail of cross-flow ventilation in a cold roof, where joists run at right angles to another building.

Roofing felt

The roof designer should specify the type of felt needed for a particular project. This will be based on a classification system of 'Types' outlined in British Standard 747. However, the categorisation was revised in March 1994, when Type 1 felts were withdrawn from the British Standard.

The roofing industry was delighted with this move, because it acknowledged that rag-based hessian felts would no longer be approved for built-up flat roofing work, and that the superiority of polyester-based felts had finally been officially recognised. It is worth noting that some manufacturers continue to produce Type 1 felts, since they are cheaper and wholly adequate on potting sheds and other small outbuildings. However, they must not be used on domestic buildings.

Although comparatively cheap, the trouble with hessian-cored felt is that it tears easily, rots and is hygroscopic. In contrast, polyester-based felts have notably better resistance to repeated movement, and are much less likely to become torn or damaged. Although they have been in existence since 1971, it has taken some time for the higher-performance materials to gain official recognition. Because of this move, many roof specifications will be for two-layer, rather than three-layer, systems – using high-performance polyester-type felts. In some developments, you may even see reference to new bituminous single-ply systems.

Some high-performance felts must be applied with a special torch.

Kits are often available for roofing small sheds, using felt and a cold bitumen compound.

Solar coatings

An essential element of a flat roof is the solar reflective layer. The heat of the sun on a dark surface is most damaging, causing continual expansion and contraction of the surface so that the layers to lose their bond. Solar gain can also affect the building itself, and uncomfortable levels of heat in rooms beneath a flat roof are not unusual.

Many roofs are covered with white reflective chippings to reduce the problem. These can be purchased through a builders' merchant and can be very effective. However, it is not unusual for them to be blown away in the course of time, more chippings being found in the guttering than on the roof itself. It is essential to check this periodically, and to add more chippings whenever necessary.

An alternative is to coat the roof with an approved solar reflective paint. Some products are pigmented with aluminium, although this type must be checked regularly, because the lustre of the surface may diminish quite quickly.

These types of coating can be applied in several ways. Some installers mount a decorator's roller on a broom stick; others use a wide brush – or even a soft-bristled broom. Needless to say, the manufacturer's advice concerning the method of application should be checked before starting work.

Pitched roofs

The roof of a building has to withstand the weather in all its fury – and faults are more likely to develop here than anywhere else. But weather damage isn't the only problem. Structural failures are not unusual either, and older houses often need the addition of bracing struts to support the rafters and purlins.

Many repairs are fairly straightforward, but in severe cases replacement of a substantial part of the structure, or even all of it, may be necessary. Therefore, it is important to understand how pitched roofs are built before venturing to cure any fault.

Identifying problems

As a general precaution, you should check a roof periodically and remedy any faults at once. It's not unusual for a slate to slip out of place if a fixing fails; similarly, tiles may become loose if the nibs that hook over a batten break away. If you don't own a roof ladder and can't make a close inspection, many faults can still be seen from the ground by using a pair of binoculars.

Safe access

Although many roof repairs are easy to carry out, the work is made more difficult because of the roof's inaccessibility. To carry out roofing work safely and efficiently, it is essential to hire or buy appropriate access equipment. Quite often, a ladder affords insufficient security, and a scaffold tower will be needed as a base from which to set up a roof ladder.

For the more ambitious projects described here, it is obvious that full scaffolding must be erected, which is a job best left to a specialist.

Whatever the job, you must be absolutely certain that safe and secure access has been arranged before any repair work is undertaken.

Ridge tiles

Damage to ridge tiles is quite common, although this is less likely on modern houses built with a dry ridge system, where the tiles are fastened to a timber batten with stainless steel annular nails. Most ridge tiles, however, rely solely on mortar for their security, and whereas this is a good gap sealer, it

On pitched roofs, ridge tiles frequently become detached in strong winds. (Photograph courtesy Redland Roof Tiles Ltd)

doesn't always offer long-term success in holding the tiles down.

You may notice cracks in the mortar bedding of a ridge tile, which is caused by the different rates of expansion of the two materials. It also occurs if the original mortar mix contained too much cement, which leads to shrinkage. Equally, a poor bond will have been achieved if the mortar dried too quickly, a problem caused by a dry tile sucking the moisture from the mortar as soon as they came into contact.

Normally, an end ridge tile will become detached first. Depending on the orientation of the house, this is usually on the westerly side, which is the source of the prevailing wind.

The mortar required for rebedding a ridge tile comprises 3 parts sharp sand and 1 part ordinary Portland cement (by volume). Clean water is required, and the mix should be fairly stiff. A plasticiser can be added to increase the workability of the mortar, although this isn't essential. Many builders, however, add a small amount of PVA bonding agent to improve adhesion between the tile and the mortar. Follow the product's instructions for mixing procedures.

At the bedding point along the peak of a roof, it is customary to insert some broken tiles into the mortar. These help to reinforce the mix, as well as prevent it from slumping around the ridge board. At the exposed end of a line of ridge tiles, these inserts are often left slightly proud of the mortar as a decorative infill.

If the ridge tile is a capping for profiled tiles, such as pantiles, small inserts are often placed in the valley of the tile, at the junction with the ridge. These are set into the mortar and are called 'dentil slips'.

Extra fixings

Because of the poor bond achieved by mortar, some manufacturers have developed ridge tiles that incorporate fixing wires. One end of the wire is attached to the underside of the tile, while the other is wound around a nail driven into a ridge batten. Mortar is still used for bedding the tiles. It is even possible to adopt a similar arrangement by carefully making a small hole in the ridge tile with a masonry

Some ridge tiles can be wired down to a ridge batten for added security. (Photograph courtesy Marley Roof Tiles Ltd)

drill. You can run a length of wire through this to an attachment point below, then waterproof the hole in the tile with a sealant. It's not ideal, but it works well on an end ridge tile that is most vulnerable to the prevailing wind.

Slate and tile problems

Water penetration, frost and thermal movement all damage tiles. Slate is not affected in quite the same way, but many slates on older properties will have become soft. If they are easily scored with a knife, creating powder, they are no longer of use.

Clay tiles tend to break down into flakes, which is called spalling. In either case, patch repairs are unlikely to provide an answer. In the long term, the roof will need a new covering (see pages 68-69).

Vegetation

Allowing moss, lichens or other vegetation to grow on a roof is unwise. They absorb moisture, which freezes in winter, damaging the surface of the tiles.

A high-pressure washer is ideal for cleaning a roof that is covered with vegetative matter. Fortunately, it's a job that will not need doing often.

Sheathing

When a slates have reached an advanced state of

deterioration, one measure is to sheath the surface, which will delay the time when the whole covering needs replacing. It involves applying a coating compound with a binding material, such as hessian or nylon mesh.

Unfortunately, the process leaves an unattractive surface, and any undamaged slates that might have been usable elsewhere will no longer be reclaimable. Also, any damp in the loft space or roof timbers becomes sealed in, and the natural ventilation afforded by gaps in the slates is lost. Periodic recoating may also be necessary, and if rain does find its way through a weak spot, it may track under the sheathing material, making the original entry point difficult to locate. On the positive side, poorly-attached slates will be prevented from slipping out of place.

Another of sealing a tiled or slate roof is to coat it with a cement wash. Again, this is not likely to prove a long-term success, and it often looks unpleasant. In reality, the only satisfactory answer will be to re-roof the property.

Replacing slates and tiles

If a slate becomes detached, it should be refixed promptly. If, however, the problem of slipping slates becomes a regular occurrence, it indicates a 'nail sick' roof. This term is used when the fixings have corroded so badly that there are frequent breakages. When this point is reached, the only practicable proposition is to re-roof the property.

Occasional breakages, however, can be dealt with individually. If a slate is broken, it is worth visiting a local supplier of reclaimed building materials to see if any slates of similar size are held in stock. Although they can be purchased through a builders' merchant, buying a single slate may prove difficult.

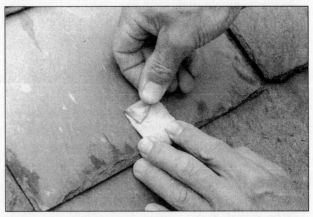

When inserting a new slate, a lead strip, or tingle, is nailed to the batten first. When the slate is slid into position, the tingle is folded upwards to keep it in place.

A different method

Originally, slates would have been fixed by nails near the upper edge (the head), or near the middle. The nails will be of a non-ferrous material, such as aluminium or copper. Unfortunately, you cannot reattach a single slate in this way, because the heads of the nails will fall directly beneath the slate above. In consequence, the slate should be reattached with the aid of a 'tingle'. This is a narrow length of lead which is nailed to the batten that will be covered by the slate. Alternatively, you can use a purpose-made copper tingle, also known as a 'strap'. Whichever is chosen, once the slate has been slid into place beneath the one above, the lower end of the tingle must be folded around the lower edge of the slate to retain it. Sliding layers of snow have a habit of unfolding lead tingles, and if you notice any sticking

upright, they must be folded down again.

If a small area of slates needs replacing, you should work from the bottom upwards, matching the overlap of the adjacent slates. In this case, it may be possible to nail some to the battens, which means that you will have to make nail holes in the slates. The craftsman will deftly form holes with the spike of a slater's axe; however, the amateur is advised to use a masonry drill.

Clay and concrete tiles are usually made with nibs that hook over the battens, although some rows will be nailed for additional security. A replacement, however, will only be hooked into place. The method of removing the remnants of a broken slate or tile is shown below. You will need a bricklayer's trowel and a slater's rip – which can usually be hired.

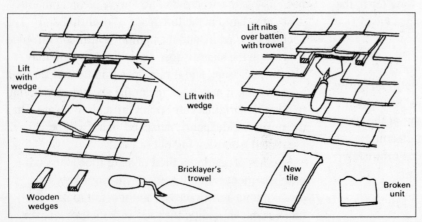

Lift with wedge

Lift nibs over batten with trowel

Lift with wedge

Bricklayer's trowel

Wooden wedges

New tile

Broken unit

When removing the remnants of an old broken tile and inserting a replacement, a trowel and a pair of wooden wedges will make the job much easier.

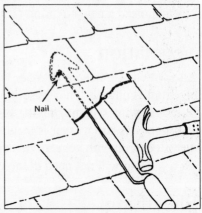

Nail

The nails holding the head of a broken tile may be removed with a slater's rip.

Reinforcing rafters

Damage to roof timbers and deflections in roof structures are not unusual. Prior to the advent of prefabricated trusses, the roofs of most houses were built from rafters, wall plates, a ridge tree (board) and purlins. Additional bracing struts could derive support from internal structural walls, and the entire structure was built on site.

The reasons for failure are various, but a common problem is the tendency for rafters to deflect outwards at the eaves. This may occur because the purlins that support the rafters are not sturdy enough. Running at right angles, a purlin supports a rafter between the ridge and the wall plate; if it begins to flex, so will the rafters it supports.

One reason for sagging can be the weight of the covering. Even if a roof structure appears sound, its integrity may be threatened if you re-roof with heavier tiles than originally specified.

Professional help

If a problem of this kind becomes apparent, you must enlist the help of a structural engineer to identify the reasons and recommend solutions. Moreover, the local authority's building control department must be consulted because of the work's structural element. However, as long as the remedial procedures are designed by a qualified person, there is no reason why a competent home owner should not carry out the work.

One method of preventing rafters from splaying out at the eaves is to add strutting braces, as shown here. In this instance, structural-grade 100 x 50mm (4 x 2in) timber was installed.

Similar work that may be easy to carry out involves the installation of additional supports beneath purlins to prevent future deflection. However, some roof problems are far more serious, and if major rebuilding or modification work is required, the task must be tackled by a reputable contractor.

TOOLS AND MATERIALS
☐ Tape measure
☐ Pencil
☐ Adjustable square
☐ Saw
☐ G-cramps
☐ Electric drill
☐ Wood bit
☐ Hammer
☐ Spanner
☐ Timber for struts
☐ Coach bolts and nuts
☐ Galvanised toothed washers

1 When adding these strengthening struts to a traditional roof, the timbers were cramped between the ceiling joists and the rafters for drilling.

2 Special galvanised steel, toothed connecting washers were sandwiched between the ends of the struts and the sides of the rafters.

3 Coach bolts were inserted through the bracing timbers and the original roof and ceiling timbers. They were tightened with a spanner.

4 Each rafter was treated in the same manner. The completed bracing will prevent any further outward deflection of the rafters.

Renewing the structure

When a roof structure, or its covering, is beyond repair, a replacement is urgently needed. Stripping the original structure will be a dirty job; you'll need to hire a skip and possibly a roof chute. There will be a lot of unwanted material to remove.

A safe means of access is essential, and scaffolding can be erected for you by a contractor. You will also need to hire tarpaulins to protect the building during wet weather – whenever possible, it's best to carry out major repairs during the warmer months.

Preliminary planning

Understandably, such a project calls for a clear knowledge of the way different types of roof are built, and professional advice is essential; working drawings for a new structure must be prepared by a qualified person. You will also need to consult your local authority's planning and building control departments. In most cases, the planning department is unlikely to have a great deal of interest in your work, unless you intend making a radical change to the appearance of the property. However, a building control surveyor will most certainly want full details of the proposals.

Although it's quite common to see houses being re-tiled, the Building Regulations recognise problems that can arise when the new covering is heavier than the old. If, for example, the original roof structure was designed to support a light asbestos slate, there would be structural implications if you wanted to replace the slate with a concrete tile, which is significantly heavier. It is quite likely that the existing structure will need inspecting to confirm that it is able to sustain the increased loading.

If there are doubts about the integrity of a structure, it will have to be strengthened (as shown on page 63). Needless to say, if you are building a completely new support structure, it will have been designed to suit the intended covering.

Further help is obtainable from the manufacturers of slates and tiles, many of whom offer technical advice services and a variety of useful publications.

Traditional structures

If a project involves building a new structure, the architect will compare the merits of a traditional construction and the use of prefabricated trusses. In a complex design, especially on an older property, only the former is feasible. However, in a simple structure, prefabricated trusses will speed the work.

The traditional approach uses rafters that rest on a timber wall plate at the eaves, and press against a roof board (or tree) at the ridge. Ceiling joists are fixed between the feet of the rafters to brace the triangle. However, the rafter span of most roofs is sufficient to need an additional support, known as a purlin, positioned approximately mid-way between the wall plate and the roof board.

Constructing a simple twin-pitched roof in the traditional manner is quite easy; the task is much more difficult, however, if you are building a hipped roof. For example, it is not easy to cut the composite angles on the ends of timbers, known as jack rafters, where they meet the hip board.

Further work occurs if a valley has to be

When building a roof structure, the traditional method of construction, using separate sections of timber may be preferable.

constructed where two pitched roof faces meet at right angles. Many manufacturers make special valley tiles for this situation, but profiled tiles need what is known as an open valley gutter. Traditionally, this was formed from boards and lined with Code 4 or 5 lead sheet. Modern practice, however, favours the use of pre-moulded, glass-reinforced-plastic valley gutters, which are supported by timber strutting.

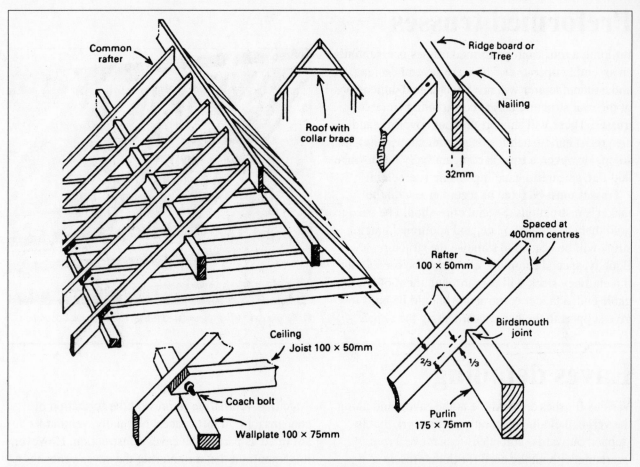

Above *The chief components in a traditional structure include rafters, purlins, wallplates, joists and a ridge board.*

Below *The structure for a hipped roof is difficult to construct, and involves making complex angled cuts on the end of each jack rafter.*

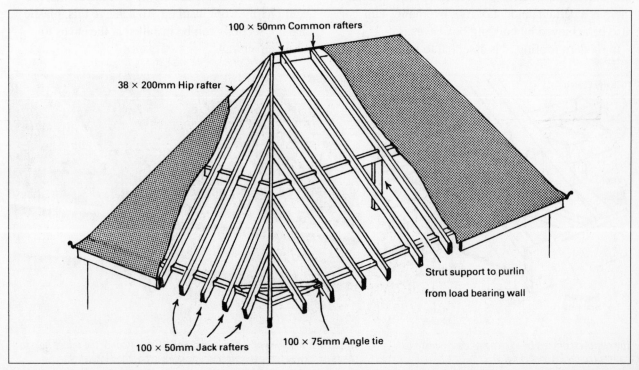

Preformed trusses

Building a roof from preformed trusses is essentially an assembly operation. There are several designs, and a manufacturer will need details and dimensions of the roof structure before constructing suitable trusses. These will support the roof covering, and also resist anticipated loadings from snow, wind, and so on. However, a truss is comparatively weak when laid flat, so careful handling on site is essential.

Trusses must be fixed in accordance with the maker's instructions. Special clips should be used to hold them to the wall plate, and additional bracing struts will be needed to stabilise the structure. Equally, special trimming work must be carried out if a chimney stack will pass through the roof. At a gable end, a ladder construction should be built to give support to the barge-board along the verge.

Building a roof with prefabricated trusses can be a quick operation.

Eaves detailing

Various finishes are possible at the eaves, and along the verge, including decorative brickwork that is stepped outwards (corbelled) to achieve a roof overhang without the need for timber fascia boarding. There's no question that the external walls of a building are better protected from the weather if there is a certain amount of roof overhang. This can also be achieved by building box eaves.

In modern roofing, it is essential to incorporate a system of ventilation to prevent the formation of condensation in loft spaces. Normally, ventilators are fitted as part of the eaves construction. However, it is important that air entering the eaves vents has a clear route past the point where the rafters rest on the wall plate. There should be no obstruction, for example, by wool insulant. To achieve this, plastic channel sections can be installed at the eaves to create an airway.

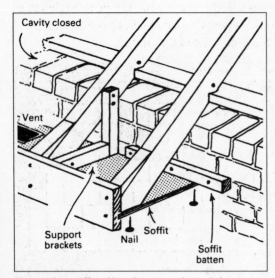

The overhang offered by a box eaves design helps to protect the brickwork below.

These black moulded plastic units laid along the bottom of the rafters help to create an airway for roof ventilation by holding back the insulation.

Felt, boarding and battens

A roof must have a secondary barrier to keep out the rain, and the usual method is to install sarking felt under the tiles or slates. This bitumen-based covering should sag slightly between the rafters, and be carried down into the guttering to discharge any water that may be driven under the tiles.

Unfortunately, in many cases, this barrier fails because hessian-based felt rots away at the eaves and no longer drapes over the gutter. In a re-roofing project, a lightweight polyester-based bitumen felt, which is unaffected by water, should be used. In an exposed location, the roof may need a barrier of boarding as well. The arrangement comprises:
● Tongued-and-grooved boards
● A layer of roofing felt
● Battens that run from the eaves to the ridge, creating a drainage route for penetrating rainwater
● Normal horizontal battens on top

The size of roof battens (also known as laths) will be specified by the tile manufacturer. Preservative-impregnated softwood battens should be used, and are available from most builders' merchants.

Choice of cover material

Some cover materials are not suitable on pitches with a modest slope. Inexpensive gauges are available to establish the roof pitch; alternatively, you can use a spirit level incorporating a swivel gauge for measuring angles.

Weight is another factor when comparing tiles and slates, and the loading will be supplied by the

These modern reconstituted slates have moulded side grooves, thus acting as single-lap coverings – just like profiled pantiles.

manufacturer. This will be taken into account by an architect if you are engaged in new work. Another issue is whether a single-lap or a double-lap product will be used, since this also affects the weight.

The method of fixing partly depends on whether the tiles have side interlock grooves. These overlap each other at the edges, keeping out the weather. There are no grooves on natural slate or plain tiles, and the only way to cover the roof effectively is to overlap them so that at certain points there will be three layers. This is known as double-lap cover.

With moulded tiles and imitation slates, the side interlock means that there will only be a single lap at the head of each unit. As a result, fewer battens are needed than for a slate or plain tile.

Single-lap tiles are made with interlocking side grooves. Double-lap slates and plain tiles do not have these grooves, and need to attain a treble thickness at their heads to keep out the rain. This necessitates many more battens.

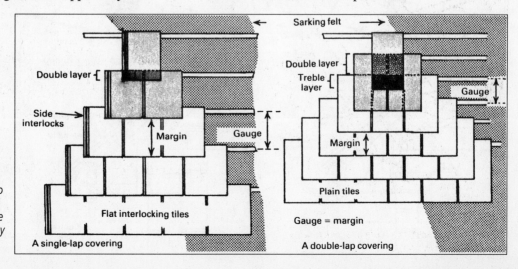

Batten spacing

As soon as the roof structure is complete, the felt should be installed, starting at the eaves and working upwards. It will be held in place by the battens, so their spacing will need calculating first.

On a simple twin-pitched roof, using single-lap tiles, the top batten must be placed so that when a tile is hung on it, the ridge tile will overlap it by at least 75mm (3in). Tiles in the eaves course should project beyond the roof so that their lowest point is directly over the centre of the guttering. This will establish the position of the lowest batten.

Next, you have to calculate how many intermediate battens are needed. The tile manufacturer will state the minimum amount of overlap needed between the tail of one tile and the head of the one below. You can increase this slightly, bringing the battens closer together, but you must not reduce it, otherwise rain may be driven underneath by strong winds. As a rule, however, the headlap should not exceed one quarter of the overall length of the tiles, although the manufacturer's figure may be slightly less.

A simple method is to measure the distance between the top and bottom battens, transfer this to the ground, and lay out the tiles as they would be on the roof. If you can't fit in an exact number of tiles, you may need to push them closer together, thus increasing the headlap. Having established the spacing, you can do the job for real on the roof.

The correct method of calculating batten positions is set out below, the 'gauge' being the distance from the centre of one batten to the centre of its neighbour. The following formula is used:

Overall length of tile – minimum lap
= maximum gauge.

Measure the distance between the top and bottom battens, then divide this by the maximum gauge to calculate the number of spaces between battens. If this won't work out exactly, increase the answer to the next whole number. Having calculated the number of spaces, subtract one to obtain the number of additional battens needed. To calculate the actual distance apart, take the distance between the centre of the top batten and the centre of the bottom batten, and divide it by the number of spaces.

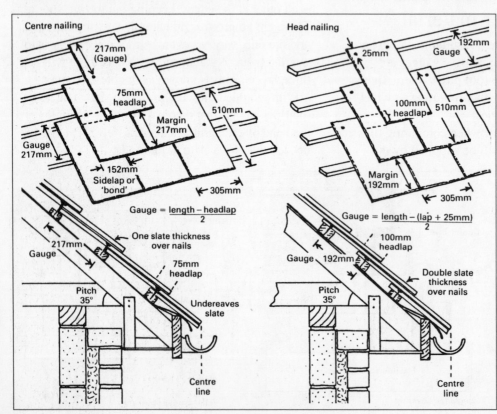

Detail of slate fixings. Welsh slate is usually centre-nailed as a precaution against damage from windlift. The thicker and heavier slates of the Lake District are usually nailed at the head.

Fixing tiles and slates

Once the roof is felted and battened, you can begin to lay the tiles or slates, following these guidelines:

● Set out the eaves course first to determine how many tiles are needed to fit from end to end. Since the overhang at the verge (the gable end) should be 38-50mm (1½-2in), begin by making the right-hand eaves tile overhang the gable by about 40mm (1⅝in), then lay out the complete row. In addition to the leeway at the verge, tiles with side interlock have a small amount of sideways movement, which will offer further adjustments.

● Stretch a chalked line between the eaves course and the ridge batten, checking its distance from the edge of the roof. Then snap the string against the intermediate battens so that the chalk leaves a mark where the edges of the tiles should align.

● Along the verge, lengths of a cement fibre strip, called the undercloak, must be slid under the battens, shiny side downwards and nailed in place. These provide a base for the mortar bedding that supports the verge tiles.

● On an exposed site, it is best to fit ridge tiles that have attachment wires. Mortar plays a very small role in holding the tile in place, and should be seen as a filling compound only.

A comparatively recent development is a system

Tiles are bedded at the verge with mortar mixed from 3 parts sharp sand and 1 part ordinary Portland cement.

for holding down ridge and verge tiles with clips, or special nails, but no mortar. At the verge, some systems include plastic cover strips; others provide a special tile, known as a cloaked verge, which wraps over the edges. Although mortar-based systems retain prominence, dry tile systems can be fixed in any weather, and are ideal for amateur installers.

● Since the ventilation system of a roof needs a high-level outlet, some ridge tiles incorporate a venting arrangement.

● A double-lap system of attachment is used when laying slates. Some are nailed near the centre to resist wind lift; others at the head. The nails must be non ferrous, alloy and copper nails being the most common. Galvanised nails must not be used, as they will rust when the coating starts to deteriorate.

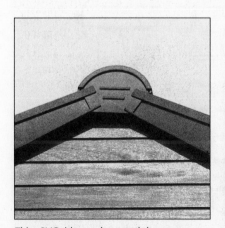

This uPVC ridge end cap and dry verge covers eliminate the need for mortar and can be installed in most weather conditions. (Photograph courtesy Marley Roof Tiles)

Battens should be fixed to run the length of a hip, and tiles will need cutting to match the angle created at the hip. (Photograph courtesy Redland Roof Tiles)

Hip tiles are laid on a mortar bedding to cover the trimmed ends of tiles in each horizontal course. (Photograph courtesy Redland Roof Tiles)

Chimneys

High winds, driving rain and frost are the enemies of chimney stacks. These can be sizeable structures, and the larger they stand, the heavier they fall. So it is essential that they are kept in good repair.

With the demise of open fires in many houses, chimney stacks have often become redundant. However, before demolishing an unwanted or insecure stack, it is necessary to seek the advice of a building surveyor or architect. Even removing a chimney pot and capping the flue can lead to problems. For instance, if you fail to provide adequate ventilation in a closed-off flue, vapour that previously vented to the outside becomes sealed within the structure. This may lead to dampness, which often appears on chimney breasts. On the other hand, normal repairs and maintenance are more straightforward, provided you carry out the work from the safety of a chimney decking.

Good design

Before repairing a chimney stack, it is useful to know what features constitute good design. The stack should be built so that rainwater is deflected efficiently outwards onto the roof. In addition, rain driving against the sides must not lead to damp in the structure below. A good design includes:

● Flaunching that slopes steeply outwards.
● Oversailing brickwork that creates an overhang to throw rainwater clear of the stack.
● A damp-proof course to prevent rainwater from percolating down through the masonry into the structure below the roof.
● Lead flashing around the base to weatherproof the point where the stack breaks through the roof.
● Additionally, in a brick-built stack, weatherstruck pointing of the mortar joints, since its shape helps deflect rainwater outwards.

▶ **SEE PAGE 72 FOR STEP-BY-STEP INSTRUCTIONS ON RENEWING LEAD FLASHING**

In addition to poor brickwork and decaying zinc flashing, cracks in the flaunching indicated this stack was in urgent need of repairs.

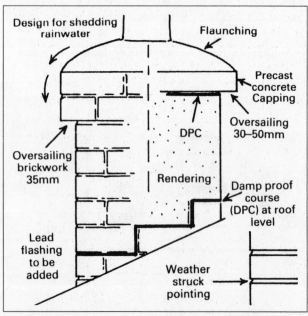

A chimney stack should be built with a DPC and a design that sheds rainwater outwards, onto the roof.

Structure

Quite often the structure of a chimney stack will need attention. Repointing is a common necessity, while on older property you may find that some of the upper bricks are loose and require re-bedding. When repointing the joints, shape them so that they slope outwards to create a weatherstruck finish.

On a rendered stack, check the soundness of the render and carefully remove any areas that are breaking away. Then re-render as described on pages 46-47.

Flues

Designing flues and chimney systems is complex, and the task should be entrusted to a qualified person. Details of the flue itself depend, in part, on the appliance concerned and its type of fuel. Considerations such as cross-sectional area, liner material and outlet position have to be taken into account. Errors in design may result in the combustion gases cooling too quickly, which can lead to condensation on the flue surface. Problems may occur if this then runs back down to the appliance or soaks through the chimney breast.

Another difficulty is that brick flues in older properties may be wholly unsuitable if you want to install a gas fire instead of the original open fire. Similarly, solid-fuel, wood-burning appliances and gas log-effect fires have their own requirements.

Given the design specifications and product recommendations of an expert, the competent DIY builder is often successful in constructing a flue in a new building. For instance, a flue built from ready-made lining units is relatively easy to construct, joints between the liner units and surrounding brickwork being filled with mortar.

However, installing a lining inside the brick-built flue of an existing building is much more difficult. The choice of liner is important, and its installation can be complex. Stainless steel ducting, passed down through the stack is one option, while another involves pumping a special slurry into the chimney around an inflated former. Once the slurry has set hard, the former is deflated and removed.

There are many products for curing flue problems, and it is worth consulting the British Flue and Chimney Manufacturers' Association for advice.

Chimney pots

Some chimney pots are surprisingly large, so take care if you have to remove one, and employ a helper when lowering it to the ground. When fitting a new pot, make sure that at least a quarter of its height, or 150mm (6in), whichever is greater, is covered by flaunching and surrounding courses of bricks. Modern buildings have a special chimney capping, which has a recess to accept the pot; in older buildings, the edges of the pot were placed on slates before being covered with mortar.

Flaunching

Cracks in flaunching are commonplace, and if this capping is loose, it's best to remove it completely and replace it. Remember that it holds the pot in place, so exercise great care, making sure that no debris tumbles down the flue.

Flaunching is formed with a 1:3 cement:sand mortar mix, and should be carefully trowelled off to a slope so that rain will be shed efficiently outwards.

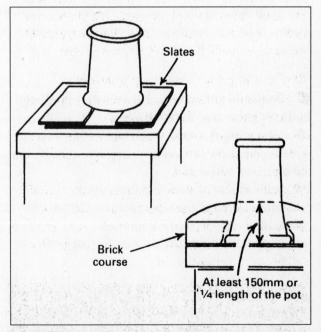

In older buildings, chimneys were supported on slates; note the amount of support needed to secure the pot.

Renewing flashing

At the base of a stack, lead flashing is the best form of weatherproofing. On older properties, zinc sheeting was sometimes used, and this may be in a poor state – especially in industrial cities where atmospheric pollution will have hastened corrosion. You may find a fillet of mortar instead of flashing, but this is seldom successful. Differential expansion causes mortar to crack and lose its bonding, so if repairs are needed, it is best to replace the mortar with lead flashing.

New flashings should be formed using Code 4 lead, which can be purchased from a builders' merchant. If the stack is situated on the slope of a roof, the sections of flashing needed are the sides, the apron (at the front of the stack) and the back gutter. A stack on the ridge will have two aprons and a saddle piece rather than a back gutter. These sections of lead are attached to the stack by folding over their upper edges and securing them in the mortar joints with lead wedges and fresh mortar. The lead sheet is easily cut with tin snips and formed with the aid of a wooden bossing mallet.

● The apron, which is the cover piece along the lowest part of the stack, is fitted first. It must be taken around the sides of the stack by 150-200mm (6-8in) and overlaps the faces of the tiles below.

● At the sides, a roof that is clad with plain tiles or slates must have separate pieces of lead, called soakers, inserted under each tile and curled over their upper edges. The soakers must also be folded up at the sides against the stack. Having done this, you then cut a stepped cover flashing to overlap the soakers. If profiled single-lap tiles are used, i.e. those that have a moulded side interlock, no soakers are needed. In this case, you fit a combined step and cover flashing that is dressed over the face of the tiles.

● Two pieces of lead are needed for the upper edge of the stack. One forms a gutter along the back of the stack, while the second is a cover strip attached to the stack. The gutter is laid on a timber base, which is built as part of the roof construction. The recommended dimensions of back gutter flashing are:

Upstand at rear of stack – 100mm (4in)
Length – width of stack plus at least 225mm (9in) at each end
Sole of gutter – at least 150mm (6in)
Extension piece for roof slope – 225mm (9in)

● The ridge saddle for a stack on the ridge of a roof will be the last section to be installed. The saddle piece should be dressed over the ridge tile, ensuring that there is a generous overlap with the side flashing. It should also be cut with a stepped edge and anchored in two courses of the stack's brickwork.

TOOLS AND MATERIALS

☐ Cold chisel
☐ Club hammer
☐ Tape measure
☐ Steel rule
☐ Scribe
☐ Tin snips
☐ Bossing mallet
☐ Wooden board
☐ Bucket
☐ Pointing trowel
☐ Code 4 lead sheet
☐ Ready-mixed mortar

The zinc flashing around the base of this chimney stack is in poor condition and needs replacing; the brickwork also needs urgent attention. The flashing should be replaced with new sections of lead, while the mortar joints should be repointed. (Photograph courtesy of Redland Roof Tiles)

1 After installing the soakers along both sides of the stack, cut lines are scored onto the new lead sheet in readiness for cutting a stepped flashing section. Each step is fixed into a mortar course, while section of lead should be long enough to dress round both upper and lower edges of the stack. If no soakers are required, a combined step and cover flashing is installed and dressed over the face of the tiles.

2 After cutting out the stepped flashing section on a board, mark the mortar joints to be chased (cut out), then remove the mortar to a depth of about 2.5cm (1in) with a cold chisel and club hammer. Fold over the top edges of the flashing steps, insert them in the mortar joints and hammer in rolled-up offcuts of lead to wedge the flashing in place. Then repoint the mortar joints to conceal the wedges.

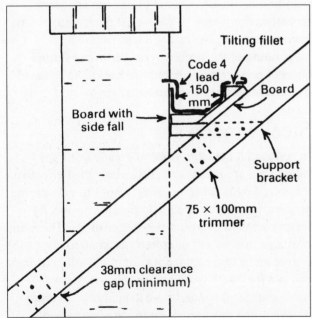

3 A back gutter is formed by preparing a timber support, which is part of the roof structure; two pieces of Code 4 lead sheet are then placed on the base and dressed into shape. One section of lead forms the back gutter itself, while the second is a cover strip attached to the stack. The tiles above the chimney are positioned so that rainwater will run off them and into the gutter, which directs it to the sides.

4 A wooden bossing mallet is used to dress (shape) the lead sheet around the chimney stack; as it is worked with the mallet, the lead will stretch and assume the required shape. Tap the lead cautiously to avoid splitting the material. Since the back gutter will receive water draining from the roof slope above, it should be constructed with the utmost care. (Photograph courtesy of Marley Roof Tiles)

Windows

There is a variety of materials, structures and methods of operation to be found in windows. Some are fixed with no opening light, whereas others are made with an opening section, which may be referred to as the 'casement' or 'sash'. Depending on the type of opening mechanism, a window can be classified as follows:

Casement This type of window has a hinged opening light – often called the 'casement sash'. If its hinges are attached to a vertical side member (a jamb), the construction is known as a side-hung casement. However, if the hinges are fixed horizontally to the top cross-member of the frame, the opening portion is a top-hung ventlight.

Pivot-hung casement Sometimes a sash is fixed in the frame using a pivot arrangement, and this may operate in either a horizontal or a vertical plane. Some pivots are made with a friction system to hold the sash in any opened position. Alternatively, there may be brackets that limit the amount of movement.

Sliding sash This type of window was often used in Victorian housing, but there are modern versions that are also popular. The sill is normally made of solid timber, whereas the jambs and the head (the top section) are of box construction. In traditional designs, the side boxes house a pulley system and cast-iron counterweights, but modern versions use a spring-loaded tape or spiral rod system.

Other types Recent developments include factory-made windows that have to be set in a separate hardwood or extruded-plastic sub-frame. Sliding patio windows fall into this category. You can also find moulded concrete sills and lintels that complement the shape of a window. Another modern window design has a sash with both side and bottom hinges; a lever selects the operating mode.

Wooden windows

Traditionally, wood is the most popular material for windows. In most cases, softwoods are used, although hardwoods such as mahogany may be found in more expensive products. The long-term performance of wooden windows is partly dependent on the quality of the timber, and the

Moulded concrete lintels and sills are available in a variety of designs to enhance the appearance of a window.

treatments used by the manufacturer. Large joinery manufacturers use chemical impregnation processes.

However, periodic maintenance is important, too, and softwood windows are most commonly painted with primer, undercoat, and gloss topcoat. More recently, other forms of stain-type preservatives have become popular. Normally, a less-rigorous preparation of the surface is needed when further coats of preservative are required, and this is one of the advantages of these products.

Steel windows

In residential housing, windows made from hot-rolled steel are robust and particularly cost-effective. Rustproofing is achieved using a hot-dip galvanising process, although it is equally possible to specify factory-applied polyester powder coatings. These are available in a variety of colours as an alternative to primer and a two-coat paint system. Powder coatings can last for 10-25 years before needing further treatment. Steel windows are available in a variety of styles, and most are designed to accept double-glazing units.

uPVC windows

In the last few decades, uPVC (plastic) windows have become very popular because they need no maintenance, apart from periodic sponging down. However, whereas there are good examples of these products, some are poorly designed and badly fitted. This is most regrettable, since when well made and correctly installed, the product has many advantages. Lengths of uPVC extrusion can be cut to size with relatively inexpensive machinery, and a wide choice of window designs can be made.

Aluminium windows

Window frames made from extruded alloy and containing hermetically-sealed double-glazing units are set within hardwood surrounds. They include vertical sash windows, casement windows, pivot systems and tilt/turn units. Some incorporate an insulant to provide a thermal break between the inner and outer portions of the frame, eliminating the tendency for condensation to appear on the inside.

Replacement windows

When necessary, it is advisable to replace completely rotted windows with standard-sized replacements, which should be in keeping with the age and character of the property. However, this assumes that the dimensions of the modern product will match the existing aperture, although a small amount of filling might be possible if the reveal is slightly larger, by using timber framing. In situations where a standard size of window will not do the job, there are four options:

● Make a custom replacement yourself
● Reduce the size of a replacement window to suit
● Use a self-assembly window frame kit
● Have a window made by a joinery company.

The first option is far from easy, obtaining good-quality pre-treated timber being difficult. Moreover, the intricate cross-sectional shapes of window components must be reproduced to make the structure fully weatherproof. Without suitable woodworking machines, this is very difficult to achieve. Even though the second option requires some skilled woodwork, it is a better strategy to follow if you want to do the work yourself.

▶ **SEE PAGE 78 FOR STEP-BY-STEP INSTRUCTIONS ON REPLACING AN OLD WINDOW**

Repairing wooden windows

Before replacing a window, make a check to determine whether remedial work may be feasible. For example, if parts of a sill are in bad condition, it may be possible to cut away the damage, and graft replacement timber into place. Similarly, it may be possible to build a new casement and fit it to the existing frame.

If rot has not spread too far, the frame can often be made good with a proprietary wood repair system. This will comprise:
● A brush-applied chemical that reinforces decayed wood and adds a moisture-repellent seal.
● A filler paste that will set into a solid material that can be planed, sanded and shaped.
● Preservative tablets that are inserted into holes drilled in the frame; dowels are glued into the holes to reinstate the surface. These tablets will subsequently dissolve and release a powerful preservative into the surrounding timber fibres.

Small areas of rot can often be made good with a proprietary wood repair system that incorporates filler and preservative.

Installing windows in new buildings

If you are building a house extension, it is important to recognise the latest procedures for installing windows. Concerns about the level of insulation at window reveals and the problems of cold spots have led to several new techniques for meeting the requirements of the Building Regulations.

Where the outer and inner skins of a cavity wall meet at the sides of a window opening – called the reveal – the traditional practice was to insert a vertical damp-proof membrane. Typically, this would be nailed to the sides of the window frame to protect it, folded outwards, and built into the brickwork that closed off the ends of the cavity. However, although the damp-proof material prevents moisture from reaching the inner skin, the continuity of masonry can act as a route for the loss of heat. The ensuing cold spot may give rise to localised condensation problems.

Eliminating the cold bridge

Several acceptable solutions to the problem have been developed, depending on where the window is located within the reveal – aligned with the inner edge, the outer edge or somewhere in between. A variety of products has been introduced to eliminate the cold bridge that's caused when brickwork is used to close the two skins at the reveal. One is a vertical DPC that comprises a flexible, flame-retardant, expanded polystyrene strip bonded directly to a polyethylene damp-proofing material. This is available in various widths, the composite strip being installed in the reveal at the point where the two skins of blockwork and brickwork meet. In effect, it replaces the conventional damp-proofing membrane. However, this is only one way of dealing with the problem.

Other products have been developed that make it completely unnecessary to use bricks or blocks to close off the cavity. For example, you can purchase plastic, channel-section cavity closers that contain a foam insulant. These are inserted into the cavity around the reveal. Not only do they close the cavity, but they also form a vertical DPC, break the cold bridge through the introduction of an insulant, and provide a fixing point for the window frame itself.

No doubt, many similar products will be introduced in the near future to achieve this objective.

Another requirement of the Building Regulations is the prevention of cold draughts from entering the property through gaps around window frames. This may be tackled by attaching draught-proofing strips to a frame so that it fits tightly in the reveal.

Fixing the frame

It is normal to locate a new window on a mortar bed, having previously placed the damp-proofing material and chosen cavity closing system under the sill. The frame is checked for correct positioning, and that it is upright and level. Then it is supported with a building board while the masonry is built up

Before installation of a window, a length of damp-proof membrane is normally attached to the sides of the frame. (BRE Crown copyright photograph)

As the brickwork is added, the vertical damp-proof membrane separates the outer and inner leaves at the window reveal. (BRE Crown Copyright photograph)

This vertical DPC includes a flame retardant, expanded polystyrene strip to eliminate a cold spot at the reveal. (Photograph courtesy TDI (UK) Ltd)

A purpose-made insulated closer and thermal break for insertion into the cavity is another method of eliminating cold spots. (BRE Crown copyright photograph)

A new window is placed on a mortar bed, checked with a spirit level, and then supported by a building board. (BRE Crown copyright photograph)

Cavity trays are recommended additions at the head of a reveal to protect the lintel. These must have stop ends, as shown. (BRE Crown copyright photograph)

around it. A different technique is to build around a temporary former, and to add the window later.

Various methods are used to anchor the frame to the surrounding masonry. One is to screw metal brackets to the frame and build them into mortar courses. The brackets may be straight or angled to allow for the different window positions within a reveal. Another approach is to install hardwood or thick plywood pads in horizontal mortar courses at 450mm (18in) centres. These provide fixing points for screws driven through the frame when the mortar is dry. Alternatively, the method of fixing may be provided by proprietary cavity closers.

However, whichever means of fixing is favoured, remember that if you use screws, these should not be overtightened. If you don't exercise caution, the frame may become distorted, upsetting the fit and operation of the casements.

Lintel requirements

At the head of the opening, a lintel must be used to comply with latest regulations. This, too, must contain an insulant. Above the lintel, cavity trays with stop ends should be installed; alternatively you can fit an angled piece of damp-proofing membrane. This protects the lintel from any condensation that might run down the cavity, and weepholes are needed in the face brickwork (see page 21).

Finally, the frame needs to be completely draught-proofed. This is achieved by injecting an appropriate mastic sealant around the outside, and a foam filler on the inside.

This type of pre-moulded lintel end stop will provide the necessary protection from cavity moisture that is currently required by the Building Regulations.

You must select the correct sealant. Here, a silicone sealer, specially formulated for uPVC windows, is being applied. (Photograph courtesy Dow Corning Hansil Ltd)

To keep out draughts, polyurethane foam is injected around the frame. This will expand to fill any gaps completely. (BRE Crown copyright photograph)

Replacing windows

It may be possible to remove an old window frame intact, but in most cases it will be too tight. In the latter situation, follow these guidelines:

- Remove all the glass
- Where possible, unscrew the casements
- Saw through all internal members at an angle, and remove them
- Saw through the head and sill of the window at both ends
- Prise away all outer sections with a wrecking bar or bolster chisels
- Try to minimise damage to plasterwork.

Any damp-proofing materials should be left intact. Check the size of the reveal, and its squareness by measuring the diagonals. There should be a minimum gap of 6mm (¼in) around the new frame.

The simplest method of fixing the frame is to cut slots in the mortar joints and insert wooden wedges. The frame can be nailed or screwed to these. Special types of fixing are manufactured for uPVC windows so that a neat finish is achieved on the inside of the frame. A mastic sealant should be injected around the frame, and the plasterwork reinstated on the inside.

Glazing

Many modern windows are provided with integral hermetically-sealed glazing units. However, these can be ordered separately for wooden frames, but you must check that the rebate is deep enough. You may be able to increase its depth with a router, provided this doesn't reduce the thickness of the casements too much. The sealed glazing units are normally held in place with wooden fillets and a butyl-based sealing compound, rather than conventional putty.

TOOLS AND MATERIALS

- [ ] Tape measure
- [ ] Pencil
- [ ] Adjustable props
- [ ] Timber needle
- [ ] Bolster chisel
- [ ] Club hammer
- [ ] Wrecking bar
- [ ] Bricklayer's trowel
- [ ] Spirit level
- [ ] Shovel
- [ ] Bucket
- [ ] Mixing board
- [ ] Hammer
- [ ] Lintel
- [ ] Wooden wedges
- [ ] Wooden blocks
- [ ] Cut nails
- [ ] New window frame
- [ ] Glass
- [ ] Glazing sprigs
- [ ] Putty

1 If the new window is a different height to the old one. Support the masonry above the opening with adjustable props and a timber needle. Then chop out the soldier arch or old lintel.

2 Remove any fixings holding the old frame within the opening, then lever it out, using a wrecking bar or bolster chisels. Cut openings in the masonry for the new lintel.

3 Lift the new lintel into place, bedding it on mortar at each end. Check that it is level, and pack out at either end with pieces of tile or slate if necessary. Then let the mortar set for at least 24 hours.

4 If the new window is wider than the old, mark the width of the opening inside. Then use a club hammer and bolster chisel to remove the masonry from the inner leaf of the wall.

5 Fill in with bricks above the lintel, then transfer the width of the new opening to the outer leaf of the wall. Make sure that the guideline at each side is perfectly vertical.

6 Remove the bricks from each side of the opening, working downwards from the lintel, chopping out alternate whole bricks to produce a toothed edge to the opening.

7 Cut bricks to fill the gaps in the sides of the opening, and set them in place with mortar. Make constant checks with a spirit level to ensure that the sides of the opening are vertical.

8 In this solid brick wall, the soldier arch is recreated in the outer leaf by laying the bricks on a timber former. Once the mortar has set, the props and needle may be removed.

9 Brick up the opening in the wall above the window where the needle was inserted. Then remove the arch former so that the new window frame can be fitted in place.

10 Traditionally, frames were nailed to wooden wedges set in the mortar joints. Decide on the positions of the wedges, cut slots with a bolster and drive the wedges into place.

11 Set the frame in position, flush with the inner face of the wall. Check that it is level and upright with a spirit level. Set it against the lintel by packing out with wooden blocks.

12 When you are satisfied with the frame's position, use cut nails to fix it to the wedges at the sides. Finally, brick up any gap beneath the frame, glaze it and replaster the wall inside.

Installing a roof window

A simple solution to the light and ventilation requirements of an attic room is to install a roof window, and you can choose between plastic-framed versions and timber windows. They are relatively straightforward to install, and in many circumstances the work can be carried out from inside the loft space, easing the problem of access considerably. The units are supplied with special pre-fixed weatherproofing flashing systems, while purpose-made blinds are optional fittings.

Check the pitch

However, before buying a roof window, you should check that the roof pitch is acceptable; for instance, some products may be suitable for pitches between 25 and 75 degrees. If you want to install such a window in a roof with a lower pitch, your only recourse is to construct a wedge-shaped box within the roof structure to house the window at the required angle. This is quite a common solution to the problem, but it is wise to discuss the construction first with the window manufacturer's technical staff.

When installing a window in an existing roof, you must check with a building surveyor that the removal of rafters and the substitution of a trimmer will not weaken the structure. This is particularly important where modifications would be necessary in a prefabricated trussed rafter roof. Since this is likely to have considerable structural implications, it might be more appropriate to install a small window unit, or two matching units, between the existing rafters. With many trussed rafters set at 600mm (24in) centres, the narrowest windows should fit within the available opening. The options are much wider in the case of traditionally-constructed rafter and purlin roofs.

TOOLS AND MATERIALS

☐ Tape measure
☐ Pencil
☐ Sharp knife
☐ Saw
☐ Hammer
☐ Bradawl
☐ Screwdriver
☐ Spirit level
☐ Soft-faced mallet
☐ Angle grinder
☐ Nails
☐ Rust-proof screws
☐ Timber for trimmers
☐ Roof window

1 Working from the inside, the felt is cut through, and the necessary tiles are removed. (All photographs courtesy The Velux Co. Ltd)

2 A rafter is removed from the opening, the remaining portions at top and bottom being linked to the adjacent rafters with timber trimmers.

3 An intermediate rafter is nailed between the trimmers to make the opening the correct width, and the battens cut to length.

4 Using special L-shaped fixing brackets, the frame of the roof window is attached to the rafters and top and bottom trimmers.

5 The frame should be checked to ensure that it is square by taking the diagonal measurements in each direction. If necessary, remake the fixings.

6 A pre-formed apron flashing section is fitted along the bottom of the frame so that it overlaps the course of tiles below the opening.

7 Next, pre-formed side flashing units are added to the frame to provide weather protection. These overlap the apron unit below.

8 Using a soft-faced mallet, the lead apron flashing is carefully dressed over the tiles below the opening. It should closely follow the tiles' profile.

9 Tiles are now reinstated along the sides of the frame. Some may need cutting to width, which can be carried out with an angle grinder.

10 With the sides completed, attention should be turned to the head of the window, where the tiles are laid to overlap the flashing.

11 The pivoting sash is installed in the frame and checked for correct operation. It rotates completely to allow cleaning of the glass.

12 The completed roof window will provide an attic room with plenty of light and ventilation, while being less obtrusive than a dormer extension.

External doors

Being exposed to the weather, an external door may become damaged beyond repair, particularly if it isn't looked after. Buying a replacement can be quite costly, and it also takes a surprising amount of time to fit the hinges and other fittings. For this reason, you should determine whether repairs are feasible before buying a new door.

There are several ways of coping with the problem of deteriorating wood. For example, there are products for repairing wood, while a number of epoxy resin wood fillers enable you to replace a rotted area of a door with a highly durable substitute.

Once rubbed down and painted, a repaired area can be scarcely discernible.

Where rot has progressed so far as to weaken the door, it may be possible to insert new sections of timber. If fixed securely, they will extend the life of the door considerably. If too much is damaged, however, the only solution is to replace it.

> ▶ **SEE PAGES 84-85 FOR STEP-BY-STEP INSTRUCTIONS ON DEALING WITH ROTTEN WOOD**

Choosing a replacement door

When a deteriorating door is beyond repair, there's no option but to fit a replacement. This may also be necessary if a door develops a bad twist. Timber can be unstable, and once a severe twist becomes evident, efforts to re-straighten it are seldom successful. If the door is only mildly twisted, thin fillets of wood can be planed at an angle and pinned in the frame's rebate to close gaps and reduce draughts. In extreme cases, however, a replacement door is the only satisfactory answer.

If your house is modern, you will find plenty of suitable doors stocked at joinery centres and major DIY stores. When making your choice, you must make sure that the door's thickness suits the depth of rebate in the frame.

However, if you own a period property, it is obviously important to preserve its character. In this situation, you will need to contract a specialist joinery company to construct a replica.

Popular material

Timber remains the most popular material for doors, and there may be little opportunity to fit anything different without replacing the frame as well. For example, there is growing interest in uPVC doors, but they are usually supplied as a complete unit with a frame to suit. Doors manufactured in uPVC are available as replacement front doors and also

traditional French doors. Their major advantage is the fact that they are virtually maintenance-free, although they are not always as attractive as traditional wooden products.

Safety considerations

Doors with large glazed panels may constitute an accident risk. Where glass is used in a lower panel, a stumbling toddler, or an elderly person losing their footing, can be placed at risk. This type of door was popular several years ago, but now the Building Regulations specify strict requirements concerning the location of such doors and the type of glass used.

In other parts of a door, decorative glass such as a fanlight can be an attractive feature. However, the position of any glass should be considered from the security angle; if a glass panel is too close to a latch, it will be easy for a burglar to break it, reach in and open the door.

It is worth noting that some manufacturers produce front doors that match the design of garage doors. If these are situated in close proximity, the pairing can look particularly appealing.

> ▶ **SEE PAGES 86-88 FOR STEP-BY-STEP INSTRUCTIONS ON FITTING A NEW FRAME AND DOOR**

Choosing and fitting hinges

If you are replacing an existing door, the positions of the hinges will already be determined by cutouts in the frame, and all that is necessary is to match those positions on the door by careful measurement. On the other hand, if your new door is being hung in a new frame, the hinges should be positioned 150mm (6in) from the top and 200-225mm (8-9in) from the bottom. If a third hinge is required, this should be placed mid-way between the two.

Medium-weight doors, which include many firecheck doors, need three 100mm (4in) butt hinges. Heavier doors, particularly those containing glazing, should be hung using three brass butt hinges that incorporate steel washers. As a rule, brass hinges are preferable for external doors, since they are not susceptible to rust.

The hinges should always be fitted to the door before the frame, and their positioning relative to the edge will depend on their type:

Pressed steel butts The full knuckle of the hinge must be placed so that it extends beyond the face of the door.

Cast butts The centre-line of the knuckle pin should align with the edge of the door.

Cutting the housing

Before cutting the housing in the door, mark the hinge position carefully, scoring it deeply with a sharp craft knife. One method of achieving accuracy when marking is to fix the hinge temporarily to the edge of the door using two or three screws. This allows you to scribe around it with perfect accuracy, and without fear of it slipping on the surface.

When you begin to remove the waste, the deep score marks will help prevent the wood from splitting accidentally as you cut with the chisel. The quality of workmanship depends on having a sharp chisel, and removing small amounts of wood at a time. The procedure is as follows:

● Using a mallet and a bevel-edged chisel with a blade slightly narrower than the hinge flap, cut down vertically through the wood along the scored lines. Hold the bevel of the blade towards the waste side of the line and drive the blade down by an amount equivalent to the thickness of the hinge flap. If the

chisel is sharp, you won't need to use a heavy blow with the chisel, even if the door is made from hardwood.

● Make a series of feather cuts across the waste wood, holding the chisel bevelled edge down and keeping the blade within the outline of the hinge flap. Try not to drive the blade below the depth of the flap outline.

● Hold the chisel bevelled edge up, and cut across the waste material to remove it. You should not need to use the mallet for this, only hand pressure. Tidy up the edges with careful chisel cuts into the corners. Check that the recess has been cut to an even depth.

● Offer up the hinge and check that its flap sits flush with the surface of the door. If necessary, make further cuts with the chisel until it does.

● Fix the hinge to the door with brass screws, starting their holes with a bradawl.

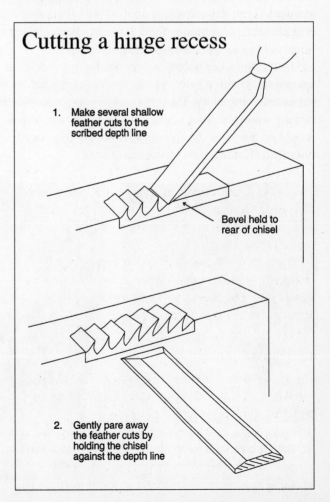

Cutting a hinge recess

1. Make several shallow feather cuts to the scribed depth line

Bevel held to rear of chisel

2. Gently pare away the feather cuts by holding the chisel against the depth line

Repairing rotten wood

Although finding an area of rot in a door can be a worry, provided the damage hasn't weakened the structure of the door, it may be possible to make a cosmetic repair using a special filler. While this is unlikely to provide a real long-term solution the problem, it should at least stave off the time when more substantial repairs, or even replacement of the door, are necessary.

The example below shows an external door in which a large area of rot had developed at one end of the bottom rail. The rot was removed with an old chisel, after which the area of the repair was allowed to dry completely before applying the treatment. The resin-based repair compound used comprises a two-part polyester filler and a paste catalyst. The latter is sometimes referred to as the hardener; it must be dispensed from its tube in a carefully measured amount if the filler is to perform as it should.

TOOLS AND MATERIALS

☐ Old wood chisel
☐ Putty knife
☐ Mixing board
☐ Sanding block
☐ Paint brush
☐ Two-part polyester filler
☐ Coarse and fine glass-paper
☐ Primer, undercoat and topcoat

Mixing board

It is easiest to mix the two components of the filler together on a piece of board. Then the mixture is applied with the aid of a putty knife. Provided the preparation of the wood has been carried out carefully, the filler will dry to form a tough protective layer.

Because the filler becomes very hard when it dries, it is better to start smoothing it with a heavy grade of glass-paper before the compound has cured completely. This removes any major undulations in the surface while the filler is still soft. The final sanding work, however, should be left until the filler has hardened. It's essential to wear a suitable dust mask if a disc sander is used.

1 Having removed all the rotten wood from the door, the polyester wood filler is mixed on a board, adding a carefully measured amount of catalyst hardener from a tube.

2 The bottom of this external door was in bad condition, and several layers of the polyester wood filler had to be applied. Each was allowed to dry before the next was added.

3 The filler was applied with a putty knife, the final layer being shaped carefully to achieve a reasonable surface before finally smoothing off with glass-paper.

Replacing rotten wood

In some cases, the bottom of a door may rot to the extent that the only solution, other than replacing it completely, is to cut out the rot and rebuild the door with new wood. In the example shown below, the uprights – called 'stiles' – were intact, whereas the plywood infill panel and bottom rail had deteriorated badly. Obviously, damage of this sort will vary from door to door, but the basic principles of the repair can be applied to any similar situation. Once the rail had been removed from the door by sawing through each end, the infill panel could be slid from its rebate and replaced with a new panel of exterior-grade plywood.

A replacement rail

Since the moulded weatherboard at the bottom of the door was sound, it was used to align the replacement rail. It also acted as a brace to ensure that the two stiles didn't splay outwards once the original rail had been cut away. Three pieces of 100 x 50mm (4 x 2in) planed softwood were then accurately cut to length and positioned between the stiles to form a new bottom rail, 300mm (12in) in height.

The new wood was secured by drilling through the stiles from the outside and driving hardwood doweling into the ends of the sections of timber. All the paint had been removed from the mating surfaces, allowing an exterior-grade PVA wood glue to be applied as well. Together with the dowel joints, the adhesive is an important contributor to the overall rigidity of the final structure. Sash cramps are useful for holding everything tightly together while the adhesive is setting. If these are not available, it should be possible to fashion a tourniquet arrangement from a looped rope that can be tightened by twisting.

TOOLS AND MATERIALS

- ☐ Panel saw
- ☐ Pencil
- ☐ Tape measure
- ☐ Try square
- ☐ Circular saw
- ☐ Electric drill
- ☐ Wood bit
- ☐ Hammer
- ☐ Sash cramps or rope tourniquet
- ☐ Paint brush
- ☐ Hardwood dowels
- ☐ Weatherproof wood glue
- ☐ Exterior-grade plywood
- ☐ Wood for frame sections
- ☐ Primer, undercoat and topcoat

1 The rotten bottom rail was removed and a new plywood infill panel fitted. However, the moulded weatherboard was left in place to prevent the stiles from splaying outwards.

2 Three lengths of 100 x 50mm (4 x 2in) softwood were cut to length and placed between the stiles to form a new bottom rail for the door. They were secured with dowels and glue.

3 The uppermost section of timber had a rebate cut in it for the bottom of the plywood panel, while the lowest section was cut to clear the metal weather bar on the sill.

Replacing a door frame

If a door frame needs replacement, the task of fitting it within a reveal is essentially similar to that of fitting a window frame (see pages 76-79). For instance, you have to be careful not to over-tighten any screws that attach the frame to the brickwork, since this leads to distortion and subsequent problems when fitting the door later. If the frame is slightly too small for the reveal, inserting timber packing pieces between the frame and opening will ensure that its uprights won't bend outwards when you tighten the securing screws.

When choosing an external frame, it is important to check that the rebate is made for the type of door you want to fit. Front doors will need one for an inward-opening door, but French doors, for example, will need a frame for outward-opening doors. The frame should also be made with a hardwood sill that includes provision for a steel strip, known as a weather bar. This is essential to keep out wind-driven rain.

There are three methods of fixing the frame in its opening:

● You can use proprietary frame fixings, or ordinary screws and wall plugs (but make sure the screws are corrosion resistant).

● You can attach galvanised metal wall ties to the jambs and mortar these into pockets cut in the brickwork.

● You can nail the frame to wooden wedges set in the mortar joints between the bricks.

TOOLS AND MATERIALS
☐ Hammer
☐ Try square
☐ Screwdriver
☐ Club hammer
☐ Bolster chisel
☐ Electric drill
☐ Wood and masonry bits
☐ Tape measure
☐ Pencil
☐ Spirit level
☐ Panel saw
☐ Nails
☐ Rustproof screws and wall plugs or proprietary frame fixings
☐ Mastic
☐ Door frame

Removing the old frame

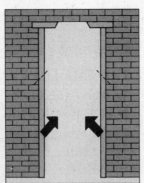

First, cut the centre portion from the head, by sawing at an angle. Then treat the lower portions of the jambs in a similar fashion, either removing their securing screws or levering them free. Finally, remove the upper corners of the frame, breaking any horns at the top of the frame free from the masonry.

1 The sill of the frame will need protecting against rising damp, so the first task is to nail a length of DPC strip to its underside, using galvanised nails. Treat the heads of the nails with a liberal coat of bituminous emulsion to prevent moisture from working its way through the holes in the DPC. Although the frame should have been treated with preservative, paint all surfaces that will contact masonry with primer, undercoat and top coat.

2 Assemble the door frame, attaching the sill between the feet of the jambs. Then secure it by skew nailing or by driving screws diagonally down through the jambs into the sill. Offer up the frame to the opening to determine if the latter will need enlarging. If it does, you can chop out up to a third of a brick's length from each side, using a bolster chisel and club hammer. Check the final fit of the frame.

3 Replace the frame in the opening, and wedge it in place so that the jambs are vertical in both planes. Both head and sill must also be horizontal. Check these with a spirit level. Also, make sure that the sill is at the right height in relation to the floor inside and any step outside. If necessary, pack the frame out in relation to the opening, using offcuts of wood, but make sure they are treated with preservative.

4 The simplest way of securing the frame to the opening is to use proprietary frame fixings. These combine a special hammer-in screw with a long plastic wall plug that passes through the frame and into the wall. Having drilled the holes in the frame, drill through them into the wall with a masonry bit. Then insert each fixing, hammer in the screw, and give it a final tighten with a screwdriver.

5 Complete the frame by fitting the weather bar to the sill. To do this, apply a good bead of mastic to the rebate in the sill and press the metal bar into the groove. The mastic will hold it in place and prevent moisture from reaching the inside. The final job is to make good the opening around the frame by applying a good bead of mastic around the outside for weather protection; inside, the plaster can be taken up to the frame.

Hanging the door

Before trimming a door, it is always wise to check the accuracy of its construction. By holding the edge of a long spirit level or steel rule along the sides, you can check that the door doesn't bow in any direction. It is worth noting that some types of hardwood front door are now being manufactured with an identical finish on both sides. However, if the door is glazed, the outer face can be determined by checking the position of the glass rebate; the rebate will be cut in the outer face of the door.

Making it fit

When the weatherproofing rebate has been prepared on the underside of the door, it should be placed on some thin ply packing to achieve about 6mm (¼in) clearance between the bottom of the door and the frame. This may seem rather a wide gap, but it allows for the fact that the door will tend to drop over a period of time.

You must ascertain any discrepancies in the fit, marking the edges of the door that may need trimming. This takes time, and the door will need to be offered up and removed on a number of occasions before you achieve an accurate fit. A clearance gap at the top and sides of around 3mm (⅛in) is recommended.

When trimming is complete, you can fit the hinges to the door. If you are fitting the door into an existing frame, careful measurement is needed to ensure that the hinge positions match those of the frame. Once that has been done, you need to support the door in the open position so that the hinges can be screwed to the frame. When an existing frame is being used, the hinges should mate with the existing recesses cut into the frame, although some final adjustments may be necessary. It's much easier, of course, to fit a door into a new frame, since there won't be any original hinge positions to match; you merely mark and make new ones.

Door furniture and locks

Finally, the door accessories – referred to as door furniture – should be installed. Some items may need to be recessed, and the cutouts should be accurately scribed, using the same technique as when mounting the hinges. When cutting mortises in the door, they should be drilled out first, with either a brace and bit or a power drill fitted with a high-speed flat bit. Then the series of holes should be squared-up with a chisel.

If you decide to fit a cylinder lock, these are usually supplied with a fitting template, and the metal operating strip of the lock will need trimming to suit the door's thickness. Incidentally, if you intend fitting a latch lock, a double-action or deadlock type is preferable, although this will cost slightly more than the standard version.

It takes time to fit all the door furniture, but since this contributes to the appearance of an external door, careful workmanship is essential.

TOOLS AND MATERIALS

- ☐ Spirit level
- ☐ Pencil
- ☐ Tape measure
- ☐ Plane
- ☐ Panel saw
- ☐ Wood chisel
- ☐ Mallet
- ☐ Bradawl
- ☐ Screwdriver
- ☐ Pin hammer
- ☐ Hinges
- ☐ Latch
- ☐ Screws
- ☐ Panel pins
- ☐ Putty or glass sealant
- ☐ Glass panes
- ☐ Glass beading
- ☐ Door

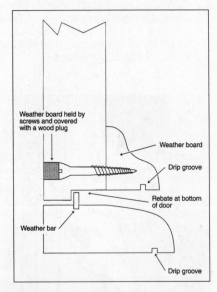

Weather board held by screws and covered with a wood plug

Weather board

Drip groove

Rebate at bottom of door

Weather bar

Drip groove

WEATHER BOARD
A steel weather bar in the sill works in conjunction with a weather board on the door to keep out driven rain, and a new door must be fitted with one – you should be able to buy it at the same time as the door. A section needs to be removed from the bottom of the door to clear the bar when it's closed. This is easily done with a portable circular saw, or a panel saw if you don't have one. The weather board can be attached to the door using screws or, for a neat finish, with glued wooden dowels.

1 In this instance, the door frame will accommodate a pair of french doors. Set them in place and check their fit. If necessary, plane the edges to ensure a narrow gap on all sides.

2 Mark out the rebate needed to clear the water bar in the sill, then cut across the door with a panel saw. A batten clamped to the door will act as a sawing guide. Chisel out the waste.

3 Determine the positions of the hinges on the edge of the door and draw around them. For most doors, two hinges will suffice, but for a heavy door it is better to fit three.

4 Cut around the edges of each hinge recess with a chisel, then make several shallow cuts across the grain. Finally, carefully pare away the wood until the hinge sits flush with the surface.

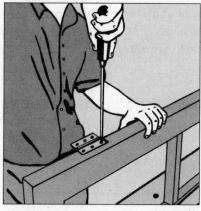

5 Check that the hinge sits square in the recess. Then push a bradawl through the screw holes to start the screws. Fit a screw to each hole in the flap and tighten them.

6 Prop each door in place in the frame, and mark the hinge flap positions on the jambs. Chisel out the recesses, as before, then replace the doors and screw the flaps to the jambs.

7 Bed a layer of putty or similar sealant around the rebate for each pane of glass, working it into the corners. Make sure you cover the entire rebate, but don't apply too much.

8 Carefully press each pane of glass into place, positioning the bottom edge first. Push the glass gently inwards to bed it properly. Then remove any excess putty or sealant.

9 Finally, secure the pane by pinning lengths of glass beading around the rebate. Mitre the corners for a neat fit. You can now prepare the door for painting or staining.

Chapter 3

Interior Work
Concrete floors

In the early 1900s, a ground floor usually comprised a suspended platform built in timber. Today, floors cast in-situ from concrete – and more recently, constructed from reinforced concrete beams with a block infill – are more common.

Whatever method of construction, precautionary measures must be taken to keep damp out of a building. Moreover, the Building Regulations require some form of thermal insulation to prevent heat loss from the building.

The options

When it comes to laying a concrete floor, there are three basic methods of construction:
● **Raft foundation** Where a building is erected on unstable ground, its foundation will be constructed using a reinforced concrete raft. This provides the base on which a thin floor screed, together with some form of insulation, would be laid.
● **Concrete slab** More conventionally, concrete strip foundations are laid in a trench, then walls built from brick or block to a level just above the surrounding ground. Within this structure, a concrete slab floor can be laid.
● **Beam and block** Using the foundation walls described above for support, the floor can be built from pre-cast, steel-reinforced concrete beams. A clear space is left beneath the concrete beams – as with a suspended timber floor. Gaps between the beams are filled with thermally-efficient blocks.

Reinforced raft floors

Where building is carried out on an infill site, the risk of subsidence is acute. The ground has poor bearing capacity and building a reinforced concrete raft is one of the options. The use of deep piles and lintels is another.

Sometimes, the raft will be a flat structure of uniform thickness, but where the ground is particularly compressible, a 'wide toe' raft is preferable. In this design, the edges of the raft, and any areas that have to support the internal walls of the building are stiffened by incorporating reinforced concrete beams.

This is an involved operation, which is best left to a specialist contractor.

Uninsulated slab floors

The ground floors of unheated outbuildings, do not need any thermal insulation under the terms of the Building Regulations. Moreover, a small extension, not exceeding 10m² (107.5ft²), needs only adopt the level of thermal insulation of the 'parent' building. However, whether the floor is insulated or not, a concrete slab is only suitable where ground conditions are stable. Its construction is as follows:
● Prior to marking a site and digging trenches, all plants, topsoil and humus must be skimmed from the surface. The actual depth removed will vary, and in rural locations it may be as much as 300mm (12in).

● An infill of hardcore, at least 150mm (6in) deep, is needed next. This will form a base for the concrete, and raise the level to the required height. Correctly selected, hardcore also helps prevent damp rising from the ground below by capillary action.

● The next task is to 'blind' the hardcore base by adding a sealing layer – usually of sand – to fill any gaps in the surface of the hardcore, to a depth of approximately 50mm (2in). This prevents the wet concrete from falling into the gaps, which is wasteful. In addition, concrete permeating through the hardcore might absorb moisture from the ground.

● A damp-proof membrane (DPM), of heavy-grade polyethylene, can be laid on top of the blinding. This is preferable on damp ground; otherwise, the membrane can be placed on top of the concrete slab before screeding. If the membrane is placed below the oversite concrete, polythene or polyethylene sheet of at least 0.25mm thickness (1000 gauge) is required; more recently, 0.3mm (1200 gauge) has been specified. If joints are necessary, one method is to create an overlap of at least 150mm (6in) and seal it with a mastic tape. Another is to create a series of folds and hold them down with bricks until the concrete is poured. The membrane must be taken up the sides of the slab to overlap the DPC.

● For a small project, it may be more convenient to hire a mixer; for a large one, however, it's best to order ready-mixed concrete. A key constituent is ordinary Portland cement (OPC), which should not be confused with masonry cement. The sand must be sharp sand (also known as concreting sand), which is coarse It must be mixed with gravel that has been graded to a specific size.

These three materials can be bought separately and mixed to the proportions in the accompanying table. On the other hand, it can be more convenient to buy 'all-in' aggregate, in which the sand and gravel is already mixed. This is often referred to as 'ballast'.

When using a cement mixer, start with a small quantity of clean water in the bowl and then add sand and gravel in measured amounts by volume. Add more water to ensure the particles are coated and damp, but not awash.

Concrete for hand or machine mixing is identified by the ratio of cement, sand and gravel, based on their dry volume. The best way of measuring this is by the bucketful. Ready-mixed concrete, however, is referred to using a British Standard specification, as measuring by volume can be inaccurate.

To calculate the quantity needed, multiply the depth, length and width of the slab. For a small shed, the slab will be no more than 100mm (4in) thick, but in a domestic building 150mm (6in) is more usual.

Steel reinforcement

The slab may need reinforcing, depending on the ground conditions. Normally, steel mesh is used and placed prior to adding the concrete. Where reinforcement is needed, the advice of an engineer should be sought regarding its positioning.

▶ SEE PAGE 92 FOR STEP-BY-STEP INSTRUCTIONS ON LAYING A CONCRETE SLAB

Application	Self-mixed - Proportions by volume		Amount per m³ (yd³)	Yield per bag of cement	Ready-mixed - BS specification
General purpose, incl. oversite slab	Cement Sand 20mm (¾in) agg. Ballast	1 2 3 4	6.4 bags 680kg (0.67 tons) 1175kg (1.16 tons) 1855kg (1.83 tons)	0.15m³ (0.2yd³)	C20P to BS 5382 medium/high workability
Foundations, footings and base for pre-cast slabs	Cement Sand 20mm (¾in) agg. Ballast	1 2.5 3.5 5	5.6 bags 720kg (0.71 tons) 1165kg (1.15 tons) 1885kg (1.86 tons)	0.18m³ (0.24yd³)	C7.5P to BS 5382 high workability

Note: One bag of cement has a volume of 0.035m³ (1.24ft³)

Information supplied by British Cement Association

Laying concrete

Although laying a concrete slab is a relatively straightforward task, the job will be easier if you follow these tips:

● When laying a slab, you will find a garden rake ideal for spreading a load of concrete and bringing it to the approximate finished height.
● Check that the concrete is worked into the corners of the slab and thoroughly bedded down, and that the polyethylene DPM doesn't lift away from the base.
● Embed a batten in the surface of the concrete if services are likely to run across the slab later. When the batten is removed, it will leave a channel for pipes, etc.
● When working in bright sun, the concrete may dry out too quickly and begin to crack. Spray the area periodically with a fine mist of water. In addition, cover the surface with damp hessian sacks or even an old carpet.
● Leave the surface rough if a screed is to be added later.
● If the slab represents the final surface,(in a garage, for example) it may be 'trowelled-up' to achieve a smooth finish. Usually, this is done using a steel trowel, but wait until the concrete has started to cure before beginning.

TOOLS AND MATERIALS

☐ Punner, plate vibrator or roller
☐ Shovel
☐ Rake
☐ Tamping board
☐ Steel float
☐ Hardcore
☐ Concrete
☐ Sand
☐ Wood for shuttering
☐ Polyethylene DPM (optional)
☐ Steel reinforcing mesh (optional)

CURING TIME

☐ Depending on temperatures, concrete takes several days to cure fully. In hot weather, it is advisable to damp down the surface periodically over a three-day period. Note, however, that the curing time for concrete is considerably greater if laid on a plastic DPM. When laid directly on top of blinded hardcore, moisture can escape downwards and the drying time is markedly shorter.

1 Clean broken bricks are often used for hardcore, but check the acceptability of an oversite material with the Building Inspector. Demolition rubble is usually unsuitable; old plaster remnants and bits of timber will hold and conduct moisture. However, many other materials are acceptable. The hardcore should be spread out in an even layer across the site, to a minimum depth of 150mm (6in).

2 The hardcore must be compressed, and whereas some materials (i.e. gravel) tend to self-compact, others, like broken bricks, need to be compacted using the appropriate equipment. On very small projects, and where access is difficult, a hand punner can be used. For larger projects, it may be necessary to hire a vibrating roller. Alternatively, a plate vibrator may be powerful enough to do the job.

3 To reduce waste through the concrete dropping down between the pieces of rubble, the hardcore must be topped (blinded) by a layer of sand. This should be raked out to an even depth of about 50mm (2in) and either rolled to compact it, or trodden down. Another reason for adding a blinding layer is to prevent the sharp edges of crushed stone or brick of the hardcore from puncturing the DPM, which quite often is added next

4 Once any DPM has been positioned, the concrete mix can be spread across the site, either by offloading it from wheelbarrows or by distributing it from the chute of a mobile mixer. It should be raked out roughly level with a rake, aiming for even distribution. Then a tamping board is used with a sawing action to skim off high points and level it with the surrounding formwork. Fill any low areas with more concrete.

5 With the concrete levelled across the site, the tamping board is used with a vertical chopping action, working steadily from one end of the slab to the other. This tamping releases trapped air from the concrete and brings excess water to the top, producing a smooth surface. Avoid over-tamping the concrete, as it will shake larger particles of aggregate to the bottom of the mix, weakening the surface.

6 If the surface of the slab is to be left in its natural concrete state, a smooth surface can be achieved by going over it with a steel trowel as the concrete begins to dry. While it is curing, the slab must be protected from frost, which could cause the concrete to crumble. This can be done by covering it with straw, sacking and a layer of polythene sheeting. Similarly, it must not be allowed to dry out too quickly.

Laying a screed

Normally, a fine sand/cement screed is applied to a concrete floor slab, forming a suitable base for carpet, ceramic tiles, vinyl and other popular floor coverings. Achieving an accurate level is essential, but this is simplified by dividing the slab into bays with wooden battens, known as 'screeding rails', and using the battens as depth guides.

If the screed is laid directly on a slab, it will bond with the surface of the concrete and need only be 38mm (1½in) thick. However, if a damp-proof membrane hasn't been installed below the concrete slab, provision must be made before screeding. One option is to apply several coats of a damp-proofing liquid, another is to lay 1200 gauge polyethylene sheeting. In this instance, the screed remains separate from the slab, so it needs to be at least 50mm (2in) thick.

The slab must be clean and dust free. First, it should be dampened, then a cement water grout applied. Mix this to a creamy consistency; many builders add a PVA bonding compound to achieve better adhesion. Apply the grout to small areas at a time – as much as you expect to be able to screed in about 20 minutes.

Although a sand/cement mix is the traditional way of screeding concrete, you can also obtain self-levelling floor screeds. Many of these cure within a matter of hours, having to be mixed and poured from a bucket, then spread with a steel float.

TOOLS AND MATERIALS

- ☐ Battens for screeding rails
- ☐ Spirit level
- ☐ Long straight-edge
- ☐ Shovel
- ☐ Short batten for tamping
- ☐ Steel float
- ☐ Small trowel
- ☐ Sand and cement
- ☐ Polythene sheeting

THE RIGHT MIX

- ☐ If the floor covering will be a flexible material, like vinyl tiling, the screeding mix should be 1 part ordinary Portland cement (OPC) and 3 parts concreting sand. However, if a rigid tile will be laid, use a 1:4 mix.
- ☐ The screeding mix should be quite dry, so little water is needed. A test is to mould it into a ball in your hand: when squeezed, hardly any water should be released. It should also retain its shape when you open your hand.

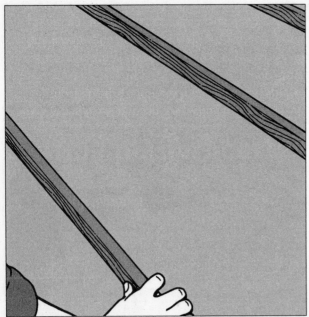

1 Place the screeding rails about 300-450mm (12-18in) apart, using battens of the appropriate width. They can either be held in place with dabs of the screeding mortar, or nailed to the floor with masonry nails. In the latter case, you must treat the nail holes with more damp-proofing liquid when the battens are removed. Set the battens across the shortest dimension of the floor, not forgetting to place them along the edges.

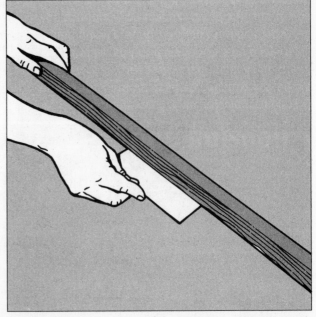

2 It is essential to make sure that the battens are level along their length and also level with each other, as they determine the depth of the screed and whether or not its surface is flat. Use a spirit level and long straight-edge to check. If necessary, insert packing pieces of hardboard or thin plywood beneath the battens to adjust their positions. These packing pieces can be left in place when the battens are removed.

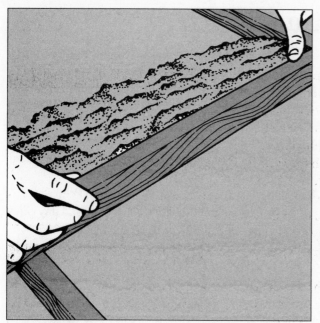

3 Having mixed the screed to the appropriate formula (see opposite), shovel some of it between the battens of the first bay, roughly spreading it out, and taking care not to disturb the battens. Use a short length of batten to level the mortar with the screeding rails, tamping it gently and adopting a sawing action to compact the mortar and remove any air pockets. Fill any low spots with more mortar and level again.

4 Go over the screed carefully with a rectangular steel trowel to produce a smooth finish, keeping the blade wet to lubricate it. Use light strokes sufficient to ensure a fine finish. Then shovel more of the screeding mix into the bay and continue as before, levelling it with the battens and polishing the surface. When you have completed the first bay, repeat the procedure for the second bay.

5 Once you have completed the first two bays, you can remove the batten separating them. Carefully lift it free, taking care not to disturb the surrounding screed. Then fill the resulting gap in the screed with more mortar, using a small trowel to pack it in. If you need to incorporate channels in the floor for services, some of the battens can be left in place until the screed has cured completely.

6 Carefully use the wet blade of the steel float to smooth the mortar added between the two bays. Continue working in this manner until you have screeded the entire floor. Once completed, the floor should be covered with a layer of polythene and left to cure for at least three days before walking on it. Then leave it to dry out completely before laying the chosen floorcovering.

Insulated concrete slab floors

In a house, a concrete slab floor must incorporate an insulating layer, and the insulation requirements are determined by its size and shape. The architect has to calculate what is known as the 'shape factor', based on the floor perimeter and area. The perimeter/area, or P/A, ratios are used to determine the type, thickness and placing of the insulation.

Adding the insulation

There are two methods of insulating a slab:
● Rigid plastic foam boarding can be placed on top of the blinding before the concrete. This presumes that the ground is stable. The foam must have a high compressive strength, a good resistance to moisture, and be unaffected by ground conditions. In addition, 25mm (1in) wide insulation layers need placing vertically around the sides of the slab and screed, unless insulating blockwork is used below the DPC, or the cavity insulant extends below the slab.
● Insulation can be placed on top of the slab before laying the screed. In this case, the DPM must be placed above the slab. This method may be used if there's a possibility that contaminants in the ground could damage insulation placed under the slab.

Several types of insulation material are available, extruded polystyrene achieving slightly lower thermal conductivity than expanded polystyrene. A typical thickness of material needed for a detached house is 50mm (2in) extruded polystyrene, or 75mm (3in) expanded polystyrene.

Care must be taken to insulate service entry ducts and drainage stacks that pass through the slab. The insulation around water pipes and soil stacks must extend below the ground, under the slab, to a depth of at least 750mm (29½in) to protect against frost.

Air must also be prevented from entering a building via the ducts. For this reason, foam should be injected where ducts pass through foundation walls – a precautionary measure that also helps to keep out rodents. Foam should be used to seal around any pipe where it passes through polystyrene insulation.

Damp-proof membranes

There are various methods of installing a DPM:
● If there's any possibility that an insulant could be damaged by chemicals in the ground, the DPM should be placed below the insulant.
● Placing the DPM above the insulating blocks, but below the slab, prevents the concrete mix from running down between joints in the insulating blocks. It is also less likely to snag when laid on a flat slab, than it is on blinding material.
● A DPM, or a liquid damp-proofing compound, can be placed above the slab if a moisture-sensitive floor finish is planned, since it could be affected by damp rising from the slab. If plastic sheeting is used as a DPM, it should be 1200 gauge polyethylene. The damp-proofing must extend up the sides of the slab, to the top of the screed, to keep out any residual dampness in the walls.

Insulation boards can be laid above a damp-proof membrane before adding concrete. (BRE Crown copyright photograph)

Tongued-and-grooved insulating panels can be laid on a DPM over a concrete slab. (BRE Crown copyright photograph)

Gaps around pipes passing through a floor should be sealed with polyurethane foam. (BRE Crown copyright photograph)

Beam and block flooring

In the last decade, there has been increased use of pre-stressed concrete T-beams for constructing ground floors in housing schemes. Together with their block infill, they form a suspended floor, which is more suited to unstable ground conditions such as subsidence, compaction or clay heave. These systems can be laid quite quickly, even in adverse weather. For small spans, a person of adequate strength and fitness can manhandle the beams into position without the aid of lifting machinery.

Ground preparation is minimal. Provided the ground has natural site drainage, the soil under the floor requires no oversite concrete. However, it should be free from vegetable matter, and the local authority may require weed killer treatment before the beams are positioned.

The void beneath the floor should be at least 75mm (3in), and this should be exceeded if ground heave is likely. With some products, a 150mm (6in) void is specified. The void must also be ventilated, and if a wall cavity is to be filled with insulant, the external and internal ventilators need linking by a duct.

Normally, the beams are laid on a DPC, on the inner skin of an external wall. However, the depth of the beams means that the DPC in the outer wall usually has to be higher. However, a mortar fill in a cavity wall should terminate at least 150mm (6in) below the lower of the two damp-proof courses.

The infill between the beams is carried out using building blocks, or purpose-made flooring blocks. More recently, however, changes in Building Regulations regarding insulation levels have led to the introduction of expanded polystyrene shutter (EPS) blocks. In some cases, these are moulded so that a lip extends underneath the concrete beams to ensure continuity of the insulation layer.

Insulating above the floor

There are two common methods of adding insulation and floor finishes above a beam and block floor. One is to lay rigid foam insulation, followed by a cement/sand screed; the other is to use tongued-and-grooved composite floor panels, made of an insulant bonded to either plywood or chipboard sheets. In both cases, the surface of the beams and blocks

Beam and block floor systems are easy to install, and it's often possible to lift the beams into place without machinery. (Photograph courtesy Marshalls Flooring Ltd)

should be flat; with some flooring systems a grouting compound has to be added to achieve continuity over the surface. Sometimes, a levelling screed is used for this purpose.

If a cement/sand screed is preferred, an insulation board of suitable compressive strength is placed first. A thin layer of insulating board should also extend around the sides of the screed. Joints should be taped to prevent wet screed from running between the panels. The screed should be 1 part cement to 3-4½ parts sand, and laid to a depth of 65mm (2½in), ensuring that it is well compacted.

If laying a composite board, a vapour control layer of 0.12mm (500 gauge) polyethylene sheet should be laid first to protect any subsequent floor finishes from residual damp that may be in the structure below. Note that a damp-proof membrane is not required with a suspended concrete floor, although a vapour control layer is important. The bonded panels are laid next, making sure that the tongues and grooves are glued with a PVA adhesive. At heavy traffic areas, such as doorways, preservative-treated timber battens are needed to support the edges of the panels.

There are several ways of providing floor finishes with this type of construction, and advice should be sought from the manufacturer on this point.

Timber floors

When comparing timber floors, you will see that there are differences between a suspended timber floor at ground level and a one built at a higher level. In particular, the ground floor structure needs ventilation to the void below the timbers, thermal insulation, and a concrete capping of the ground below. Specifications relating to these elements are clearly laid down in the Building Regulations.

Changing practices

The construction of ground floors has undergone a number of changes. Originally, they were built on compacted soil, and damp problems were commonplace. This prompted the introduction of elevated timber floors in the late nineteenth century, while air bricks helped to disperse dampness that developed in the void below.

However, floors were still built over exposed ground, so the problem of moisture rising from below wasn't completely solved. In consequence, the Health Bylaws, 1936, required a layer of concrete to be laid over all ground within the external walls of the building. Air bricks were still

included in the design, and clearances were standardised to give good cross ventilation below the timber structure.

Today, concrete ground cover is still obligatory, acceptable mixes being specified in the Building Regulations. Moreover, the layer of concrete should either be at least 100mm (4in) thick laid over hardcore, or 50mm (2in) laid on 1200 gauge polythene. If the finished level is not above the highest point of the surrounding land, the surface must be sloped and drainage points constructed. In addition, a space of at least 150mm (6in) is required between the surface of the concrete and the underside of the joists or insulating materials.

The Building Regulations also recognise the part that floors can play in providing lateral support to external walls. This can be achieved by using purpose-made metal straps.

Ground floor structures today must also include the provision of insulating materials to minimise heat loss. Without insulation, the ventilation system below the floor introduces cold air into the building, and heat loss is substantial.

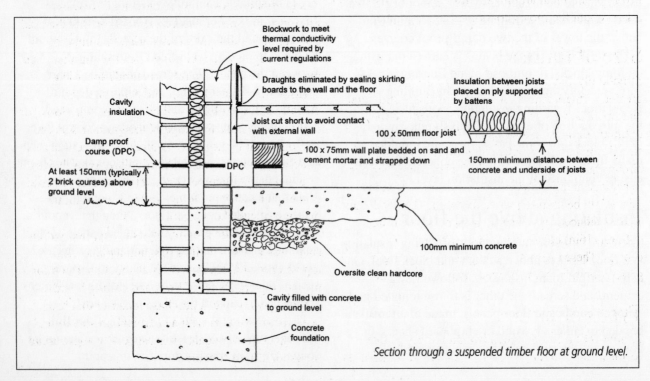

Blockwork to meet thermal conductivity level required by current regulations

Draughts eliminated by sealing skirting boards to the wall and the floor

Insulation between joists placed on ply supported by battens

Cavity insulation

Joist cut short to avoid contact with external wall

100 x 50mm floor joist

Damp proof course (DPC)

100 x 75mm wall plate bedded on sand and cement mortar and strapped down

150mm minimum distance between concrete and underside of joists

DPC

At least 150mm (typically 2 brick courses) above ground level

100mm minimum concrete

Oversite clean hardcore

Cavity filled with concrete to ground level

Concrete foundation

Section through a suspended timber floor at ground level.

Design points

Like many aspects of self-build work, it is best to leave the design of a floor, and the structural calculations, to an architect or building surveyor. In upper floors, the joists may need to span quite large rooms, and are properly referred to as bridging joists. In some cases, the floor may also need to provide support for a dividing wall in an upper room. This is often achieved by placing a double bridging joist directly below the position of the wall, the two lengths being held together by coach bolts and double-sided, tooth plate connectors. This technique makes it possible to build partitions using lightweight blocks instead of timber.

Joist spacing

This is partly governed by the standard sizes of boards that will be attached to the joists later, such as plasterboard to form a ceiling below, and chipboard for the floor above. Therefore, the distance from the centre of one joist to another may be 400, 450 or 600mm (16, 18 or 24in).

Spacing is also linked to the width and depths of the material used for the joists which, in turn, are related to the span between the points of support. Information on an architect's drawings will also take into account the most economical use of timber.

Size of timber

Structurally, the depth of a bridging joist gives it greater stiffness than its width. From solely structural and financial viewpoints, it might appear that the optimum dimension and disposition of joists is straightforward. In practice, however, there may be circumstances where cost and efficiency are sacrificed to achieve another objective. For instance, a wider joist might be used to reduce its depth. The depth may also be reduced significantly by spacing joists at 400mm (16in) centres instead of 600mm (24in) centres. These alternatives may need exploring if greater room height is needed in an existing building.

Types of timber

Timber for building comes from a variety of tree species, and in a range of qualities. On account of its

The centre span of this upper floor construction employs a double joist, coachbolted together, to provide the necessary extra strength to support a dividing wall above.

structural role, timber is given different strength classifications (i.e. SC3 and SC4) by the Building Regulations. Timber is also graded differently, and this is usually shown on the drawings. If you see reference to 'Special Structural' (SS) or 'Mechanical Special Structural' (MSS) material, this must be acknowledged when ordering from the supplier. You may also see GS (General Structural) specified.

Timber designated as GS and SS is checked visually and verified by skilled graders, who look for defects like knots, the slope of the grain and so on. Machine grading involves subjecting timber lengths to deflection tests, and is a particularly reliable way of evaluating structural characteristics. The material is stamped with its grading, and it is essential to purchase the timber specified.

As a rule, timber used for joists is supplied with a rough sawn finish on its sides, and a planed finish top and bottom. This provides a smooth surface for the subsequent fixing of floor and ceiling boards.

Nowadays, you can purchase material that has been factory treated with a chemical preservative. This vacuum impregnation is especially appropriate for ground floor timbers.

Suspended ground floors

A key feature of the suspended ground floor is that it avoids contact with any source of damp. At their extremities, the joists are mounted on timber wall plates measuring 100 x 75mm (4 x 3in). Sometimes, galvanised steel joist hangers are used instead. Whatever method is used, checks must be made to ensure joists finish level with each other.

Additional support is provided by sleeper walls, which are topped with a DPC and a wall plate of 100 x 75mm (4 x 3in) timber. This intermediate support helps to distribute the load of the floor and allows joists of smaller dimension to be used. They also provide fixing points so that the joists can be cross-nailed in position.

The wall plates are bedded on mortar with a damp-proof strip. Usually, this is a pitch polymer material, sold in rolls by builders' merchants.

Sleeper walls are built directly from the mandatory concrete slab. Since it is impossible to create a mechanical bond between a plate and its wall, using mortar alone, metal straps keep the plate in place.

Sleeper walls are constructed with a honeycomb bond so that cross draughts can pass easily through the underfloor area. Moreover, the outer sleeper walls, supporting the ends of joists, are built slightly inboard of the external brickwork, providing additional protection against damp. The joists are usually cut to leave a small gap between their ends and the external walls. While it is possible to build joists into an inner wall (as in an upper floor), this is not recommended for ground floors due to the greater likelihood of damage from damp.

Sleeper walls are usually built at 1.8m (6ft) centres across the entire run of the joists, and the frequency of these supports means that, in many cases, the timbers need not exceed 100 x 50mm (4 x 2in). Each sleeper wall must be built so that the upper face of the wall plate remains level throughout its length.

Ventilation

Cross ventilation is essential in a suspended ground floor, because the timber can be damaged by moisture accumulating in the void. This provision also eliminates the need for laying a vapour control membrane as part of the floor structure.

For good ventilation, a space measuring at least 75mm (3in) from the concrete ground cover to the underside of any wall plates must be provided, and at least 150mm (6in) to the underside of the joists.

The ventilators themselves must provide an actual open area of either 1500mm^2 (2.4in^2) for every metre (3ft) length of the external wall or 500mm^2 (0.8in^2) for every 1m^2 (9 ft^2) of ground floor area, whichever is greater. They should be located in at least two opposite walls and must not be obstructed by insulation materials on the inside, or soil on the outside. The ventilators are normally placed within 450mm (18in) of the corners of the floor, and at no greater spacing than 2m (6ft) centres.

Although many buildings are correctly constructed with air bricks in outside walls, their long-term success is wholly dependent on the vents remaining unblocked. Soil from flower beds must be kept clear of the apertures. The cast-iron grilles often seen in Victorian properties do not always stand the test of time and should be replaced. If they become broken, they provide easy access for vermin.

In some instances, straight-through ventilators cannot be installed, and in this situation, stepped units – sometimes referred to as periscopic vents – are required instead. In new properties, the vents are installed below the DPC when the walls are built. (Illustration courtesy Rytons Building Products Ltd)

Insulation

Given that a good flow of air between joists is essential for dispersing any damp and stagnant air, traditionally-built suspended floors are often cold in winter. The heat loss can be appreciable.

Therefore, in new work, it is necessary to incorporate insulation into the structure. This can also be done if an older property is being renovated. A degree of improvement can be achieved by laying a composite board of block foam, bonded to plywood, directly on top of the original floorboards. Inevitably, this reduces room height and necessitates modifications to doors, but it is easier than lifting floorboards to install insulant between the joists.

The latter procedure is easier when building a new floor, mineral fibre quilt or block materials, such as expanded polystyrene or extruded polystyrene, being equally suitable. However, a support system is needed, and heavy-duty plastic netting may be stapled to the joists for this. It is better, however, to attach battens to support solid block insulant, or to fix boarding on battens nailed low down on the sides of the joists to provide a base for a quilt insulant.

The thickness of the insulant depends on the floor area, and this should be specified by the architect. The level of thermal efficiency required by Building Regulations is normally achieved by installing a mineral fibre quilt to a depth of 60mm (2½in). Alternatively, if polyurethane foam is used, this would typically be 25mm (1in) thick in a terraced or semi-detached property, and 40mm (1¾in) in a detached house.

It is essential that there are no gaps in the insulating material itself, or around the perimeter of the floor structure. This means that a quilt insulant should be inserted between the external walls and the outermost joists. Care must be taken to ensure that there is continuity in insulation at the threshold of external doors. Precautions must also be taken to prevent air entering from the void below. This can occur in several places, including:

● Around the outside of the floor
● Where pipes or other services penetrate the floor
● Around access panels built into the floor.

These gaps can be closed with sealants and draught stripping material.

Services

Since effective insulation prevents heat from rooms escaping into the void beneath the floor, any water pipes below the insulant may be damaged by frost. Accordingly, they should be well lagged. Central heating pipes should run above the insulant, whereas gas pipes should be below.

Another important point is that electricity cables must not rest against polystyrene insulant, so it is best to run them in conduit. Moreover, if cables are closer than 50mm (2in) to the top of each joist, they should be run in a metal conduit.

Boards resting on edging struts provide a firm base for quilt insulant. (BRE Crown copyright photograph)

A good depth of quilt insulant can be placed under a suspended floor. (BRE Crown copyright photograph)

To keep out cold air from the void below, insulant should be placed around pipes. (BRE Crown copyright photograph)

Upper floors

Floors for upper rooms involve a number of different constructional elements, partly because the joists have to bridge much larger spans. Additionally, it is important to achieve accurate levels on both sides of the joists, since they have to provide a level surface for floor boards above and ceiling boards below.

For economy, joists are normally laid across the narrower span.

Timber is rarely perfectly straight, and twisted material should be rejected, since it can become progressively worse, leading to serious distortion later. However, a slight bow over the length of a joist is less of a problem, although you should ascertain the straightness of all timbers before beginning construction.

The procedure is to look along the length of each joist, then to lay it on the ground so that the cambered edge is uppermost. Having done this, the joists should be compared, and those that have the greatest camber placed in the middle. The straightest joists should be placed near the edges. This is how the timbers will be installed, thereby producing a slight rise in the middle of the platform, rather than a sag. When furnishings are added to the room later, there will be a natural tendency for the floor to revert to a flat surface under their weight.

Support

Joists are generally installed when exterior walls are being built. Normally, one end of the joist rests on the inner skin of the external wall, and the other on a loadbearing internal wall. Joist ends should be treated with preservative and cut so as not to project into the cavity.

The difficulty with this method lies in achieving a consistent level on the bearing points. Constant checks are required, using a spirit level and a length of timber with a good straight edge. Joists should be levelled by adding small packing pieces of slate or tile under the bearing points.

An alternative is to bed a mild steel bar in the wall, measuring 75 x 6mm (3 x ¼in) and being tarred to give good protection. This approach provides a better chance of achieving a level base, and ensures that the weight of the floor is better distributed.

Joist hangers

An alternative method of supporting joists is to build galvanised steel joist hangers into the inner skin. The advantage of these is that the timber isn't built into the wall, so it is less susceptible to damp rot. It is easy to pack pieces of plywood into the bottom of hangers to level the joists. If a floor needs to incorporate horizontal support to stabilise the walls (in houses of more than two storeys, for example), joist hangers are available that include a hook, which rests within the cavity.

First floor joists are bricked into place on an internal wall. Temporary struts nailed across the top provide stability.

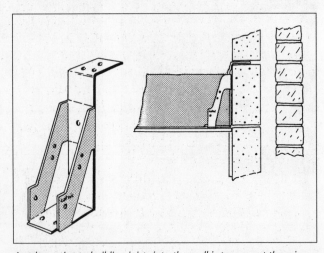

An alternative to building joists into the wall is to support them in galvanised joist hangers.

Bracing

The floor structure in modern buildings usually acts as a bracing element to prevent movement in the external walls. Where needed, bracing can be achieved using special joist hangars, or by the addition of galvanised mild steel straps. These straps tie the floor structure to the brickwork, forming a cohesive structure.

Struts between joists

It is inevitable that floor joists will twist as shrinkage occurs in the material. This can lead to distortion of the floorboards and damage to the ceilings below. To prevent this, some form of bracing is needed between the joists.

Where the span is 3.5m (12ft) or less, one line of strutting is needed,but for each additional 1.5m (5ft) in span, further struts are required. The simplest method is to cut lengths of joist to fit tightly between the joists. These are either skew nailed in place, or offset so that nails can be driven into both ends. The problem with this method of bracing is the fact that it's very difficult to cut timber accurately enough to fit tightly in each recess. Herringbone strutting is usually preferred.

Fitting herringbone struts between joists is a traditional method of preventing them from twisting. Modern construction may make use of purpose-made galvanised steel straps instead.

Traditionally, each herringbone strut is made from 50 x 38mm (2 x 1½in) batten, being nailed top and bottom. This has the effect of bracing the joist and preventing twisting. To complete the bracing, the outermost joists must be prevented from flexing outwards by driving wedges against the wall. A modern alternative is to use galvanised steel struts with forked ends for gripping the sides of the joists.

Trimming

Frequently, apertures are needed in upper floors: on a landing, an opening is needed for the stairs, while in buildings with a chimney, a frame must be constructed around an internal flue so that the joists are not in direct contact with the masonry.

The shortening of joists and construction of a frame around an aperture is known as trimming. The timber that forms the frame will be thicker than the normal bridging joists, and is usually 75mm (3in) in width. At least one of the sections, known as trimmers, will carry the combined weight of the shortened joists that butt against it.

The traditional way of constructing the frame was to form joints between each trimmer, and also between the shortened joists that connect with the structure. Usually, these took the form of some sort of housing joint. Today, however, the timbers are normally joined by galvanised steel joist hangers.

First floor joists have to be trimmed to produce a stairwell. The joists and trimmers are normally connected with special galvanised joist hangers, instead of traditional joints cut in the timber.

Flooring

In very old houses, lengths of floorboard with square edges were used, and there was no interlock between them. This means that you can easily lift a board for inspection. However, as shrinkage occurs, large gaps develop between the boards. Similarly, it is more likely that a single board will twist, pulling out its nails and shaking loose.

Tongued-and-grooved (T&G) boards are much better. The tongue is usually machined slightly off-centre, and the wider portion should be laid uppermost. This provides an allowance for wear before the T&G section is exposed.

Where the boarding will be left exposed, treated and polished, the tongues and grooves are cut on a slight splay so that the nails can be driven into the tongues. Once a board is fixed, the next board hides the heads of the nails.

Although softwood boarding is still used, flooring grade chipboard panels are now more common.

Panel sizes are typically 2400 x 600mm (8 x 2ft) and 18mm (¾in) thick. They are manufactured with tongues and grooves. Installation is comparatively fast, and another advantage of the material is the fact that it is not affected by woodworm; nor, for that matter, does it shrink like softwood floorboards. However, when any inspection is needed below the boards, sections have to be cut away and replaced with the addition of supports under the cut edges.

The thickness of boarding adds to the strength of the floor. Softwood boards should have at least 16mm (⅝in) finished thickness where joists are spaced up to 500mm (20in) centres; at up to 600mm (24in) centres, 19mm (¾in) finished thickness is required.

▶ **SEE PAGE 106 FOR STEP-BY-STEP INSTRUCTIONS ON REFURBISHING A TIMBER FLOOR**

T&G boarding

For a traditional-looking floor, tongued-and-grooved softwood boarding should be chosen. When laying the boards, follow these guidelines:

● T & G floorboards tend to shrink as they dry out. To avoid this becoming a problem after they have been laid, it is always best to store the boards for as long as possible in the room where they are going to be installed.

● Another precautionary measure is to ensure that when they are finally laid, a large number of boards will be placed on the joists and then cramped together tightly so that the tongues are forced deeply within their grooves. This is done prior to nailing, and it is not unusual for a dozen or more cramped boards to bow slightly during this process.

● Cramping is carried out with special flooring cramps that grip the joists with serrated cams. They are extremely effective, and can be obtained from tool hire companies.

● The nails used for securing softwood boarding are known as floor brads, and typically are 55mm (2¼in) long. They are designed so that the head will become embedded in the board as the nail is driven home with a hammer, thereby eliminating any need for punching-in afterwards.

● In the case of secret nailing through the board tongues, each board has to be fixed individually, and the cramping procedure cannot be applied to more than one length at a time. Moreover, an oval brad or a lost-head round wire nail will be necessary. Fixing requires an accurate hammer action, and the head of each nail must be punched below the surface of the tongue so that it does not interfere with the adjacent board when it is positioned.

● The ends of boards should be staggered across the floor, and an accomplished joiner will mitre the ends at 45 degrees to form a scarf joint. This should occur directly on top of a joist, allowing both boards to be fixed by the same nails.

Flooring grade chipboard

Using tongued-and-grooved chipboard panels will provide a quick and simple means of laying flooring. However, there are a few points to consider:

● Particle boards are unlikely to shrink, but it is still sensible to ensure that the tongues of the boards locate deeply in the adjacent grooves. Never hammer directly on the edge of a board; instead, use a panel offcut, about 300mm (12in) long and 75mm (3in) wide, with a groove along one side.

● Use lost-head round nails to secure the panels, driving them into the joists at 75mm (3in) centres. To save time in spacing the nails, cut a batten to the appropriate length. Alternatively, mark the spacing on your hammer handle with adhesive tape.

● Flooring grade chipboard is very dense, so you may find it useful to drill pilot holes for the nails.

● It is not unusual for boards to spring away from joists at a later date, producing a creaking floor. To reduce the likelihood of this occurring, use screws for some of the fixings – about four per board should suffice. Alternatively, annular nails can be mixed with the other nails, as the rings on the shank provide better anchorage.

● Generally, the interlock of tongues and grooves on particle board panels is good and creates a stable, continuous platform. However, you can provide an even stronger bond between the boards by applying a thin coat of PVA wood glue to the tongues. When

When laying tongued-and-grooved floorboarding, it is a good idea to glue the joints with PVA wood adhesive. (Crown Copyright photograph, used with permission from Energy Efficiency Office's Good Practice Guide, Ground Floors)

laying the boards, make the large dimension span the run of joists, and ensure that the joints are staggered.

● Chipboard is notorious for blunting tools, so bear this in mind when panels need cutting. Moreover, sharp particles can often fly out when using a circular saw, so eye protection is essential.

Acoustic boarding

Noise transmission through wood floors can be extremely aggravating, but finding a remedy is far from easy. However, in addition to conventional manufactured chipboards, recent developments in flooring materials have led to the introduction of a range of products that have been designed to reduce noise transmission.

A typical example of the special noise attenuation boards now available is the range known as Ecomax

Acoustics. This includes boards such as Reduc flooring units. These panels are designed to be laid on top of existing floorboarding during refurbishment work.

The unusual acoustic sandwich construction of Reduc units incorporates air gaps and special sound deadening elastic strips. The boarding is available in three thicknesses for different situations, and installation is not difficult.

Refurbishing a timber floor

Replacing a floor completely is a substantial undertaking, but in some instances repairs can be carried out to floorboards without their removal and replacement. Typical problems are loose, twisted and shrunken boards.

Re-attaching loose boards is quite a common job – particularly in areas where there's heavy traffic, such as across a landing. In general, it is better to re-fix loose boards with wood screws rather than nails, because these will effectively draw a deflected board back against its joist. A screw with a shank will pull a board down more effectively than one that is threaded along its full length. It is important, however, to remember that water pipes and electrical cables may run below the boards. Before driving in fixings indiscriminately, lift a board and make a preliminary inspection of the void.

Gaps can be the sources of draughts and can also damage the underside of carpets. If they appear between square-edged boards, the problem can often be solved by filling them with timber inserts. Another remedy is to apply a latex-based levelling compound, products being available that can be trowelled onto the surface.

Twisted boards are rather more difficult to remedy. One method is to drive the fixing nails deeply below the surface, then plane down the edges of the boards that stand proud. An industrial belt or rotary sander may be suitable for this, but if a lot of material needs removing, a plane will more effective.

A new surface

These precautions must taken prior to laying a new carpet, but where the surface is very poor, a cure is to lay hardboard on top of the boards. This forms a smooth surface and evens out small irregularities. Use conventional hardboard if carpeting is to be laid. However, if ceramic tiling is planned, an oil-based hardboard will be more suitable, because it is more resistant to water-based adhesives. It should also be laid rough side uppermost to provide a better key for the tile adhesive.

When working on large areas, it is often desirable to condition hardboard sheets by brushing them liberally on the reverse side with water. The boards should then be stacked for 48 hours, back-to-back, in the room where the work is being carried out. The effect of conditioning is that once it's fixed, the board dries out and tightens up on the nails.

When attaching hardboard, a quick method of fixing is to use long staples driven in by an electric stapler. However, annular ring nails achieve a better grip. Either way, this type of repair work should always be regarded as a patching-up exercise. Where are large number of boards are in poor condition, it is much better to replace them with new boards or chipboard flooring panels.

TOOLS AND MATERIALS

- ☐ Bolster chisel
- ☐ Claw hammer
- ☐ Cold chisel
- ☐ Spirit level
- ☐ Tape measure
- ☐ Pencil
- ☐ Bradawl
- ☐ Electric drill
- ☐ Wood bits
- ☐ Countersink
- ☐ Screwdriver
- ☐ Plane
- ☐ Electric stapler
- ☐ Screws
- ☐ Staples
- ☐ Hardboard sheets

LIFTING FLOORBOARDS

☐ To lift a square-edged board, carefully push the blade of a bolster chisel into the gap between the board and its neighbour. Lever the board upwards to loosen the fixing nails. Then insert the bolster on the other side of the board and repeat the process. Continue levering until you can insert the claw of a hammer under the board on one side and lever with the hammer until the board lifts sufficiently to slip a cold chisel beneath it. Lay the chisel across the adjacent boards so that it holds the end of the board clear of the joist. Repeat the procedure for the remaining nails until you can lift the board free.

☐ Lifting a tongued-and-grooved board requires a similar procedure, but first the tongues on both sides must be carefully cut with a tenon saw.

☐ Where the end of a board is trapped beneath the skirting, it should be possible to free it by lifting the other end and holding the board at a steep angle to prise the nails from the joist adjacent to the wall. Alternatively, drill a starting hole through the board and use a pad saw to cut through the board parallel with the skirting.

1 When refurbishing a boarded floor, begin by removing any loose boards. If the nails have pulled through the boards, simply lift them. Otherwise, prise them up with a pair of bolsters.

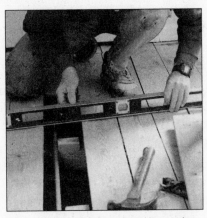

2 Use a long straight-edge or even a long spirit level to assess any unevenness in the floor boards. Mark those that stand proud of their neighbours with a piece of chalk.

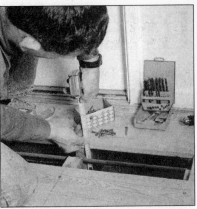

3 It is essential to determine the positions of any pipes and electrical cables that run under the floor. Measuring how far down they are will help in selecting the size of fixing to use.

4 Lift other boards to ensure that you know exactly where all the underfloor services run. Considerable damage can result from accidentally puncturing a pipe or cable with a screw or nail.

5 Mark the positions of any pipes and cables you find on the face of the floorboards. This will ensure that you don't drive in any of the board fixings at these points.

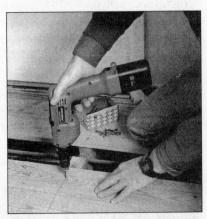

6 Regardless of whether you are using nails or screws to secure the boards, drilling pilot holes through them will make the job easier. It will also prevent boards from splitting at their ends.

7 In this instance, screws were used to secure the loose boards to the joists. They pull the boards down better than nails, making it unlikely that they will become loose again.

8 Countersinking the holes will allow the screw heads to sit below the surface of the boards. This also permits boards that have proud edges to be planed flush with the surrounding boards.

9 The original carpet acted as a template for marking out the hardboard sheets. Once cut to shape, these were fixed into place using long staples and an electric stapler.

Internal walls

The removal or construction of an internal wall is a structural matter, and Building Regulation approval is needed before work can begin. When open-planned ground floor rooms became popular a few years ago, there were instances when owners had sought neither approval nor advice before indiscriminately removing walls. As a result, some structures became seriously unsafe, putting the occupants at risk.

At the design stage, you must seek the help of an architect or structural specialist. Not only will a qualified person look at the structural implications of the work, but also issues like ventilation and precautionary measures in the event of a fire.

Structural internal walls

Walls that support floor joists are structural and must not be confused with non-loadbearing partition walls.

Some internal walls may only divide the available living space into smaller units. These are non-structural walls. Other walls, however, provide support for floor joists and may brace the roof structure as well. These are structural internal walls. Such a wall must be built on a suitable foundation, just like an external wall.

To discover if a wall has a loadbearing function, it's often necessary to inspect it from above. This may involve removing floorboards to see if it provides support for the joists. Similarly, an inspection from a loft may establish whether the roof has bracing struts supported by an internal wall.

Walls built from timber frameworks may also have a structural function. In a timber-framed house, the roof is wholly supported by its external walls, while the floors will also rest on timber-framed walls.

Adequate support

Where an opening is required in a loadbearing wall, important dimensional criteria must be considered. This is because any construction built above the opening needs adequate support. The weight of the structure above the opening is borne by a reinforced-concrete or steel lintel. This is inserted in the wall first and projects beyond each side of the opening, where it is supported by the remaining portions of the wall or by specially-constructed piers.

▶ **SEE PAGES 110-113 FOR STEP-BY-STEP INSTRUCTIONS ON MAKING AN OPENING IN A WALL**

Non-structural internal walls

A non-structural wall can be built in a number of ways and from a variety of materials. This type of construction is sometimes referred to as a partition wall. Obviously, it will need adequate support at its base, taking into account the loading imposed by the material from which it is built. For instance, an internal wall constructed in 75mm (3in) blockwork imposes a greater load than a timber-framed wall.

While an internal wall might not be required to support any of the building's structure, this does not mean that it can be removed without forethought. For example, adjoining non-loadbearing walls may support each other, so removing one may cause adjacent walls to become unstable.

At first floor level, many modern houses have few, if any loadbearing walls, on account of the advent of trussed roof design. In contrast with a traditionally-built roof, a modern trussed roof is designed to span between the exterior walls without any intermediate support. In consequence, all the first floor rooms can be divided by non-loadbearing walls, since they provide no support for the roof. It's not unusual, therefore, to find that in a modern house, all first floor walls are made from timber frames clad with plasterboard – referred to as stud walls.

More recently, partition walls have been constructed using lightweight metal frames.

Alternatively, they may be made from 75mm (3in) concrete blocks. Some modern houses have partition walls built using prefabricated wall units comprising two layers of plasterboard separated by a cardboard cellular core.

No continuity

Consistent with this feature of modern houses is the fact that upstairs walls have no upward continuity with walls built at ground floor level. In older properties, this isn't always the case. Quite frequently, a wall providing a division for ground floor rooms continues upwards into the bedrooms. This is almost always a structural wall.

The construction of additional non-loadbearing walls is relatively straightforward. In particular, stud walls are often preferred, since they are light and usually can be built directly over a timber floor. A disadvantage, however, is their relatively poor soundproofing characteristics – even when the void is filled with wool insulant.

> ▶ **SEE PAGES 114-116 FOR STEP-BY-STEP INSTRUCTIONS ON BUILDING AN INTERNAL PARTITION**

A wall built with a timber framework, like this one, is unlikely to have a structural function – but there are exceptions.

Installing a lintel

Provided modifications have been approved by a structural surveyor, and the size of the opening has been strictly agreed, making an opening in a loadbearing wall is a relatively straightforward procedure. The description given here concerns the construction of a small opening – perhaps a double doorway to link two rooms, but the techniques are the same regardless of the size.

The first task is to insert a lintel above the proposed opening to bear the weight of the masonry above, and the wall must be supported temporarily while the lintel's slot is cut. For this, you will need adjustable steel props and some sturdy timbers to act as supports, known as 'needles'. These should be measure 150 x 50mm (6 x 2in) and be no longer than 2.7m (9ft).

Holes for the needles must be carefully knocked through the wall just above the lintel's position. They should no further apart than 900mm (3ft) centres; where possible, 600mm (2ft) centres are preferred. Once inserted, the needles have to be supported at each end by an adjustable steel prop. The props should stand on a plank to spread the load. On an uncertain timber floor, it may be necessary to remove the floor boards to check joists and establish a stronger support.

With the needles installed, you can prepare the opening for the lintel. Make sure that the ends of the lintel will rest on good bearing points projecting at least 150mm (6in) beyond the intended opening. If you have any doubts about the strength of the masonry, construct bearing points using engineering bricks.

Purpose-made steel or pre-stressed reinforced concrete lintels are normally used for internal openings. Having made the aperture in the wall, bed the lintel on mortar at each end, making sure that it is level. Additional mortar should also be spread along the top of the lintel before it is placed in the aperture to provide a bed for the masonry above. Then wait at least 24 hours for the mortar to dry completely before removing the props and needles and proceeding further.

TOOLS AND MATERIALS

☐ Bolster chisel
☐ Club hammer
☐ Timber needles
☐ Adjustable steel props
☐ Concrete or steel lintel
☐ Heavy-duty dust sheets
☐ Step ladder
☐ Spirit level
☐ Tape measure
☐ Pencil
☐ Thick gloves
☐ Safety goggles
☐ Mortar and trowel
☐ Engineering bricks (optional)

BEARING POINTS

☐ In this straightforward example, it is presumed that the bearing points will be able to carry the weight of the structure supported by the lintel. However, in some cases, a building surveyor may recommend that a pier be built at each end of the opening to provide extra support. These would require a suitable foundations. Proper advice regarding this strengthening work must be sought, as well as the approval of the local authority, before going ahead.

A lintel must have a good bearing point at each end, and quite often a hard engineering brick is employed.

Pre-stressed concrete lintels, containing a reinforcing core of steel cable, are frequently used over openings in internal walls.

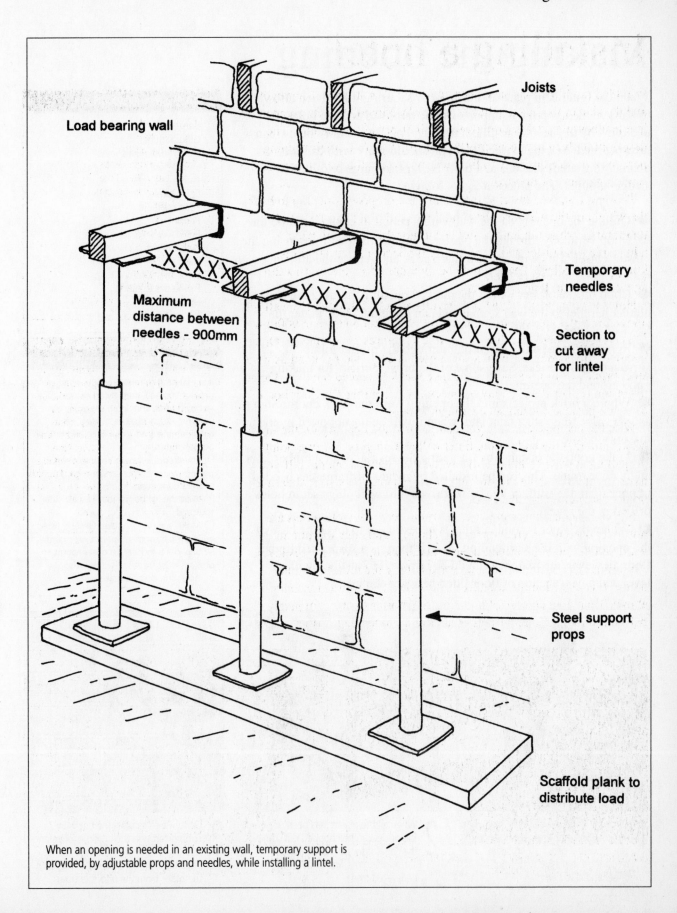

Joists

Load bearing wall

Temporary needles

Maximum distance between needles - 900mm

Section to cut away for lintel

Steel support props

Scaffold plank to distribute load

When an opening is needed in an existing wall, temporary support is provided, by adjustable props and needles, while installing a lintel.

Making the opening

When the lintel is in place and the mortar securing it has been allowed to harden, the temporary supports can be removed and the holes occupied by the needles re-filled. Removal of the masonry below can now proceed, bearing in mind that you should work with caution, dismantling small sections at a time. Never take large bites with a sledge hammer. The procedure is as follows:

● Outline the opening on the wall with a pencil or chalked plumb line.
● Chop vertically through the plaster along the marked lines, using the bolster chisel. This will ensure a sharp edge and reduce the amount of making good necessary later.
● Chop off the plaster within the marked opening, holding the chisel almost parallel to the wall so that you can drive the blade under the layer of plaster.
● Remove the masonry by cutting through the mortar joints surrounding the bricks. Save some of the broken bricks for making good around the opening.
● Where a brick projects into the opening from the wall, cut through it as you come to it rather than later when it will be unsupported by the masonry below.
● Make good the opening by plastering the reveal, or fit a timber liner and a door frame. This can be installed by means of frame ties bedded in pockets in the wall, or by screws driven into wall plugs set in holes drilled in the reveal.
● Where the floor is solid, all that is necessary is to level the base of the opening with the surrounding floor. If there is a suspended timber floor, however, the masonry should be removed to just below floor level and a new section of floor fitted between the joists.

TOOLS AND MATERIALS

☐ Bolster chisel
☐ Club hammer
☐ Heavy-duty dust sheets
☐ Step ladder
☐ Plumb line
☐ Spirit level
☐ Tape measure
☐ Pencil
☐ Bricklayer's trowel
☐ Plasterer's trowel
☐ Hawk
☐ Door liner (optional)
☐ Frame ties (optional)
☐ Mortar
☐ Browning and finishing plaster

SAFETY POINTS

It is essential to take precautions to protect yourself from flying debris while removing masonry from the wall.
☐ Wear old clothes or overalls, as a considerable amount of dust and dirt will be generated.
☐ Equip yourself with thick gloves to protect your hands and safety goggles to protect your eyes.
☐ Wear heavy boots, ideally with steel toe caps.
☐ Make sure your bolster chisel is fitted with a mushroom-shaped hand guard.
☐ Seal off the doors to other rooms to prevent dust from spreading. Also, dampen the dust to make it settle.

1 Once the lintel has been installed, mark out the extent of the opening on the plaster with a pencil. Then begin removing the plaster with a bolster chisel and club hammer.

2 When all the plaster has been removed, the bricks can be chopped out. Drive the chisel into the mortar joints surrounding the first brick until it can be levered free.

3 Continue to remove the bricks by cutting through their mortar joints and levering them out. If the wall is a full brick thick, remove one leaf first, then the other from the opposite side.

4 Try to cut the edges of the opening as cleanly as possible, as this will save a lot of making good later. Drive the chisel into the brickwork at right angles to the face of the wall.

5 When removing a second leaf of brickwork from a 225mm (9in) thick wall, take care when chopping through the joints, as there will be nothing behind to support the bricks.

6 Once the opening has been completed, it can be prepared for plastering. However, if a door is to be fitted, prepare the timber liner by attaching three metal frame ties to each side.

7 Using the bolster chisel and club hammer cut pockets in the sides of the opening to accept the frame ties and the projecting ends of the head. Offer up the frame to check the fit.

8 Use a spirit level to ensure that the sides of the frame are truly vertical and that the top is horizontal. Make any necessary adjustments with the aid of wooden wedges.

9 Secure the frame ties by filling the pockets with mortar and brick offcuts. Similarly, fill any gaps between the frame and opening. Then cover the exposed masonry with more mortar.

10 Once the mortar has hardened, spread browning plaster over the masonry around the frame. Fit timber thickness guides around the opening for plastering the reveal.

11 When the browning plaster has hardened sufficiently, apply a second layer if necessary, keying the surface first with a devilling float. If not, trowel on a layer of finishing plaster.

12 Keep the finishing plaster as thin as possible, but make it flush with the wooden door liner. Allow it to stiffen, then polish the plaster to a smooth finish with a wet trowel.

Building a stud partition

Where the floor plate of a stud partition is built over a timber floor, fixing is straightforward provided it crosses at right angles to the joists. If it is aligned with them, but not directly above a joist, you will need to install supporting noggings between the joists. The same situation applies at the ceiling for the head plate.

Having completed the floor and ceiling fixings, you must calculate the positions of the studs, bearing in mind that the frame would normally be clad with standard 1220mm (4ft) wide plasterboard sheets.

When constructing the frame, skew nailing is by far the quickest method of joining the various pieces. For the less experienced, who may find it difficult to drive home an angled nail, it often helps to drill a pilot hole first. To prevent the uprights from sliding sideways out of position when driving the nails home, it's helpful to support them with an offcut of timber temporarily nailed to the head or sole plate.

Noggings can be fixed in a similar fashion if they are to be aligned. However, they can often be staggered, allowing you to drive nails through the stud directly into the ends, which is much easier.

At openings for doors, you should allow for the width of the door and the dimensions of the lining. For additional strength, the cross-member at the head of the opening should be attached to the uprights by cutting housings for its ends with a chisel. At the foot of the opening, the studs can be skew nailed, but it is preferable to cut housings for them in the floor plate.

Before cladding the structure, any electrical wiring should be taken through holes drilled in the centres of the studs and noggings. Similarly, metal boxes for sockets or switches should be attached to the framework. Lastly, it is worth filling the void with a quilt insulant to reduce sound transmission through the wall.

TOOLS AND MATERIALS

- ☐ Tape measure and pencil
- ☐ Plumb line
- ☐ Panel saw
- ☐ Tenon saw
- ☐ Try square
- ☐ Electric drill, wood and masonry bits
- ☐ Hammer and nails
- ☐ Screwdriver, screws and wall plugs
- ☐ Spirit level
- ☐ Wood chisel
- ☐ Bradawl
- ☐ Wood for frame
- ☐ Plasterboard

THE FRAMEWORK

- ☐ A stud partition is based on a wooden framework comprising a floor plate, a head plate, the uprights (studs) and intermediate horizontal pieces known as noggings. This is clad with plasterboard.
- ☐ Sawn softwood is normally used for the framework, measuring 100 x 50mm (4 x 2in) or 75 x 50mm (3 x 2in), according to the situation.
- ☐ The studs are normally set at 610mm (24in) centres, although a 400mm (16in) spacing can be used with particularly thin cladding materials.
- ☐ Noggings should be placed centrally between the studs. If the partition is taller than a standard sheet of plasterboard (2440mm/8ft), additional noggings will be needed to support the edges of the sheets.

1 Having determined where the top plate is to be fixed to the ceiling, use a plumb line to transfer the position of the centre of the top plate onto the adjacent wall.

2 Use the mark on the wall and the plumb line to centre the sole plate exactly beneath the top plate position. Nail it to a wooden floor, or use screws and plugs on a solid floor.

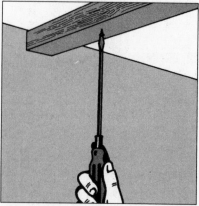

3 Drill clearance holes through the top plate for the fixing screws. Then hold it against the ceiling and mark the screw positions. Drill pilot holes and screw the top plate to the ceiling.

4 Measure the distance between the top and sole plates at each end, then cut the end studs to length, making sure they will be a tight fit. Drill and plug the wall, and screw the studs in place.

5 Mark off the stud positions along the sole plate with a try square, setting them at 610mm (24in) centres. Use an offcut of stud material to mark the width of the stud on the sole plate.

6 Align each stud on the sole plate. Nail an offcut at one side to support the stud while you skew nail it to the sole plate. Remove the offcut and nail the other side. Then nail it to the top plate.

7 Mark the nogging positions on the studs. Then support one end of each nogging with an offcut nailed to one stud while you drive a nail through the other, into the end of the nogging.

8 Skew nail through the other end of the nogging into the stud. Prise off the offcut and fit it to the next stud, repeating the process until all the noggings have been installed.

9 If the partition is to incorporate a door opening, the ends of the nogging at the top of the opening should be set in housings cut in the studs with a tenon saw and chisel.

10 Having cut the nogging housings in the studs, cut the nogging to length and tap it into place. Then drive nails through each stud into the ends to secure it.

11 When the framework of the partition has been completed, you can remove the portion of the sole plate at the foot of the door opening. Simply cut it out with a saw.

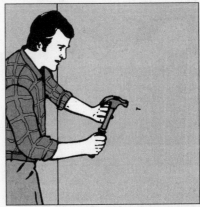

12 Drill the studs and noggings for any pipes or cables and install these before cladding the framework with sheets of plasterboard. These should be nailed directly to the timbers.

Metal stud partitions

A modern variation on traditional timber stud walling is the Lafarge Cormet metal stud partition. Using this system, partition walls can be erected quickly by means of friction-fit channelling made of lightweight galvanised steel. The sections are available in five widths, from 50mm (2in) to 146mm (5¾in), so you can produce an internal wall to suit your needs.

The system is extremely easy to assemble: once the metal framework is in place, it is clad with standard plasterboard panels that are held with screws. Provision is made for securing insulation material within the framework, and the system includes accessories such as clip-in electrical boxes, obviating the need for supporting noggings.

1 With the Lafarge Cormet system, ceiling and floor U-track sections in galvanised steel are secured with screws fixed at 600mm (24in) centres. Additional steel sections are fixed between them as uprights at the same spacing.

2 Where a door is to be installed, a U-track section is fitted between the adjacent uprights to form the head of the opening. Then the timber door frame drilled and installed with the aid of special screws.

3 Plasterboard is screw fixed to the metal framework at 300mm (12in) centres. After cladding one side, insulation material is fixed in place. Then the partition is completed by cladding the remaining side with plasterboard.

Lightweight block walls

In modern buildings, you will sometimes find non-structural internal walls built from lightweight concrete blocks. Normally, a 100mm (4in) block is used at ground floor level, while a 75mm (3in) block is often preferred at first floor level.

On the first floor, support can be achieved in several ways. For instance, in a new building, it is not unusual for a double joist to be bolted together to provide support for a block wall that will be constructed directly above it. Alternatively, if the wall runs at right angles to the joists below, the blockwork is built off a timber sole plate measuring 75 x 75mm (3 x 3in).

Internal walls built in concrete block can be constructed quite quickly and tend to have better sound insulation than stud walls. Provided the construction has been designed by a qualified person, the work itself is relatively straightforward.

Plaster wall systems

In addition to more traditional systems, there have been several developments in the area of pre-formed walling units. For instance, prefabricated wall panels, called Paramount dry partition, are made by British Gypsum. Each board comprises a plasterboard sandwich with a cellular core.

On the Continent, large pre-formed plaster blocks are often manufactured with tongued-and-grooved edges for the construction of partition walls. These are fixed together using an adhesive, and when the excess from the joints has been smoothed down, the resulting fair face finish can be sufficiently smooth to receive wall paper without the need for any further surface preparation.

Together with other similar innovative partition wall systems, these products have been used in many commercial buildings, such as banks and offices. However, they seem slow to gain a foothold in domestic buildings, where more traditional techniques are still preferred.

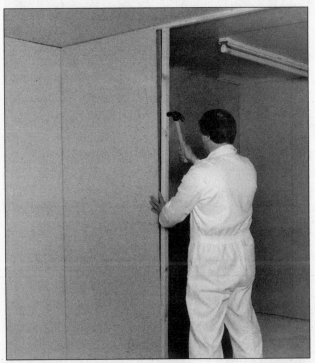

Lengths of connecting batten are tapped into the core of British Gypsum Paramount dry partition boards.

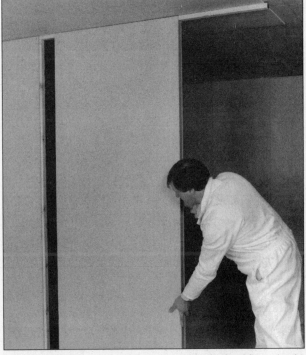

With the aid of locating battens fixed to the ceiling and floor, the dry partition board units are slid into place.

Plastering

Acquiring plastering skills is not something you can accomplish in a couple of weekends, and most self-builders sensibly enlist the help of a professional to carry out this important finishing operation. However, plastering a walk-in wardrobe or similar small area offers a splendid training ground if you are keen to give it a try. If your efforts are far from perfect, at least they won't be too obvious.

Changes in plaster materials

Considerable changes have occurred in the materials used for plastering. In the early part of this century, interior walls were finished with a lime, sand and cement plaster. This was applied on a base of wooden or metal laths that provided a good bond. The use of expanded metal as a replacement for the traditional 25 x 6mm (1 x ¼in) pine laths began in the last century, and even today metal plays an important part as a structural binder. For example, external corners are formed using metal beading with a meshed edging.

Before the advent of cement, plaster was made from lime with a binder to provide strength. Accordingly, ox or horse hair was added to the mix, and anyone renovating an old property may find evidence of this. Wattle-and-daub plastering, using clay, straw and dung, is an even older technique.

Compared to earlier finishes, cement-based plaster is very impact-resistant, which is why it's also used for external rendering. It's comparatively heavy, and on interior walls a cement/sand basecoat is finished by applying a layer of Sirapite. This is a hard finishing coat that can be trowelled off to produce a very smooth surface, which is ideal if you want to paint the walls with emulsion. Sirapite begins to harden after 15-20 minutes; but it can be re-tempered without detriment by adding more water, thus extending its working time by an hour or more.

Although traditional sand/lime/cement plaster provides a tough surface, most tradesmen use a modern gypsum plaster containing perlite or vermiculite. These materials are fire-resistant and enhance the thermal insulation properties of the

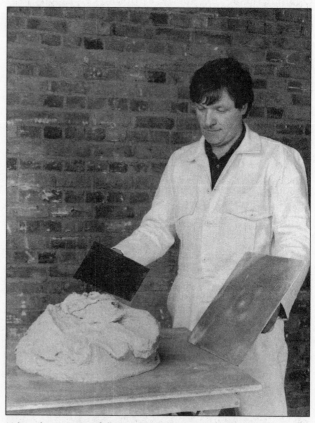

Using plaster successfully requires skill, practice and patience.

plaster. In addition, modern plaster is lighter and very much easier to work. Unfortunately, it doesn't fare well in damp conditions. If you are doubtful about the integrity of a damp proof course (DPC) in a building, use a traditional sand/lime/cement plaster finished with Sirapite. Some builders also prefer to use this traditional plaster in bathrooms.

The information given in this section provides a guide to plastering techniques and the products available for those who want to try their hand. There is no substitute for practice, and you must follow the manufacturers' instructions when using any plaster products.

▶ **SEE PAGE 122 FOR STEP-BY-STEP INSTRUCTIONS ON PLASTERING A BARE WALL**

Modern plasters

Even though the constituents of modern plasters are different from lime-based plasters, they are compatible. In other words, you can use a modern product to carry out repairs to an old surface finished with a traditional plaster. There are four types of modern plaster:

Browning This is for backing coats and should be applied quite thickly – up to 10mm (⅜in) – to smooth off undulations in the wall.

Bonding An alternative backing coat for use on surfaces that don't readily absorb moisture, such as engineering bricks.

Finishing A surfacing coat that is applied on top of the backing coat once it has hardened, to a depth of no more than 5mm (¼in).

One-coat Instead of requiring a day between coats of conventional plasters, one-coat plasters allow the work to be carried out in one operation. However, there are disadvantages. Trowelling-off a one-coat plaster can be difficult. Since the product doesn't begin to dry with a 'snap' finish, like conventional products, the action of trowelling can shift the material around. While there's a benefit in

using this for repair work, it isn't as easy to use as many DIY builders expect.

Several points should be born in mind when using these products:

● Never use two layers of bonding plaster. This can lead to the top layer shrivelling and crazing. Instead, apply a layer of browning plaster over a layer of bonding.

● An alternative to using a bonding plaster is to coat a moisture-resistant surface, like a concrete lintel, with a liberal application of a PVA adhesive, such as Unibond. This creates the adhesion needed by browning plaster.

● Never use old plaster; it dries too quickly. Modern plaster contains a retardant, but this becomes less efficient after a long storage period. Store a bag of plaster in a stout polythene outer bag to prolong its working life.

● Buy a fine plant sprayer from a garden centre for dampening surfaces. Professional plasterers typically flip a wet brush over the surface, but a hand sprayer will distribute water far more efficiently and accurately.

Essential tools

There is a range of specialist plastering tools available. Not all of them are essential for every plastering job, and some can be made at home. These are the basics:

Hawk A wooden, metal or plastic square attached to a handle for carrying plaster to the wall. You can make your own from a 30cm (12in) square piece of chipboard or thick plywood screwed to a length of broom handle.

In addition to being a convenient way of transferring plaster to the wall, the hawk also acts as a safety net. By placing it directly below the area being plastered, any plaster falling from the trowel as you press it onto the wall will merely fall back onto the hawk.

Plasterer's trowel A thin rectangular steel blade with a plastic or wooden handle for applying plaster to the wall and polishing the surface. Also known as a steel float.

Wooden float A rectangle of wood with a handle for giving a flat finish to the plaster.

Devilling float Used for keying the surface of the backing coat ready for the finishing coat. A wooden float can be converted into a devilling float by driving a couple of nails through one end so that their tips just protrude underneath. Passing the float over the surface of the plaster produces scratches that a subsequent layer of plaster can adhere to.

Rule A long, straight wooden batten used for levelling a backing coat of plaster when applied between wooden grounds nailed to the wall.

Spot board For keeping the plaster close to the job. You can make one yourself from a 1m (3ft) square of exterior-grade plywood. Support it on trestles, or similar, so that it is at a convenient height. One edge should overhang the support so that you can hold the hawk below as you scoop plaster onto it.

Making patch repairs

In an old building, the plaster may be in a particularly bad way, and areas of it may have broken away from the backing, moving when you press against them. If several areas of a wall are loose like this, it is better to strip all the old plaster off and replaster the wall completely (see pages 122-123). If only one or two weak areas are found, they can be patched.

Patching a small area of damaged plaster is not difficult, and the first job is to discover the extent of the damage. Rap the wall with your knuckles – loose plaster will produce a hollow sound. Use a pencil or piece of chalk to mark out the area of damage, then begin to remove the plaster with a bolster chisel and club hammer. Work inwards from the edges of the damaged area, carefully chipping the plaster away. This will ensure that you don't remove any more sound plaster than is absolutely necessary, keeping the size of the repair to the minimum.

Once all the old weak plaster has been removed and the masonry or laths below cleaned and dampened, you can begin to apply a backing coat of plaster. This is brought up to just below the level of the surrounding plaster, allowed to harden and then the repair is completed by applying a coat of finishing plaster.

TOOLS AND MATERIALS

- ☐ Bolster chisel
- ☐ Club hammer
- ☐ Brush
- ☐ Water spray
- ☐ Hawk
- ☐ Plasterer's trowel
- ☐ Devilling float
- ☐ Wooden batten
- ☐ Bucket and mixing stick
- ☐ Spot board

HOW MUCH?

☐ An area of repair, measuring 1m (3ft) square needs around 6kg (13lb) of basecoat and 2 kg (4½lb) of finish coat. Builders' merchants normally sell plasters in 50kg (27lb) bags, but smaller quantities can often be found in large DIY stores.
☐ Mixing a small quantity is usually done in a bucket, and a surprisingly large amount of plaster is needed to produce a modest working quantity.

1 Use a bolster chisel and club hammer to remove the damaged plaster from the wall, taking it right down to the masonry or laths underneath. Make sure you remove all the weak and loose plaster, cutting it back to sound material. Square-up the area of the repair, straightening the edges, and undercut the edges slightly to aid the grip of the new plaster. Wear goggles while doing this to protect your eyes from flying debris.

2 Remove all the dust and debris from the area of the repair, using an old paint brush. Make sure all loose material is removed, otherwise the new plaster will not adhere to the wall as well as it should. Going over the masonry with a vacuum cleaner will also ensure that it is perfectly clean. Then dampen the wall with water, either using a brush to apply it, or a plant water spray.

3 Hold the hawk bearing a small amount of plaster firmly against the wall below the damaged area. Insert the trowel blade into the plaster, angle it at about 45 degrees, and push it firmly towards the wall. Press the plaster upwards on the trowel, pressing firmly inwards at the same time. As the plaster is transferred to the wall, flatten the trowel to an angle of about 30 degrees, increasing the inwards pressure.

4 Level the plaster with a wooden batten, using a sawing action. Then, as the plaster begins to harden, cut it back with the trowel so that it sits slightly below the surrounding plaster. The backing coat should be about 1mm (¹⁄₁₆in) below the surface. If the original plaster is too thick to allow this with a 10mm (⅜in) basecoat, you will need to apply a second coat after a couple of hours. Key the first coat with a devilling float.

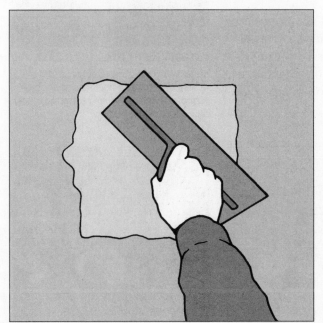

5 When applying the finishing coat, make sure that the mix is creamy and completely free of lumps. Transfer a quantity to the hawk and use your steel trowel to press it hard into place, holding the trowel so that the blade is at an angle to the wall. Again, hold the hawk firmly against the wall immediately below the area of attention. Cover the entire area of repair as quickly as possible, keeping the trowel moving.

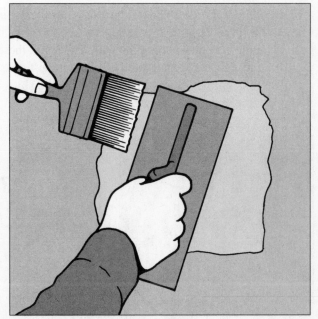

6 Use the trowel to smooth the finishing coat upwards, then from side to side. Polish the plaster by resting the blade flat against the surface, with slightly more pressure on the trailing edge of a sweep. If the surface begins to dry before you have finished, wet it very lightly with a plant spray, or flick water onto it with a brush. A polished finish is surprisingly easy to achieve, but don't over-polish, as emulsion paint may not adhere properly.

Plastering a wall

Plastering a new wall follows the same broad principles as patching plasterwork. The main difference, however, is the need to recognise surface depth and undulations while you work. It is essential to prepare the wall, or walls, with depth guides so that a minimum thickness of plaster can be applied, leaving a flat, smooth, vertical surface.

Any door linings should be positioned carefully to suit the required depth of plaster; similarly, metal boxes for sockets and switches should be set into the masonry, but project a little so that when the plastering is completed, they will be flush with the surface. In a new building, door linings should project about 12mm (½in) prior to plastering.

Fit metal corner beadings to any external corners of walls, door openings and window reveals, setting them in dabs of plaster and aligning them carefully with a spirit level. Alternatively, they can be anchored with masonry nails.

To ensure the correct depth of plaster across the expanse of a wall, it should be divided into manageable sections, or bays, using vertical wooden battens temporarily nailed in place. These are known as grounds and provide a useful guide to the plaster's depth. They should be set with the aid of a spirit level to ensure that they are truly vertical. As the floating coat (the initial layer of plaster) in each bay is completed, the right hand ground is repositioned to form a fresh bay ready for plastering.

Plastering a wall needs care and patience, as plaster is not the easiest of materials to work with. It may readily slip from the hawk or trowel, or may slump perilously down the wall. However, these faults can be overcome if your are prepared to persevere. Don't take on to ambitious a project to begin with; where possible, learn the skills on an area that will not come under critical gaze.

TOOLS AND MATERIALS

- [ ] Spot board
- [ ] Hawk
- [ ] Plasterer's trowel
- [ ] Devilling float
- [ ] Wooden batten (1.5m/5ft long)
- [ ] Water brush
- [ ] Bucket and mixing stick
- [ ] Timber grounds (10mm/⅜in thick)
- [ ] Spirit level
- [ ] Masonry nails
- [ ] Hammer
- [ ] Browning or bonding plaster
- [ ] Finishing plaster

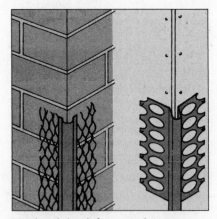

Metal angle beads for external corners are designed to accept a floating and finishing coat on masonry walls, and a finishing coat only on plasterboard walls.

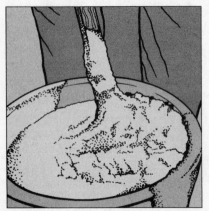

1 Mix equal amounts of plaster and water, stirring it with a stick until thoroughly blended. Both Browning and Bonding plaster should have a stiff consistency, resembling porridge.

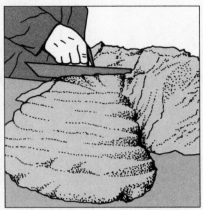

2 Tip the plaster out onto a spot board, placed close to where you are to work. Then knead the mixture with your trowel, sprinkling on more plaster if the mix appears too wet.

3 Scoop some plaster onto the hawk and practice loading and unloading the trowel. Hold the trowel at right angles to the hawk, push the blade forwards and rotate the hawk.

4 Continue tilting the hawk until it is vertical and scoop off the plaster. Keep the trowel blade horizontal with the plaster on top. Then level the hawk and tip the plaster back onto it.

5 Next, practice applying plaster to the wall. Rest the trowel blade against the timber ground and push upwards, steadily reducing the angle of the blade as the plaster is spread onto the wall.

6 Keep the blade on the ground, reducing the angle until it is almost parallel with the wall. Finish by pressing the lower edge in slightly to squeeze the plaster against the wall.

7 When you are confident, scrape off your practice plaster and begin applying the floating coat to the first bay. Work from the bottom right hand corner and apply the plaster in strips

8 Level the plaster with the grounds, using a wooden batten with a sawing motion, working upwards. Fill in any low spots with more plaster and level them off with the batten.

9 Use a devilling float to key the floating coat of plaster before it sets, keeping the bottom wet. Reposition the right hand ground to form the next bay and repeat the procedure.

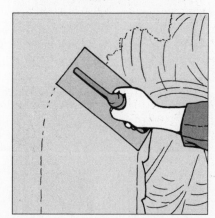

10 Spread a thin layer of finishing plaster over the hard floating coat, working from top to bottom. Then use wide sweeping movements of the trowel to produce a smooth surface.

11 Any ridges or splashes in the finishing coat can be lightly trowelled off, stroking the blade lightly downwards. Keep the trowel blade at a shallow angle to the wall.

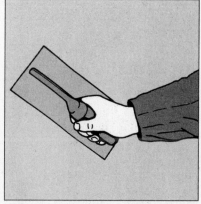

12 Allow the finishing coat to harden, then go over it with the trowel again, keeping the blade wet. This will polish the surface, producing a nice smooth finish.

Plasterboard lining

Since the advent of manufactured plasterboard, interior finishing work has changed significantly. For instance, modern plasterboards can be used to clad an internal timber stud partition, speeding the job considerably. Similarly, the material is used for the construction of ceilings. No longer are walls and ceilings constructed from wooden laths coated in plaster that has been mixed on site.

As can be seen, plasterboard is an invaluable product for the builder. In addition to stud walls and ceilings, plasterboard can also be used to line a brick or block wall, instead of using a traditional plastering technique. This is of particular interest to DIY enthusiast, who justifiably has misgivings about conventional plastering.

Another advantage is that there are insulating plasterboards, which are ideal for use in older properties. Where the lack of a cavity wall causes considerable heat loss, the addition of insulated plasterboard can increase the thermal performance of external walls significantly. However, insulating plasterboard can be used in modern properties, too, improving the normal level of insulation still further.

The potential of plasterboard is considerable, and it's important to be aware of the different types, so that the best can be selected for the job in hand.

An insulating plasterboard is often fitted to new properties, but it's ideal for increasing the insulation levels in older houses, where solid walls cause considerable heat loss. (Photograph courtesy British Gypsum Ltd)

Modern plasterboards

Plasterboard panels are made by sandwiching a layer of gypsum plaster between two sheets of thick paper. They are available in two standard thicknesses: 9.5mm (⅜in) and 12.5mm (½in). The former is used where the supporting timber members are spaced at 450mm (18in) centres. If the timber supports are set at a wider spacing – for example at 600mm (24in) centres – the thicker plasterboard should be employed. Board sizes vary, too. The most popular measures 2400 x 1200mm (8 x 4ft), although a smaller panel at 1829 x 900mm (72 x 35½in) is also available and is easier to handle, particularly when working alone.

Differences

Some boards are finished with an ivory paper on one side, while the other side has a grey finish. Where the intention is to skim the surface with a finish plaster, the grey finish gives a better bond. On the other hand, the ivory surface should be used when wallpaper will be applied directly to the surface. In the event, plasterboard with a grey surface on both sides tends to be more common, since most professional installers prefer to apply a final skim coat to the surface.

Other variations include the edge finish. Some boards are manufactured with a square edge, whereas others have a tapered edge. The latter produces a shallow recess on both sides of a joint, which can be filled with jointing compound and scrim tape that won't stand proud of the adjacent surfaces, making it easier to conceal the joint.

Important developments

Another important development is the production of plasterboard that's bonded to an insulating layer of polystyrene or phenolic foam. This is particularly useful in refurbishment work where the thermal insulation level of a property needs to be improved.

Also of interest is the availability of a 6mm (¼in) contour wallboard, which is quite flexible, allowing curved features to be formed. Other products include plasterboard with additional fire resistance, and plasterboard that is moisture-resistant. The moisture-resistant product is especially appropriate for installation in bathrooms and kitchens.

The manufacturers of plasterboard invariably offer technical help on installation methods and product selection, and it is worth consulting them and their technical literature before commencing a project.

Brick or block walls

The use of plasterboard for lining brick or block walls is preferred by many builders to the traditional approach of applying a plaster finish. There are several advantages to this, quite apart from the fact that a 'wet trade' such as plastering inevitably introduces a significant amount of damp material into the building. A long drying-out period is then needed before the building can be occupied.

With careful installation, plasterboard panels fixed to a brick or block wall will produce a particularly flat, true surface. To a degree, they will also improve the level of thermal insulation, although where this is a key requirement a special insulating plasterboard should be chosen instead of the standard product.

A flat surface

In the refurbishment of old an property, drywall techniques are easily carried out. For example, if the walls have unattractive irregular surfaces, the supporting framework can be packed out where necessary to produce truly vertical and flat surfaces when boarded. Such problems can also be accommodated by a proprietary metal support frame system that incorporates special wall brackets. These allow adjustments to be made so that the supporting sub-frame for the plasterboard can be constructed with a level surface.

In addition, another metal framing system enables you to erect a new inner wall without even making contact with the masonry wall behind. This is particularly advantageous where the existing wall suffers from persistent damp problems. The supporting structure consists of a friction-fit framework that is adjusted to mount tightly between the floor and ceiling.

▶ **SEE PAGES 125-129 FOR STEP-BY-STEP INSTRUCTIONS ON INSTALLING PLASTERBOARD**

Fixing plasterboard

The traditional method of mounting plasterboard to a wall is to construct a sub-frame, using wooden battens measuring approximately 25 x 19mm (1 x ¾in). The centres of the uprights should be coincide with the edges of the boards. In addition, you should add horizontal battens at the bottom of the wall to support the plasterboard and provide a firm fixing for the skirting board. Similarly, horizontals are needed near the ceiling, and at any point where the panels need additional support. It is best to use a preservative-treated timber for the framework. Follow these guidelines for success:

● It is essential that the supporting framework offers a truly vertical surface on which to attach the plasterboard panels, so each upright must be positioned with the aid of a spirit level. If necessary, packing pieces of hardboard or plywood should be placed behind the battens to bring them into line.

● The simplest way of mounting the battens is to use frame fixings, which combine a special hammer-in screw with a plastic wall plug. A hole is drilled through the batten and into the wall. Then the plug and screw are pushed through the batten, and driven home with a hammer. Any final tightening can be done with a screwdriver. Alternatively, normal screws and wall plugs can be used.

● When offering up plasterboard panels, a foot lifter will be useful for raising the bottom edge of each panel so that the top can be pushed hard against the ceiling. You can make one from a scrap of wood, cutting it to give a shallow triangular profile. Working single handed, you can see-saw the lifter on its apex to elevate the board. If the wall is significantly taller than a standard panel, it is best to add an extra strip of board at the bottom, as the skirting board will hide any slight irregularities in the surface where the boards are joined.

● Proper galvanised plasterboard nails should be used to fix the boards to the battens. They should be placed about 13mm (½in) in from the edge of the board, and spaced at intervals of no more than 150mm (6in). You can make a mark on your hammer handle to aid correct spacing. Drive each nail in until its head just dimples the surface of the board, without causing a tear in the paper binder.

● An alternative to nails for fixing plasterboard panels is to use countersunk wood screws. Their length should be double the thickness of the board. However, this method would be quite time consuming and would only be viable on a small project. If you do choose screws, make sure they are a non-rust type.

Cutting plasterboard

When dealing with plasterboard, occasionally you will have to cut panels to fit around obstructions. The material is easily sawn with an old fine-tooth saw, but don't press down too much – let the saw do the work. Alternatively, you can cut panels using a straight-edge and a sharp knife. A proprietary cutting guide is also available for this. Several passes will be needed with the knife to deepen a groove through the plaster. Moreover, to preserve the paper binder, you should also scribe another groove across the reverse face. Depending on the finish needed, you can often achieve an acceptable edge by snapping off the waste without having to cut through the board completely.

Plasterboard can be cut to size and shape with an old panel saw, or a sharp knife used with a proprietary cutting scale.

Direct-bond method

In contrast to attaching plasterboard to a framework, it's also possible to bond panels directly to a brick or block wall. This approach is often favoured in new work, since it's quick to complete. However, it requires a little more skill than fitting the boards to a sub-frame.

The wall must be in good condition and not susceptible to damp. Equally, it should be reasonably flat, because the dabs of adhesive can only accommodate minor surface irregularities. Special types of plasterboard are made for the direct-bond method, and the accompanying photographs show a thermal check type of board being installed. Patience, care and confidence are required when tackling this process, since subsequent corrective measures can be exceedingly difficult to carry out.

TOOLS AND MATERIALS

- ☐ Tape measure
- ☐ Pencil
- ☐ Chalk
- ☐ Chalked line
- ☐ Spirit level
- ☐ Long straight-edge
- ☐ Hawk
- ☐ Rectangular steel trowel
- ☐ Spot board
- ☐ Foot lifter
- ☐ Direct-bond adhesive
- ☐ Direct-bond plasterboard panels

1 The floor and ceiling are marked with a chalked line, allowing for the thickness of board plus at least 10mm (⅜in) of adhesive. (All photographs courtesy Lafarge Plasterboard Ltd)

2 Next, the walls are marked with vertical lines to indicate the positions of the rows of dabs. Use a long straight-edge, spirit level and a piece of chalk, or a chalked plumb line.

3 Mix up the special adhesive plaster and scoop some of it onto a hawk. Then use a steel float to place them on the wall. They should be 250mm (10in) long and 50-75mm (2-3in) wide.

4 Dabs are needed at 600mm (24in) centres, plus 50mm (2in) below the ceiling. A continuous line is needed above the floor. Apply enough for one panel at a time.

5 While being lifted clear of the floor with a foot lifter, the plasterboard panel is pressed firmly onto the dabs of adhesive. Then it is wedged in place at the bottom.

6 Finally, the plasterboard is tamped into place with a long straight-edge, aligning it with the marks on the floor and ceiling. Repeat the process for subsequent panels.

Installing a metal frame system

With the rising costs of timber, many builders prefer to mount plasterboard panels onto a metal framework. In addition, if a section in a timber sub-frame starts to develop a twist as it dries, distortion can occur in the plasterboard. A surface skim finish might also begin to show cracks. If the timber for a stud wall or support framework is stored in a room long enough for it to dry out, this is less likely to happen, but if it does, there is no easy cure other than taking out a section of the plasterboard to remove the twisted wood. Obviously, this problem doesn't occur with metal frame systems.

Quick to fit

Another advantage of using purpose-designed metal channelling is that it's quick to fit, using special fixing brackets. These are designed to accommodate undulations in the wall's surface, while special versions are made to space the framework further from the wall so that pipes can be hidden behind the plasterboard. The clip-together assembly method allows a support frame to be speedily erected.

With the steel frame system, special self-drilling screws are used to secure the plasterboard panels, obviating the need to prepare any pilot holes in the framework.

TOOLS AND MATERIALS

- ☐ Tape measure
- ☐ Pencil
- ☐ Plumb line
- ☐ Spirit level
- ☐ Electric drill and masonry bit
- ☐ Hacksaw
- ☐ Screwdriver
- ☐ Craft knife
- ☐ Screws
- ☐ Wall plugs
- ☐ Damp-proof membrane
- ☐ Metal framing
- ☐ Plasterboard panels

1 The first step is to install lengths of metal channel to the floor at 600mm (24in) centres. They are secured with screws and fixed over a length of damp-proof material. (All photographs courtesy Lafarge Plasterboard Ltd)

2 Next, additional lengths of metal channel are attached to the ceiling, again with screws, making sure that they are aligned vertically over the sections attached to the floor. This can be checked with a plumb line.

3 Standard-reach brackets are attached to the wall with screws, spacing them at 600mm (24in) centres. Longer brackets are also available to space the frame further from the wall to accommodate pipework.

4 Using the special clips provided, the upright portions of the framework are attached to the floor and ceiling channels. They should be fixed so that they are aligned with the wall brackets and are vertical, checking with the aid of a spirit level.

5 The legs of the brackets are folded out and fixed to the channelling with screws. They are long enough to accommodate any unevenness in the wall. Any extra material on the bracket legs can be folded back out of the way.

6 Finally, the plasterboard panels are screwed to the metal channels at 300mm (12in) centres. The screws used are special self-drilling types that bore holes directly into the metal, speeding up the operation considerably.

Finishing the boards

One method of finishing plasterboard lining is to skim the surface of the boards with a finishing plaster, keeping this layer to a maximum thickness of 5mm (¼in). If this method is chosen, the boards should be mounted as closely together as possible. Products like Thistle Board Finish are often used for this work; alternatively, Artex can be used where a textured appearance is required. Both of these finishes are also used for surfacing a ceiling. However, with care, you can fill and blend-in the joints between the boards, then simply decorate the surface with emulsion paint, or hang wallpaper.

Taped joints

Covering joints between plasterboard panels is carried out with a jointing compound, used in conjunction with a paper tape, a cotton scrim or a hessian scrim. Any internal corners need a similar treatment, using paper tape.

External corners, however, need more careful attention, because they are more likely to receive the occasional hard knock. To achieve a more robust finish, you can apply a special cross-fibre tape, which incorporates bonded, zinc-coated steel strips. This is attached to the boards with jointing compound, in the usual manner, and provides a rigid, impact-resistant nosing to the corner.

Jointing compounds

Various jointing compounds are available, many of which are gypsum-based and have a setting time of around 90 minutes. A band of compound is usually applied along the length of the joints with a taping knife, and the tape or scrim is pressed into this bedding with the knife. When the compound has dried, a further coat of jointing compound is added, although a steel trowel is best for this, because the material needs to be feathered at the edges to blend into the surface of the plasterboard on each side. This should be done with care so that the area of the joint is completely disguised. Going over the edges with a damp sponge often helps.

When the second coat has been allowed to dry, a final finishing coat should be applied, again feathering out the edges with your trowel, but taking even more care. Although it is possible to remove any blemishes with a final rubbing down later, using 120-grit glass-paper, the less tidying-up needed, the better.

Finally, a sealing coat is recommended prior to applying emulsion paint. Although you can use a wash coat of heavily-diluted emulsion paint for this, you can also apply a specially-formulated sealer, which is likely to be much more effective.

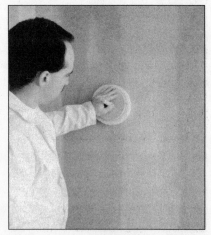

3 Where necessary, the edges of jointing compounds can be smoothed with a special round feathering sponge.

7 Jointing tape and further coats of jointing compound are added in the same manner as before.

TOOLS AND MATERIALS

- ☐ 100 & 150mm (4 & 6in) taping knives
- ☐ Rectangular steel trowel
- ☐ Tin snips
- ☐ Sanding block
- ☐ Jointing compound
- ☐ Finishing compound
- ☐ Joint tape or scrim
- ☐ External corner tape
- ☐ 120-grit glass-paper
- ☐ Drywall sealer
- ☐ Finishing plaster (optional)

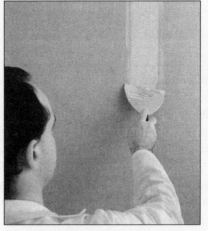

1 Jointing compound is applied with a wide taping knife. (All photographs courtesy Lafarge Plasterboard Ltd)

2 Paper joint tape is bedded in the compound, covered with more and struck off flush with plasterboard face.

4 When set hard, a second coat of jointing compound is added with a trowel and feathered off at the edges.

5 When the compound has set, a finishing coat of air-drying compound is added and feathered out at the edges.

6 At an internal corner, jointing compound is applied to both boards, using a 100mm (4in) taping knife.

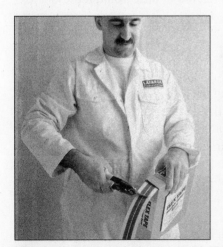

8 For an external corner, flex tape is cut with tin snips so that the integral metal strips face in towards the plasterboard.

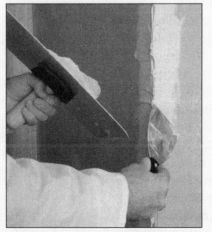

9 A 50mm (2in) wide band of fast-setting jointing compound is applied to each side of the corner.

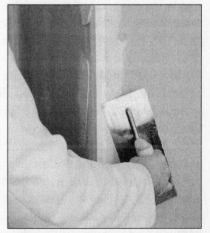

10 The tape is bedded and covered with layers of jointing compound in the normal manner.

Ceilings

The traditional method of constructing a plaster ceiling involved nailing closely-spaced wooden or metal laths to the joists and coating them with plaster. Adhesion was achieved because the wet plaster was pressed through gaps between the laths.

The lath-and-plaster method is very different from present-day practice, which makes use of plasterboard. Where joists are placed at 450mm (18in) centres, it is usual to fit plasterboard that is 9.5mm (⅜in) thick; 12.5mm (½in) plasterboard is preferred where joists are spaced at 600mm (24in) centres. If a vapour control layer is needed above the ceiling, foil-backed plasterboard can be used. However, to ensure this fulfils its function correctly, any breaks in the foil at joins in the board should be sealed, which necessitates access from above.

Making repairs

Where a traditional ceiling is in poor condition, improvements can be made by adding a textured wallpaper, such as a woodchip or embossed covering. This will disguise superficial irregularities quite effectively. However, this is not a viable solution if the plaster is loose and likely to fall away from its backing.

Where the laths are sound and still in place, you can reinstate the damaged area using gypsum plaster. Modern products are fully compatible with older lime plasters and will adhere well to the laths. First, all the old damaged plaster must be removed and raked from between the laths. Then an undercoat of browning plaster should be applied, pressing it into the laths well. When it has started to harden – in 2-3 hours, the surface should be scratched to achieve a key. It should be left for around 24 hours to harden completely, after which you can apply a thin coat of finishing plaster, using a steel trowel to produce a smooth, level surface.

In very old properties, you may need to experiment with repair strategies. For instance, if the plaster looks crumbly, you will need to stabilise the surface before adding a further skim layer. This can be done by painting a PVA bonding product directly onto the surface, using a wide brush. When it has dried, apply a thin layer of finishing plaster. Provided the laths are sound, this is usually very successful.

Decorative finishes

For many years, a popular way of finishing a ceiling has been to apply a textured coating, such as Artex. Many pattern effects can be produced in this material, some of which are quite easy to reproduce if they become damaged.

More recently, however, there has been renewed interest in plain surfaces, many home owners wanting to remove the textured finish and reinstate a smooth surface. Regrettably, this can be quite difficult. An industrial steam stripper may help, but it is still difficult to scrape away a textured finish without damaging the surface below. Sometimes a plaster coating can be added directly on top, but in many cases it is best to remove and replace the plasterboard completely. One thing you must not do is try to remove the finish with any kind of abrasive tool. Some early textured finishes contained asbestos, so the creation of dust would represent a serious health hazard.

Open-joist finish

An attractive cottage-style look can be given to a ceiling by leaving the joists exposed. Plasterboard panels can be nailed to battens fixed to the joists, or directly to the underside of the floorboards above.

The plasterboard should be skimmed with a finishing plaster. The problem you may experience lies in preventing the plaster from splashing the sides of the joists. The splashes can be difficult to remove cleanly.

The plaster can be decorated with emulsion paint, and the joists with a dark wood stain. Overall, the installation takes longer to finish than a conventional ceiling, but the result can be most attractive.

Patching a plastered ceiling

If a small section of a lath and plaster ceiling becomes damaged, the simplest remedy is to patch it with a section of plasterboard. This may be coated at all contact points with a plaster product, such as Thistle, manoeuvred into the hole and pressed into place, where it should remain because of the adhesive properties of the plaster. However, this will only work for a very small area of damage, as any substantial piece of plasterboard will fall away under its own weight. It is much better to cut the damaged laths back to the nearest joists and nail the plasterboard to them. Having closed off the hole, you can use the plasterboard as a backing for layers of fresh plaster. Where a small area is involved, you should be able to purchase a repair pack of one-coat plaster from a major DIY store.

TOOLS AND MATERIALS

- ☐ Saw
- ☐ Tape measure
- ☐ Pencil
- ☐ Hammer
- ☐ Bucket
- ☐ Mixing stick
- ☐ Hawk
- ☐ Plasterer's trowel
- ☐ Wooden batten
- ☐ Plasterboard
- ☐ Plasterboard nails
- ☐ Bonding plaster
- ☐ Finishing plaster

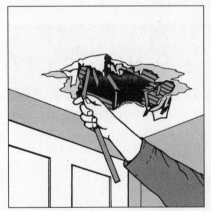

1 If the damage to the ceiling includes broken laths, the first job is to pull them out and cut the ends back with a saw. Saw them off at the centres of the adjacent joists.

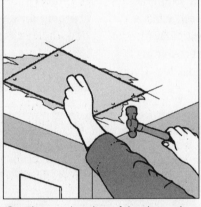

2 Clean up the edges of the plaster, then cut a piece of plasterboard to fit tightly in the hole. Nail this in place, grey side down, using 30mm (1¼in) galvanised plasterboard nails.

3 Treat the plaster around the edge of the hole with PVA adhesive. This will not only ensure good adhesion between the new plaster and old, but also reduce water staining.

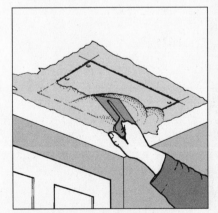

4 Mix up some bonding plaster and trowel a layer onto the plasterboard patch with a steel float. Make sure that it is pressed into the edges of the hole well.

5 Level plaster by ruling it off with a straight wooden batten. Leave the plaster to stiffen slightly, then flatten it below the surrounding plaster and key its surface with a devilling float.

6 Finally, spread two coats of finishing plaster over the patch, carefully levelling it with the surrounding plaster. As it begins to set, wet the trowel and polish the surface.

Plaster coving

A decorative plaster moulding at the junction of the walls and ceilings was very popular in quality houses erected during the last century. The plaster finish was often intricate. Today, a similar, less ornate feature, known as coving, is sometimes used.

Coving adds a smart finish to a room, but it also has another important function – it can be used to cover cracks. Differential expansion between plasterboard ceilings and plastered walls often leads to an unsightly crack between the two. Although a filling compound may initially overcome the unsightly finish, the cracks invariably reappear. Adding plaster coving is much more effective.

Coving is available in two standard sizes: one has a girth of 127mm (5in) and will extend 83mm (3¼in) onto both wall and ceiling; the other has a girth of 100mm (4in) and extends 67mm (2⅝in). Various lengths are made, and it's best to avoid creating joins in long runs wherever possible. Even

with the most careful workmanship, the joint is difficult to disguise.

Decorative mouldings

Although modern coving is far simpler in design than the ornamental versions preferred in the last century, there are signs of a revived interest in more decorative plasterwork. Techniques of manufacture are modern, however, although the end-products bear similarities with earlier designs. Hence you can purchase an ornamental plaster ceiling rose as a manufactured unit to place around a central light fitting. Similarly, there are also manufacturers who specialise in making decorative cornices.

▶ **SEE PAGE 134 FOR STEP-BY-STEP INSTRUCTIONS ON FITTING PLASTER COVING**

Ornamental ceiling roses are now available as pre-made units, and are ideal when carrying out renovation work in an older property.

Measuring and cutting coving

Cutting internal and external mitres on lengths of coving needs careful consideration; it's all too easy to get the cutting angle wrong. All measurements also need taking and marking out with care.

This type of coving is made from fire-resistant gypsum plaster, encased in a paper liner that must not be removed. Cutting should be carried out with an old tenon saw, as the plaster will soon blunt a new blade, and DIY coving kits often include a paper template that is laid on the face of the coving to mark the cutting line. A more accurate approach is to make up a mitre cutting block, as shown on page 134. While it's true that small gaps in adjoining sections can be filled reasonably successfully using the adhesive, it's always best to cut the material correctly in the first place.

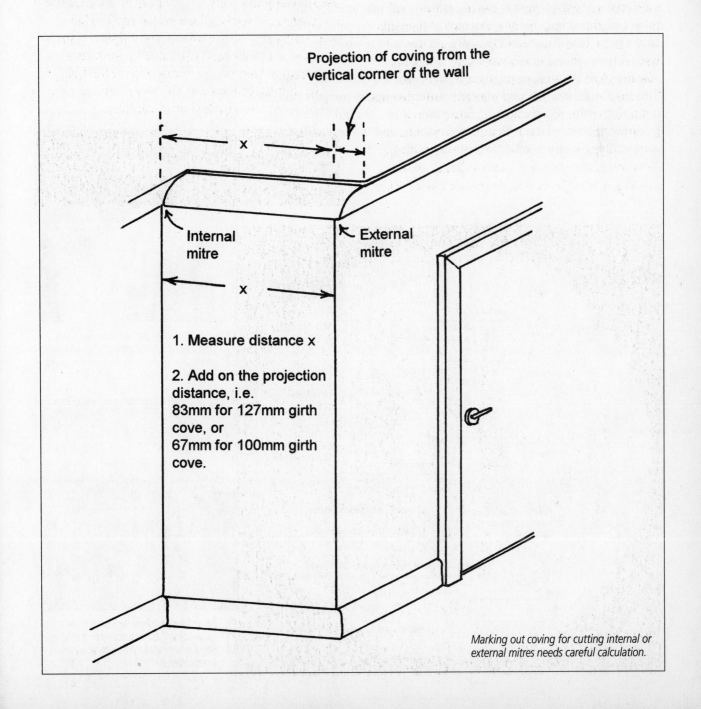

Projection of coving from the vertical corner of the wall

Internal mitre

External mitre

1. Measure distance x

2. Add on the projection distance, i.e.
83mm for 127mm girth cove, or
67mm for 100mm girth cove.

Marking out coving for cutting internal or external mitres needs careful calculation.

Fitting plaster coving

Installing coving is a relatively straightforward operation, provided you take care in measuring and cutting the lengths of plaster moulding. The techniques are shown in the accompanying step-by-step photographs.

When working with a long section, it is best to have assistance in supporting the material when it's offered up to the wall. As soon as the adhesive touches the surface of dry plaster, moisture will be drawn away quite quickly, and the setting process will begin at once. If you accidentally jog the length of coving while holding it in place, the developing bond may become fractured. Once this happens, adhesion cannot be re-established, and the only answer is to remove the coving, scrape off the adhesive and start all over again.

Bearing this in mind, on a longer run, it is a good idea to tap 25mm (1in) panel pins into the wall plaster to offer temporary support beneath the coving while you are holding it in place. When the adhesive is dry, the pins can be removed with a pair of pincers, and the holes filled with coving adhesive or a normal filling compound.

TOOLS AND MATERIALS

☐ Tape measure
☐ Pencil
☐ Wooden template
☐ Filling knife
☐ Mixing container
☐ Mixing stick
☐ Old tenon saw
☐ Mitre jig
☐ Fine glass-paper
☐ Coving adhesive
☐ Coving

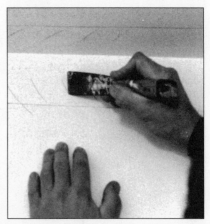

4 To ensure that the adhesive achieves a good bond, the plaster of the wall and ceiling should be scored with the blade of a filling knife.

8 Adhesive is applied liberally to the edges of the coving, spreading it with a filling knife. Make sure you achieve an even coverage.

Mitre jig

plan view

direction of saw cuts for coving placed in section
A

dotted line shows fillet position for 100mm girth cove

A

A

50

67   83

B

50

100 x 50mm deal

B

67   83

12mm ply base

fillets of 12 x 12mm deal

|← 300 →|

direction of saw cuts for coving placed in Section B

Section A for internal mitres

Section B for external mitres

The mitre should be marked on 50 x 50mm deal with a combination square and then sawn with care.

Sketch of mitre jig

NOTE: All dimensions are metric

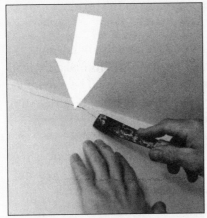

1 Cracks often develop at the junction of the wall and ceiling. You can fill these with conventional filler, or hide them completely by fitting coving.

2 Coving adhesive should be mixed in small quantities only, since it dries quickly. An old ice cream tub is ideal for this purpose.

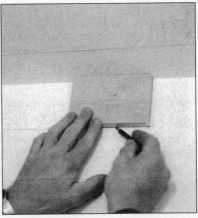

3 Cut a block of wood to the same depth as the coving and use it as a template to mark off the contact points on the wall and ceiling.

5 Using a cutting jig (see illustration opposite), the mitres at the ends of lengths of coving can be cut with an old tenon saw.

6 Make sure that the mitred cut runs in the correct direction. Provided you don't force the saw, you should be able to obtain a clean cut.

7 Carefully smooth any ragged edges on the paper binding with fine glass-paper. However, take care not to remove any of the plaster.

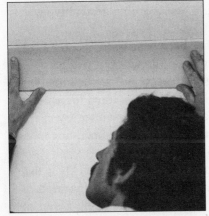

9 Press the coving gently, but firmly, into the angle between the wall and ceiling. Then hold it in place for a minute or so to allow the adhesive to grip.

10 Draw the blade of the filling knife along the edges of the coving to remove any surplus adhesive before it has a chance to set fully.

11 When the adhesive has set, the ceiling and wall can be decorated. The finished coving will add a smart finish to the room.

Timber-clad ceilings

A completely different finish can be achieved by cladding a ceiling with strips of tongued-and-grooved timber. Carefully selected wood can look most attractive; moreover, once the work has been completed, future maintenance is minimal.

However, wood cladding has fire characteristics that are quite different from plaster. This means that if you add timber cladding on top of a plaster ceiling, you will be downgrading its fire resistance properties. In certain locations, such as a kitchen, this could be unacceptable.

Fire retardance

The whole subject of fire precautions is complex, and the Building Regulations contain a wide range of measures that must be complied with. The issues do not merely relate to the combustibility of different building materials, but to other aspects as well, such as the surface spread of flame. The ability of flames to track across surfaces and to cause ignition at some distance from the original source of a fire is a well-known phenomenon.

For this reason, any plans to clad rooms with a timber finish rather than a plaster product should be discussed with your local authority building control surveyors. The proposals must gain formal approval and, in some instances, the builder will be required to apply an intumescent flame-retardant finish to the cladding after its installation. In many instances, some types of polyurethane varnish will be unacceptable. The point about an intumescent treatment is that it reacts in a fire, starts to foam and forms a dense insulation barrier. Intumescent treatments do not spoil the appearance of the cladding, and some are specially formulated for this kind of construction. Advice on intumescent finishes is available from a variety of sources, including the Timber Research and Development Association (TRADA).

Fire safety is a complex matter, and although timber clad surfaces can be very attractive, you must seek expert advice before installing one. If the cladding is installed in an inappropriate location and coated with an unsuitable finish, it could have serious implications for the safety of the occupants in the event of a fire.

Materials

There are many fine cladding materials available, especially exotic hardwoods, but the cost is often prohibitive, so most home improvers are likely to select a softwood like pine, as this is relatively inexpensive. The choice of profiles is also varied (as shown opposite), but since the cladding is decorative rather than structural, the boarding need only be 13mm (½in) thick.

Once the wood has been purchased, it should be stored on trestles in the room where it will be installed. The longer it can be left, the less likely it is to shrink when fixed. If it can be stored for as long as a month, so much the better. In winter, try to arrange for the central heating to be operating in the room where it will be used.

The penalty of installing wood too quickly is that it will shrink in the warmth of a house; in serious cases, the tongues and grooves will begin to separate and the fixings distort. On the other hand, if you use wood that has been stored indoors for lining an unheated porch, you'll be amazed at how the cladding strips will swell and buckle.

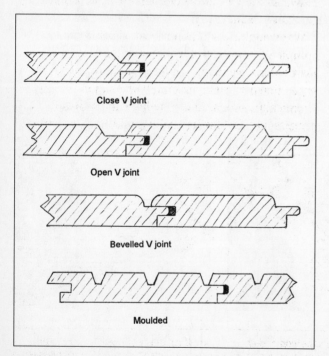

Close V joint

Open V joint

Bevelled V joint

Moulded

Wood cladding is available in a number of different profiles.

Installing timber cladding

Assuming a plaster ceiling is already in place, the first job is to attach 50 x 25mm (2 x 1in) softwood battens to the ceiling, screwing them securely to the joists. The cladding will be fixed to these. When match boarding is nailed directly to plasterwork, if a fire breaks out, the burning timber might distort the plaster, hastening its destruction and causing rapid penetration to the room above. For this reason, a building surveyor might require plasterboard to be installed before the cladding, because of its better fire resistance.

To locate the position of the joists, you can either tap the ceiling and probe with a bradawl, or you can use one of the proprietary joist detection meters. These are available from major DIY stores.

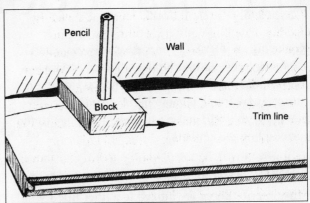

A board that runs along a wall needs marking and trimming to match the shape of the wall. Use a pencil and block, as shown.

Fitting the boards

Where boards meet on a long run, the ends of both lengths need supporting by a batten. Normally, a butt joint is used, but it is much better to mitre the ends to form a scarf joint. The overlapping ends prevent an ugly gap from opening up if the boards shrink along their length.

Boards that run along a wall will need trimming to match any undulations in the wall. These are easily transferred to the board with a marking block and pencil (see diagram). At the preparatory stage, use some board offcuts to calculate progression across the ceiling. You must make sure that the last board to be placed isn't ridiculously narrow.

The boards should be held in place by secret nailing through their tongues. This isn't possible, of course, on the first and last boards to be placed, but you can often disguise nail heads by positioning them alongside knots in the timber.

Before nailing a board, you should make sure it is pushed fully home on the tongue of the adjacent board. You can tap it home, using a short offcut of board to fit over its tongue. Some builders use 25mm (1in) lost-round-head wire nails for fixing the boards, but sherardized (rust-resistant) panel pins of the same length are less likely to split the tongues. However, they need to be driven home with care, since they bend easily.

When applying an intumescent finish to the completed ceiling, follow the manufacturer's instructions. Ventilation, a face mask and eye protection are usually essential when applying this chemical treatment. It can be quite an involved process, but the finished ceiling will look delightful.

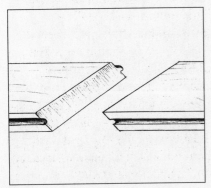

The use of scarf joints at the ends of boards will help to disguise any gaps that might appear through shrinkage.

Nailing into the tongued portion of each board ensures that the heads are concealed by the following board.

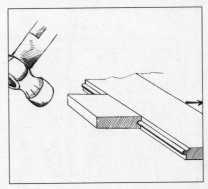

An offcut of board should be used with a hammer to tap the boards tightly together prior to nailing them to the battens.

Internal doors

Replacing an internal door is relatively easy, and changing trends in interior decor have encouraged many home owners to fit replacements. However, fitting a new frame is more involved, since inevitably this will cause a degree of damage to the surrounding plasterwork.

Fitting the frame

Most interior doors are hinged to a liner fitted with separate wooden strips that act as door stops, as opposed to a rebated frame used for exterior doors. There are exceptions, of course, and occasionally interior doors may be found pre-hinged and manufactured with an integral rebated frame as a combined unit.

Typically, however, a frame is made from planed softwood, measuring 130 x 30mm (5 x 1¼in) for installation against 100mm (4in) internal walls, or 105 x 30mm (4⅛ x 1¼in) for 75mm (3in) walls. This width of this liner is greater than the width of the blockwork to take account of the plaster depth.

Although door liners are sold in stock sizes to accept doors of standard heights and widths, the simple joints between the sides and top can easily be altered to produce a narrower opening.

Where the internal walls of a house are built from bricks or blocks, liners are often fixed using cut nails driven directly into the masonry. This is done prior to plastering. However, it's much better to use screws driven into wooden pads set in the mortar courses, or normal wall plugs. These are less likely to cause damage, and by adjusting the screws you can place thin packing behind the frame to achieve a perfectly straight edge, instead of replicating any unevenness in the brickwork. The screws should be fitted in pairs to prevent the frame from twisting in the aperture. A liner is easier to fit in a stud wall, since it is screwed directly to a timber sub-frame.

Once the liner has been fitted and plastering completed, the door can be hung on either edge of the framework, to open inwards or outwards. In addition, it can be hinged on the right or left side of the liner. This versatility is possible when there's no pre-formed rebate. Instead, you are supplied with loose stops of 30 x 12mm (1¼ x ½in) softwood.

The remaining part of the construction consists of a length of moulding to hide the joint between the liner and the plaster. This cover strip, known as architrave, is available in many decorative profiles. In older properties, architrave may be particularly ornate and much wider than that fitted in modern houses. If you are refurbishing a Victorian or Edwardian house, for example, it's likely that you will have to obtain replica architrave. This is something that small joinery specialists can often custom-make to order.

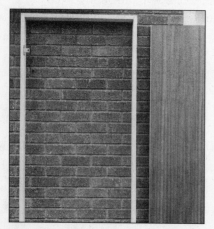

Most internal doors are fixed into a liner, rather than a rebated framework. Loose stops are provided for nailing on later.

If a liner needs reducing in width, the head can be removed and cut with a new housing joint, or drilled for nailing.

The modified door liner is glued and nailed together before being installed in the aperture with screws and wall plugs.

Selecting a door

The range of doors currently available is extensive. Ultra-light and inexpensive hollow doors, filled with a honeycomb core of cardboard, are acceptable in many situations. However, heavier fire-check doors may be needed in other locations. For instance, a fire door offering at least 30 minutes fire resistance is required between habitable rooms and a garage. Moreover, special requirements in respect of door closures are needed for loft conversions in two-storey dwellings. These requirements are contained in the Building Regulations. Accordingly, you should seek advice before purchasing new doors, since the requirements concerning fire safety are most stringent.

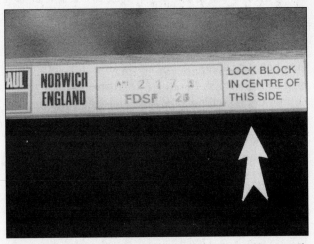

Hollow cellular-cored doors are often marked to show where a catch block is located. Similarly, the hinge edge may also be indicated.

Changing styles

Styles of internal doors are continually changing. After a number of years in which plain doors were popular, there's a renewed interest in panelled doors. In the event, many modern doors having a traditional panelled appearance are hollow, and merely bear a decorative surface that copies the panel style.

Technological development has also influenced surface materials. Many inexpensive doors bear an attractive woodgrain finish, although in fact this may be printed paper affixed to a hardboard base.

In the refurbishment of older properties, the task of selecting doors is far less easy. The openings may be wider than normal, and it may be necessary to employ a joinery company to custom-make doors. Alternatively, it may be possible to obtain reclaimed doors from an architectural salvage supplier.

Even when selecting a door for a comparatively modern house, you may find difficulties in matching the size. This is because of the change from imperial to metric sizes. During the early 1900s, doors of certain widths tended to be installed in particular locations:

2ft 0in – Airing cupboard
2ft 3in – Bedroom doors
2ft 6in – Ground floor doors
2ft 9in – Front door.

After metrication, many joinery specialists continued to manufacture doors to these dimensions, but expressed them in metric measurements; for example, 762mm instead of 2ft 6in. However, the introduction of true metric doors, around 20 years ago, saw the arrival of new widths and new heights. For instance, one of the metric widths is 724mm (28½in), while the height of a metric door is 1968mm (77½in), instead of the old imperial size of 6ft 6in (1980mm).

Check carefully

Imperial sizes are still manufactured, recognising the fact that in refurbishment work one is often faced with imperial-sized openings. Therefore, joinery catalogues should be checked carefully, and replacement doors selected accordingly.

Similar caution needs to be exercised with regard to door thicknesses. For instance, a good-quality heavyweight door is often 45mm (1¾in) in thickness, whereas a lightweight budget door may be only 35mm (1⅜in) thick. If a door is replaced by one of a different thickness, the stops may need to be prised away from the liner and repositioned.

Before fitting a hollow door – which nowadays represents the majority of factory-made units – you need to check the location of a solid wood block that will house the catch mechanism. Similarly, it is quite normal for the frame member on the hinge side to be slightly thicker to accommodate the screws. Accordingly, a door is often marked 'hinge side' along the edge.

Hanging an internal door

When hanging an internal door, follow these steps to ensure a successful job:

● Check the sides and top of the door liner for straightness, using a long straight-edge. In old houses, there may be a slight bow in the head of the liner,which must be duplicated by trimming the top of the door.

● Offer up the door to the frame, fitting small wedges underneath to keep it tight against the top of the liner. Pencil around the perimeter to transfer any undulations in the liner onto the face of the door.

● Place the door on edge for trimming, supporting it well. Plane the sides down to the pencil marks, working on the hinge side first; it is important to get this right before dealing with the other edges. At the top of the door, plane inwards from each edge. This prevents the wood from splitting at the corners. If you find that the face of the door splits when you are planing across the top, scribe the pencil line deeply with a sharp knife.

● Keep offering up the door to check progress; there's no easy remedy if you remove too much material. The gap at the top and sides needs to be about 3mm (⅛in), but since central heating may cause shrinkage, begin with a slightly smaller clearance. The gap at the bottom should be 3mm (⅛in) or just over, taking the floor covering into account.

● Normally, the edges should be trimmed square. However, on a thick heavy-duty door, you may find that the leading edge clips the liner as the door begins to close. The hinge side of the door may also bear against the frame when it's fully closed. In both cases, the problem can be solved by bevelling the edges slightly.

● Most internal doors can be supported by a pair of butt hinges. Brass hinges are preferable, especially in a bathroom or kitchen, since they won't rust. However, steel hinges are much cheaper. Position the upper hinge 150mm (6in) from the top of the door, and the lower one 200-225mm (8-9in) from the bottom. The centre-line of the spindle in a brass butt should align with the edge of the door. However, when pressed-steel butt hinges are used, the whole of the hinge knuckle should project beyond the face of the door.

● Scribe carefully around the hinge plate with a sharp knife. This will be easier if the hinge is fixed temporarily to the door with a couple of screws. Make several shallow feather cuts with a chisel before carefully paring away the waste wood. If you accidentally remove too much material, insert pieces of cardboard beneath the hinge plate.

● With the hinges attached, offer up the door in an open position, standing it on thin plywood to create the required clearance underneath. Scribe the hinge positions on the liner. When the recesses have been cut in the liner, screw the door into place, using only two screws per hinge. This allows you to check the closing action, while leaving fresh wood if you need to make slight alterations to the hinge positions. Only when the door closes correctly should all the screws be fitted.

TOOLS AND MATERIALS

- ☐ Long straight-edge
- ☐ Pencil
- ☐ Sharp knife
- ☐ Plane
- ☐ Bevel-edged chisel
- ☐ Bradawl
- ☐ Screwdriver
- ☐ Hinges
- ☐ Screws
- ☐ Door

When trimming the edges of a door to fit the liner, you can support it firmly for planing by making a pair of wedged supports such as this.

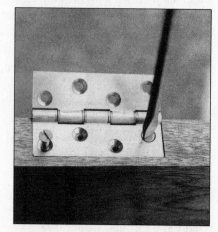

Having cut the hinge plate recesses, attach each hinge with only two screws. Then offer up the door; if necessary, you will be able to adjust the hinge positions, driving the screws into fresh wood.

Fitting the catch

In relatively modern properties, the catch and its handle are often fitted half-way between the top and bottom of a door. However, in older properties the position is slightly below the mid point. To prepare a door to accept the catch mechanism, a cutout is made by boring a number of overlapping holes in the edge with a hand brace and bit. Alternatively, a flat drill bit can be used in an electric drill. Then clean up the cutout with a bevel-edged chisel.

Insert the catch into the prepared hole, so that the plate portion sits flat on the edge of the door. Now you can score deeply around this with a sharp knife to outline the recess needed so that the plate will be flush with the edge of the door. Pare the wood from within the outline with a bevel-edged chisel. Similar techniques are used for setting the striker plate in the liner. When the catch fits properly, you can bore a hole through the door for the operating shaft.

Take care not to let the door close accidentally before you've fitted the square shaft and handle. It's all too easy to shut yourself in a room with no means of escape.

Fitting the handle and the operating shaft is self explanatory, although you may find that the shaft needs cutting down with a hacksaw; this will depend on the thickness of the door. On some designs, screws securing the plate to the door face are hidden by a clip-on cover plate for a neater appearance.

Door stops and architrave

When the door swings smoothly on its hinges, and the catch operates correctly, the loose stops can be nailed in position on the liner. These are normally fixed with small oval nails so that the heads will bury easily below the surface in readiness for filling.

Architrave is also fixed with oval nails, and is usually set back about 6mm (¼in) from the edge of the liner. In modern properties, it is should be thick enough to cover the projection of the skirting board. However, in older houses you may find an ornately-shaped block fitted at the bottom of a frame to cover the ends of both the architrave and skirting boards.

At its foot, architrave is skew-nailed into the skirting board. At the sides, it is nailed into the wooden pads that hold the liner against the wall; additional nails are driven into the liner itself at an angle, taking care not to shake it away from the plaster. At the top corners, the architrave is mitred and pinned. When fitting architrave, be most careful not to bruise the surface with the hammer head, since this damage will be difficult to disguise later. Finally, fill the nail holes and prime the wood ready for painting.

1 When the door closure position has been established and it swings freely on its hinges, the loose stops can be nailed to the liner. Use oval nails and punch their heads below the surface.

2 The architrave is usually set back from the edge of the liner by approximately 6mm (¼in). It should be thick enough to conceal the end of the skirting board at the bottom.

3 Architrave is attached in several ways; one method is to drive lost-head nails into the liner at an angle. As with the door stops, they should be punched below the surface.

Fireplaces

Two elements are discussed in this section. Firstly, there are the points to take into account when a fireplace and its accompanying hearth are constructed to accommodate an open fire, or a heating appliance such as a gas fire. Secondly, there is the decorative element, where a fireplace is principally intended as a design feature.

Constructional requirements

When considering the provision of an open fire, or the installation of a heating appliance,, you should check what implications this has for the flue. Different arrangements are needed for different types of heating system. For example, an existing flue designed for an open fire, may not be suitable for use with a gas-fired appliance. If you are in any doubt about this, consult the supplier of the appliance or fuel.

Regardless of the form of heating, the structure must also comply with the relevant sections of the Building Regulations. These require the following:

● The provision of an adequate supply of air for combustion, and for the efficient operation of the flue or chimney.
● An adequate provision for discharging the products of combustion to the outside.
● A construction in which the materials used protect the building from catching fire as a result of the heating system.

Designing the operational elements of a fireplace so that there is full compliance with the regulations is something that should be carried out by a qualified specialist. However, working from specifications and drawings, a skillful home improver may be able to carry out some of the constructional work. The Building Regulations give detailed information on the form and dimensions of the base unit, referred to as the constructional hearth; fireplace recesses are similarly detailed. There is also a British Standard (BS 8303) that concerns the installation of domestic heating and cooking appliances burning solid mineral fuels.

Additional guidance is available from the trade associations concerned with the promotion of heating products. In particular, the National Fireplace Council is very active in its promotion of products from member companies. It helps members of the public as well as tradespeople, and publishes a free yearbook, which is very informative. In addition, the Council publishes several technical leaflets. These are inexpensive publications that deal with range of relevant topics.

A number of specialists are also able to supply and arrange the installation of fireplaces. These are offered in a wide range of designs, many of them quite decorative and suitable for forming an impressive centre-piece for a room.

Some purpose-made fireplaces can form a distinctive centre-piece for a room. (Photograph courtesy Modus Design Ltd)

A new fireplace

Reinstating a fireplace that has previously been closed off may not always be as straightforward as it first seems. Elements like the provision of ventilation may be overlooked, but they must be included in the plans. You should check the requirements laid down in the Building Regulations.

The constructional hearth should be made of a solid, non-combustible material and be at least 125mm (5in) thick. No combustible materials are permitted below a hearth, except at the extreme perimeter to provide support. The only exception is where there is at least 50mm (2in) of air space between the underside of the hearth and the combustible material. In reinstatement work, however, a constructional hearth is likely still to be in place, despite the fact that the opening to the flue has been closed off. This is because the removal of a constructional hearth can be quite difficult.

A fireback needs to be installed in the fireplace opening. Then a suitable fire surround should be added to finish off the opening.

Complex design

The design of the complete system is quite involved. For example, faults in the design of a flue for an open fire can lead to downdraughts and smoke-filled rooms. A good draw on a flue is essential. Overall, the construction is complex and far more difficult than building the decorative features of the fireplace itself. In some instances, it may even be better to leave the construction of the operational part of the structure to an expert, and to devote your attention to the non-functional parts of the construction.

> ▶ **SEE PAGE 144 FOR STEP-BY-STEP INSTRUCTIONS ON REPLACING AN OLD FIREBACK**

Fireplace construction

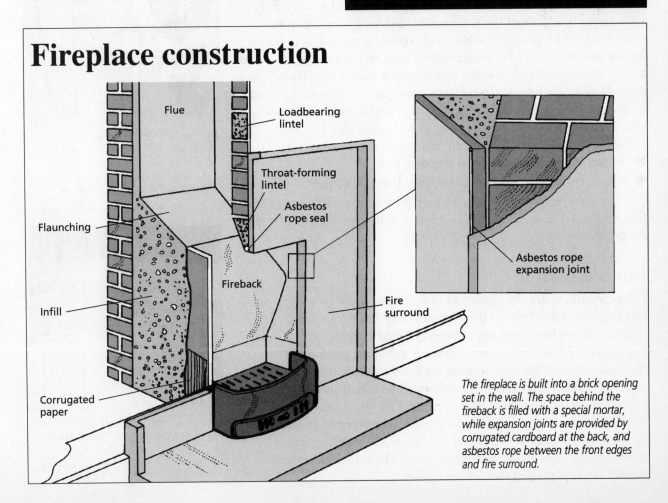

Flue

Loadbearing lintel

Throat-forming lintel

Asbestos rope seal

Flaunching

Fireback

Infill

Fire surround

Corrugated paper

Asbestos rope expansion joint

The fireplace is built into a brick opening set in the wall. The space behind the fireback is filled with a special mortar, while expansion joints are provided by corrugated cardboard at the back, and asbestos rope between the front edges and fire surround.

Replacing a fireback

With age and use, it is not uncommon for a fireback to develop cracks, and if these open up it will be dangerous to continue using the fire. If the cracking is relatively minor, a repair can be made with fire cement. Once all the soot has been brushed away, the crack should be raked out with the point of a trowel, undercutting it slightly, then soaked in water. Fire cement should be trowelled well into the crack and given a smooth finish by going over it with a brush soaked in water.

The safe solution

If there are large cracks in the fireback, or a piece of it has broken away, the only safe solution is to install a new one. Once the grate has been removed, the old fireback can be broken up with a bolster chisel and club hammer. Then the rubble infill behind must be chopped out to leave the original brick-lined opening.

Firebacks come in a variety of sizes, so it is essential to get the right one; measure the opening of the old fireback before you remove it. They are intended for installation in two sections to allow for expansion under the influence of heat, but are likely to be supplied in one piece, which must be separated along the moulded-in split line. The lower section should be located centrally in the opening, bedded on a special mortar mix and checked to ensure that its front face is vertical. The void behind the fireback will be filled with the same mortar mix. However, this will expand when hot, so normally corrugated cardboard is placed around the back of the fireback before the mortar is added. This will char away when the fire is lit, leaving an expansion gap.

The mortar infill should be damp, and one of these two mixes:
● 4 parts vermiculite with 1 part hydrated lime.
● 6 parts vermiculite with 1 part ordinary Portland cement.

If necessary, temporary shuttering may be needed at each side of the fireback, at the front, as it is unlikely that it will achieve a close fit in the brick opening.

Fire cement

Once the infill is dry, the upper part of the fireback can be located next, bedding it on a thin layer of fire cement. Then the edges of the fireback, where they meet any surround, should be pointed with more fire cement. When the fire cement has set, the upper portion of the fireback will need the same infill as the lower portion. However, at the top of the fireback, additional mortar should be added and sloped backwards to meet the rear of the opening. This flaunching should match the slope of the throat-forming lintel over the front of the fire opening. It should be trowelled off to achieve a smooth surface. Similarly, the sides above the fireback should be trowelled off to a smooth slope to prevent soot accumulating.

3 The new fireback will be supplied as one piece. However, to make it easier to fit, you can split it in two with a hammer and chisel. A break line will be moulded in for this purpose.

7 Use a weak mortar mix and some of the rubble removed from behind the old fireback to fill in behind the new one. Tamp it down well, bringing the level up to the top of the fireback.

TOOLS AND MATERIALS

- ☐ Club hammer
- ☐ Bolster chisel
- ☐ Pencil
- ☐ Bricklayer's trowel
- ☐ Pointing trowel
- ☐ Spirit level
- ☐ Paint brush
- ☐ Clean jar
- ☐ Fire cement
- ☐ Mortar
- ☐ Corrugated cardboard
- ☐ Fireback

1 The first job is to remove the old fireback by breaking it up with a club hammer and bolster chisel. Begin by working on one of the top rear corners, then work your way down.

2 Once the fireback has been removed, clean up the opening with your chisel, removing any fire cement. Then break up the rubble behind the fireback and lift it out.

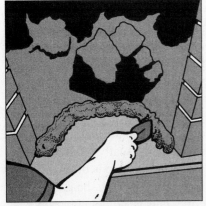

4 Offer up the fireback to check its fit. Mark its position on the floor, then remove it, and trowel a bed of weak mortar mix around the sides and back of the opening.

5 Place the lower portion of the fireback on the bed of mortar. Gently tap it into position, making sure that it is central in the opening. Check that the sides are vertical.

6 Cut two pieces of corrugated cardboard to size and push them down behind the fireback. When the fire is lit, they will char away, leaving an expansion gap for the infill behind.

8 Trowel a layer of fire cement onto the top edge of the lower portion of the fireback. Lift the upper section into position, aligning it carefully and bedding it on the fire cement.

9 Neaten the joint with your trowel, then go over the cement again with a paint brush and water to produce a smooth finish. Next, point the sides of the fireback with more fire cement.

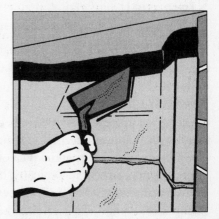

10 The final job is to fill in behind the top section of the fireback with mortar and rubble. Top this with more mortar, trowelling it off parallel with the throat-forming lintel.

Stairs

Of all the timber structures in a house, the stairs are usually the most complex. Building a flight of stairs is a major joinery project, involving a considerable amount of material, calculation, setting out, construction and assembly work. Traditionally a craftsman built a staircase that relied wholly on joints and contained no nails or screws at all. Today, there are still skilled tradesmen who build high-quality staircases in this way, and in some building work custom designs are needed. However, in most of today's housing developments, mass-produced units are used.

The construction and installation of a staircase involves close co-ordination between architect, constructor and installer, because the finished product has to comply with the Building Regulations. Some requirements relate specifically to the construction of the stairs. For instance, the rise on a stair must be 155-220mm (6⅛-8⅝in); the going must be 245-260mm (9⅝-10¼in). The gaps between the treads of an open-tread stair must be partially closed so that a 100mm (4in) sphere will not pass through. Further details, such as the minimum dimensions of tapered treads, are also dealt with. Other matters covered in the Building Regulations relate to the installation of the staircase.

Stair well

At first floor level, a structure known as a stair well is needed. Nowadays, this is relatively easy to construct; the availability of metal joist hangers has eliminated the need to cut joints in the timbers (see pages 100-101).

The top of a flight of stairs will need good support, and the joists forming the frame around the stairwell are normally more substantial than other joists used in the floor construction. Typically, the well is framed with 75mm (3in) thick timber, whereas 50mm (2in) timbers are used elsewhere. The construction also provides a sound fixing point for the newel post at the top of the stairs. This should be fixed securely, since it provides support for the handrail. Often, 8mm (⁵⁄₁₆in) coach screws are used to attach a newel post to the stair well timber. They have square heads so that they may be tightened with a spanner.

Encased construction

Although a flight of stairs can be designed in different ways, the enclosed staircase is the most common. In this construction, the stair treads and risers are housed in recesses cut into boards that run up each side of the stairs. These are known as 'strings'. In effect, the construction is encased – hence the term 'staircase'. Sometimes, however, the strings are cut with a toothed profile along their top edge, the treads resting on the horizontal portions of the teeth, and the risers being attached to the vertical portions. These are known as 'cut strings'. Often, a staircase flight is bought as a complete unit, and its installation is straightforward.

The strings afford a means of attachment, since at least one side of a staircase is usually mounted against an internal wall. Fixing here is often achieved by driving cut nails through the material and into the blockwork. This is a quick, but rather crude, method of doing the job; cut nails damage the surface of the string. If time isn't critical, it's much neater to use wall plugs and screws. In good quality work, wood pellets are prepared so that a countersunk screw can be hidden completely by an insert of matching wood. This is particularly important if the stairs are to be treated with a clear finish rather than paint.

Fixings top and bottom

At the top of a flight, the strings and final riser can be coach bolted or screwed into the timbers forming the stairwell. At the bottom, you can fix the base to blocks of wood screwed to the floor, or you can use steel brackets. These can be positioned on the inside of the strings so that they will be hidden from view. The newel post must be secured carefully, and with a timber floor, it is worth finding a fixing point against the support joists under the floorboards. On a

Staircase construction

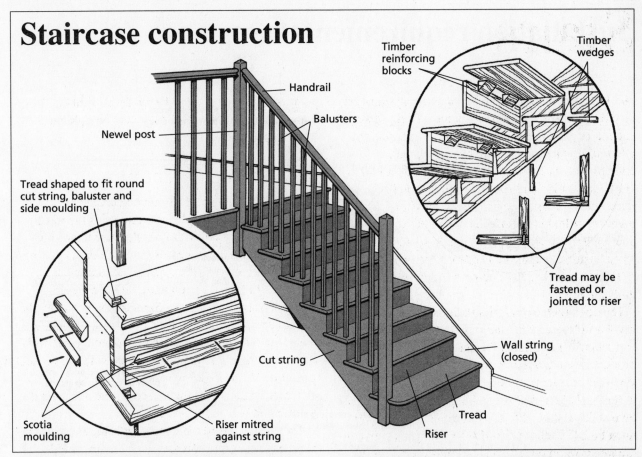

Labels on the illustration:
- Handrail
- Balusters
- Newel post
- Tread shaped to fit round cut string, baluster and side moulding
- Timber reinforcing blocks
- Timber wedges
- Tread may be fastened or jointed to riser
- Wall string (closed)
- Cut string
- Tread
- Riser
- Scotia moulding
- Riser mitred against string

The traditional method of constructing a staircase is to wedge the treads and risers into tapered grooves cut in the strings. The treads will be attached to the risers below by glued blocks, and to the risers above by means of nails, screws or some form of housing joint. This construction is known as 'closed string'. If the treads and risers are attached to a toothed string, the assembly is called 'open string'.

Newel posts at top and bottom provide fixings for the handrail, which is supported by balusters. These may be simply nailed to the underside of the handrail, or housed in a groove and secured by filler pieces. A similar arrangement is used at the foot of the balusters on a closed string staircase, but on open string stairs the baluster are fixed into cutouts in the ends of the treads.

concrete floor, a steel peg set into the screed can provide valuable stability to supplement the strength of the screws driven through the string. However, in some designs, the bottom tread extends with a curved bullnose, providing further support at the base of the newel post.

Open-tread stairs

If you are installing an open-tread stairway, rather than a staircase, the treads will be mounted on two longitudinal carriage pieces that have to bear the entire load. At the top, these need to be notched to bear against the trimmer of the stairwell. Normally, the attachment is made with fixings like coach screws or coach bolts; decorative trim pieces are added later to hide their heads.

Bearing in mind that this type of stairway has no strings for side support, a good attachment at the bottom is essential to ensure stability of the structure. Where the ground floor is of suspended timber construction, it is best to lift the boarding to identify any sub-floor members that may offer support or bracing. Additional noggings may be needed between the joists as well, but with care, a firm system of attachment can be achieved.

If you have a concrete floor, one approach is to drill it and insert 13mm (½in) steel dowels into a bedding of mortar. The dowels should protrude above the floor surface by 25mm (1in) or more, and the mortar must be perfectly dry before proceeding installing the stairs. Corresponding holes must be drilled into the bottom of the carriage bearers to produce a sturdy pegging arrangement. The installation of specially-prepared plates is another approach, but these can be unsightly.

Installation requirements

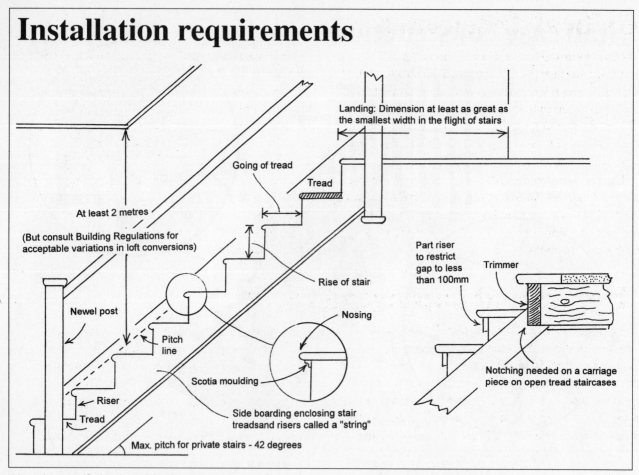

Landing: Dimension at least as great as the smallest width in the flight of stairs

Going of tread

Tread

At least 2 metres

(But consult Building Regulations for acceptable variations in loft conversions)

Rise of stair

Part riser to restrict gap to less than 100mm

Trimmer

Newel post

Nosing

Pitch line

Scotia moulding

Riser

Tread

Side boarding enclosing stair treadsand risers called a "string"

Notching needed on a carriage piece on open tread staircases

Max. pitch for private stairs - 42 degrees

Dimensions specified in the Building Regulations relate to both the construction and installation of a staircase

Handrails and side protection

Protection at the side of a staircase is mandatory, although it's up to you whether to erect a handrail and then to add a balustrade, or to board-in the sides. Either way, the structure is governed by the Building Regulations, and if there are openings along the sides – as is the case with decorative wrought ironwork – no aperture should be large enough to allow a 100mm (4in) sphere to pass through. In effect, this current regulation means that many stairways previously built fail to provide the protection now required. Building Regulations are not retrospective, of course, and stairs constructed before the relevant regulation was introduced do not have to be updated – although in some cases improvements are worth considering.

The height of a handrail alongside the stairs and the provision of guarding around a stairwell are both covered. The regulation height of a guard rail on a landing is 900mm (35½in). In addition, the top of the handrail alongside the stairs must be mounted 900-1000mm (35½-39⅜in) above the pitch line, as shown in the diagram above.

Critical dimensions

When you install stairs in a new house, it is important to provide the necessary headroom above them. This will have been taken into account by the architect when preparing drawings of the stairwell. There must be at least 2m (78¾in) clearance above the pitch line of the stairs. You should also ensure that this height exists over a landing.

The regulations are a little more lenient in respect of a loft conversion. Here, it is acceptable to achieve 1.9m (74¹³⁄₁₆in), measured above the centre of the stairs, and 1.8m (70⅞in) at the side if there's a slope in the ceiling above.

The Building Regulations also lay down certain minima for the dimensions of landings, which include intermediate landings in stairs that take a quarter or half turn. The structure of a landing consists of fully supported joists; the trimmer that provides the bearing point at the top of a flight of stairs is usually made of 75mm (3in) thick timber. Neither the length nor breadth of the landing should be less than the width of the flight at its narrowest point. In most situations, all the treads are of equal width, and this dimension will dictate the minimum size of the landing.

Repairs and improvements

In some locations, a staircase can be more than functional; it can also be an attractive design feature in its own right. In refurbishment work, it is relatively easy to improve the appearance of a conventional staircase, as a number of woodworking specialists can supply new components. These may be used in renovation work, as well as for adding important finishing touches to a conventional staircase purchased from a builders' merchant.

Equally, they can be used in a new construction.

The parts include newels, handrails and balusters. They are sold in a variety of designs and can be purchased as individual components. Moreover, a range of short handrail sections are available to make turns, rises, angled corner details and so on. Being able to purchase components individually means that you can assemble a handrail system to suit your needs.

Spiral staircases

In some projects, the installation of a spiral, or helical, stairway is very appropriate. An advantage is its economic use of space. In addition, spiral stairs have an attractive appearance, although they are less practical than a conventional straight flight. Moving furniture up or down a spiral stairway can provide considerable difficulties.

▶ SEE PAGE 152 FOR STEP-BY-STEP INSTRUCTIONS ON INSTALLING A SPIRAL STAIRCASE

Where space is at a premium, spiral stairs can be more useful than a conventional straight staircase. (Photograph courtesy of Crescent of Cambridge Ltd)

Replacing a damaged tread

All staircases suffer from a lot of wear and tear during their lifetime, and this often becomes apparent when the treads begin to creak as the joints loosen. The obvious solution is to improve the fixings of the treads, ideally by driving screws through the back edge of the tread into the riser above, and gluing reinforcing blocks into the angle between the underside of the tread and the riser below. Unfortunately, it is not always possible to gain access to this area beneath the stairs without ripping out plasterwork, and in a situation like this it may be better to live with the problem unless the tread is seriously loose.

However, on a cut string staircase – even if only one side has a cut string – it is possible to remove and replace a tread, or a riser, from above, so repairs and reinforcement are quite possible. Once the moulding across the end of the tread has been removed, and the baluster tapped out with a mallet, you can begin to remove the tread. First you need to discover whether the tread and riser above are joined by a housing joint, or by screws or nails. If there is a gap between the two, the fixings are likely to be the latter and can be cut through with a hacksaw blade; if there is no obvious gap, the tongue of the riser will have to be cut with a padsaw. Once the tread is free from the riser, it should be possible to split it from the riser below with an old broad-bladed chisel. Then, if necessary, you can remove either of the adjacent risers.

When fitting the new tread, you will not be able to wedge it into the groove in the closed string. The solution is to glue and pin a support block to the string so that it overlaps the groove to allow for the thickness of the wedge. The same applies when refitting a riser, which should be pinned and glued in place. The new tread should be glued and screwed to the strings and the riser below.

TOOLS AND MATERIALS

- ☐ Old broad-bladed chisel
- ☐ Mallet
- ☐ Padsaw with hacksaw blade
- ☐ Pencil
- ☐ Rip saw
- ☐ Tenon saw
- ☐ Bevel-edged chisel
- ☐ Plane
- ☐ Glass paper
- ☐ Hammer
- ☐ G-cramps
- ☐ Wood glue
- ☐ Screwdriver
- ☐ Nail punch
- ☐ Timber for new tread
- ☐ Panel pins
- ☐ Screws
- ☐ Wood filler

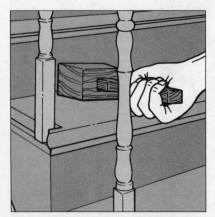

1 The first job is to prise off any moulding across the end of the tread, using an old chisel. Then take a mallet and carefully tap out the end of the baluster, lifting it away.

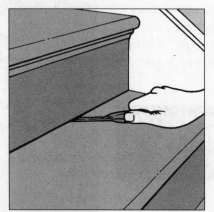

2 There may well be screws or nails holding the back of the tread to the riser above. Fit a hacksaw blade to a padsaw handle and slide the blade through the gap to cut them.

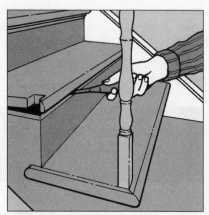

3 Carefully prise the front edge of the tread from the riser below, using an old chisel. Once it is free, remove the tread, collecting any wedge holding it to the wall string.

4 Lay the old tread on a new piece of timber of the same thickness, using it as a pattern for the new one. Draw around the tread, then cut it out, following the lines exactly.

5 To make the recess for the foot of the baluster, saw down both sides with a tenon saw. Then remove the waste with a wide bevel-edged chisel. Offer up the baluster to check the fit.

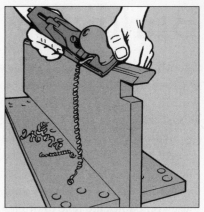

6 Carefully round off the front edge of the tread with a plane, aiming for a uniform shape from one end to the other. Use glass-paper to give the edge a smooth finish.

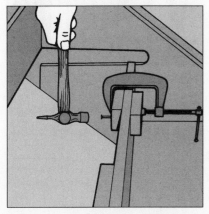

7 Cut new reinforcing blocks to fit behind the riser and support the tread. Apply wood glue and hold them flush with the top edge of the riser, using G-cramps. Then nail them to the riser.

8 Glue and pin another supporting block to the wall string, below the tread groove. Then apply glue to the tops of the blocks, the top edge of the riser and the outer string.

9 Drill screw clearance holes through the outer end of the tread. Then fit the tread in place, inserting it into the groove in the wall string. Secure the tread to the outer string with screws.

10 Fit the top of the baluster back into its recess in the underside of the handrail. Gently tap the foot of the baluster back into the cutout in the end of the tread.

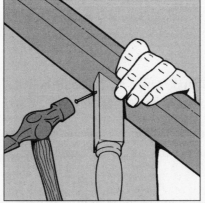

11 At the top of the baluster, drive a pin into the underside of the handrail to secure it. It may help to drill a pilot hole first, as this will prevent the wood from splitting.

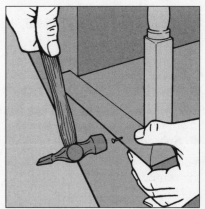

12 Finally, replace the moulding across the end of the tread, securing it with panel pins. Punch the heads of the pins below the surface and fill the holes with wood filler.

Building a spiral staircase

There's no doubt that a spiral stairway bestows a special character on a building, although if you want to install one, you must make sure that it will fit into the proposed location before ordering the components. Whilst these products are economical in their use of space, the installation implications need to be considered carefully.

Fortunately for those with a need for a spiral staircase, several manufacturers offer them in kit form, making both delivery and construction of the stairway a relatively straightforward task. Some of these companies are able to offer a service whereby they can tailor the staircase to a specific situation and requirement, using computer-aided design programmes. This will ensure that the structure fits in perfectly with its surroundings. However, there are standard products, too, which take into account the most common situations.

Spiral staircases are available in both modern and classic styles. Some manufacturers specialise in producing cast-iron spiral staircases. These designs are often ornate, and are extremely robust. They may be available as standard units, or with separate risers to accommodate varying height requirements. Some products are available in both clockwise and anti-clockwise versions. Spiral staircase manufacturers usually offer a design and technical advisory service, and will make plans available when applying for Building Regulations approval.

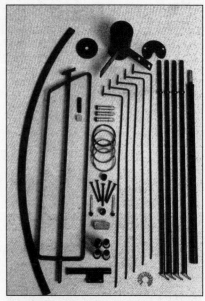

In addition to the treads, a spiral staircase kit will include all the necessary components: central column, balusters, newel posts, handrail, tread supports, tread guards, and all nuts and bolts. (All photographs courtesy Crescent of Cambridge Ltd)

Assembling a kit

The method of constructing a spiral staircase will vary with the product, but most kit versions will follow this sequence:

● The central supporting column is positioned on the floor, its bolt holes marked and drilled. Then the column is bolted to the floor with expanding bolts.

● If metal treads are provided, they are placed one at a time over the central column; wooden treads must be attached to special metal supports that fit over the column.

● The first tread will have a floor support, which must also be bolted to the floor. This will probably incorporate a newel post.

● Subsequent treads will be joined at their outer ends by some form of support, which will also ensure the correct spacing of the treads around the central column.

● A second newel post is attached to the top of the column. Then the balusters are added to the assembly, bolting them to the treads.

● Finally, the handrail is attached to the balusters.

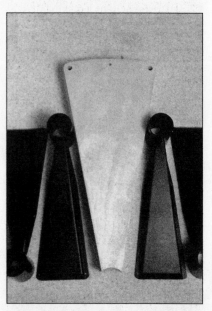

Where wooden treads are used, steel supports will be provided to mount on the central supporting column.

TOOLS AND MATERIALS

- ☐ Tape measure
- ☐ Pencil
- ☐ Electric drill
- ☐ Masonry bit
- ☐ Wood boring bits
- ☐ Bradawl
- ☐ Screwdriver
- ☐ Adjustable spanner
- ☐ Spirit level
- ☐ Step ladders
- ☐ Spiral staircase kit

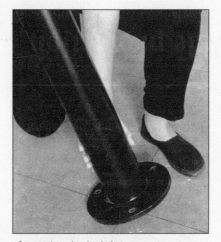

1 Having checked clearance measurements, the central column of the staircase is fixed to the floor.

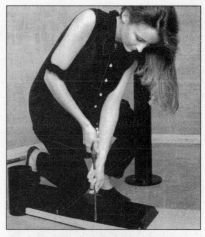

2 Steel supports are attached to the wooden treads, using the screws provided in the kit.

3 The support for the outer end of the bottom tread has to be fixed to the floor, using expansion bolts.

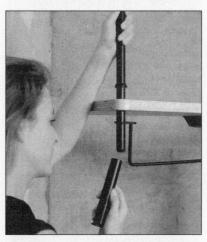

4 Adjacent treads are supported by tubes, which also carry the protective bar that fits between the treads.

5 The baluster sections are fitted into holes drilled in the outer ends of the treads, then secured with bolts.

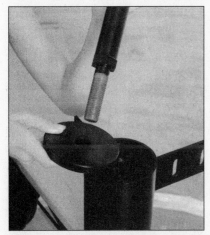

6 On reaching landing level, the joist attachment bracket and newel post are fitted to the top of the central column.

7 Hand rail locating plates are loosely attached to the tops of the balusters with their bolts.

8 The handrail is slid over the locating plates, which are then tightened. Finally, a plastic capping is added.

Glossary

Access tower A self-contained structure built from prefabricated tubular metal sections to provide a high-level work platform.

Apron A section of lead sheeting, fitted at the base of a chimney to make a waterproof seal with the roof.

Architrave A decorative timber moulding that conceals the join between a door opening liner and the adjacent plasterwork.

Back gutter Lead sheeting formed to provide a waterproof seal along the top edge of a chimney where it breaks through the roof.

Ballast A mixture of sand and gravel used for concreting.

Balloon A wire or plastic mesh fitting to prevent leaves from entering the top of a downpipe.

Baluster A narrow wooden spindle that fits between the handrail and string of a flight of stairs.

Barge-board A section of timber that finishes the edges of a gable-ended roof.

Blinding A layer of sand spread over hardcore to fill cavities before laying concrete.

Bolster chisel A wide-bladed tool for cutting masonry.

Boning rod A graduated pole used in conjunction with sight rails to measure the fall of a pipe.

Bossing mallet A special mallet for shaping lead flashing.

Butterfly tie A wire connector bedded in the mortar joints to link the two leaves of a cavity wall.

Cavity tray Fits inside a cavity wall to collect moisture running down the cavity and direct it to the outside.

Cavity wall A wall built from two separate leaves of bricks with a cavity between them to prevent moisture penetration. In modern houses, the cavity is usually filled with thermal insulation material.

Chasing Cutting a narrow channel in plaster or brickwork, usually for a cable or pipe.

Club hammer A small, very heavy hammer used with a bolster or cold chisel for cutting masonry.

Cold chisel A stout, heavy chisel used for breaking up masonry.

Collar coupling A joint for connecting lengths of drain pipe.

Concrete A mixture of sand, gravel and cement for foundation work.

Cross-cut saw A hand saw used specifically for cutting across the grain of large timber sections.

Cross ventilation Natural ventilation through a floor or roof void, achieved by installing vents at each end of the structure.

Damp-proof course (DPC) A waterproof layer in a wall that prevents moisture penetration.

Damp-proof membrane (DPM) A waterproof layer beneath a floor to prevent rising damp.

Double-skin wall *See Cavity wall.*

Dressing Shaping lead sheet for aprons and flashing.

Electro-osmotic process A method of providing a DPC in a wall that makes use of an electric current to prevent rising damp.

Fall A slope on a pipe or surface to ensure water run-off.

Fascia board A board that conceals the ends of rafters along the lower edge of a roof.

Firrings Tapered sections of timber attached to the joists of a flat roof to ensure that the decking has a fall for efficient drainage.

Flashing Sections of lead sheet that make a waterproof seal between a roof and a wall, or a chimney.

Flaunching A shaped layer of mortar that secures a chimney pot and ensures rain run-off.

Flooring cramp A special tool for pushing floor boards together tightly prior to nailing down.

Flue A tubular duct through which exhaust gases from a fire can be directed to the outside.

Frog A V-shaped recess in the face of a brick.

G-cramp Used for clamping a variety of materials together.

Gauge board A wedge-shaped board for use with a spirit level to check the fall of a pipe or surface.

Ground A timber depth guide used when plastering.

Hardcore A mixture of broken masonry used as a base when laying concrete, or for filling a soakaway.

Hopper head A funnel-shaped collector often seen at the top of a downpipe to collect waste water from an upstairs basin or bath.

Jambs The vertical members of a door or window frame.

Joist Horizontal section of timber that supports flooring above and a ceiling below.

Ladder stand-off A special bracket to prevent the top of a ladder leaning against a gutter.

Laths Narrow strips of wood, or metal, used to support plaster.

Lintel A steel or concrete beam that bears the weight of a wall over a door or window opening.

Moisture meter A special device for detecting moisture in walls and other structures.

Mortar A mixture of sand and cement used for brickwork.

Mortise A slot cut in a section of wood for the corresponding tenon of another section, or a door latch.

Nail sick A roof where the fixings have corroded, allowing many of the slates to slip.

Needle A length of timber used to support a wall while a lintel is fitted.

Newel post A decorative section of

wood that supports each end of a handrail on a flight of stairs.

Nib A lug on a clay tile that fits over the supporting batten.

Nogging A short timber brace that fits between the uprights of a stud wall or a pair of joists.

Oil stone Used for sharpening chisel blades and plane irons.

Padsaw A saw with a narrow blade.

Panel saw A hand saw used for cutting sheet materials.

Plasticiser Added to mortar to make the mix more workable.

Plate vibrator A machine used for compacting large areas of hardcore.

Plugging chisel A special cold chisel used for removing mortar prior to repointing brickwork.

Plumb line A weighted line for marking a true vertical.

Pointing Shaping the mortar joints between bricks for a neat, water-shedding finish.

Prefabricated truss A ready-made roof frame comprising rafters and associated bracing.

Punner A heavily weighted hand tool for compacting hardcore.

Purlin A horizontal timber brace that reinforces a run of rafters.

Rafter A section of timber that runs from the top of the wall to the ridge of the roof to support the covering.

Render A layer of mortar applied to the surface of a wall to provide a weatherproof, decorative covering.

Residual current device (RCD) A safety device to prevent electric shock, previously known as an earth leakage circuit breaker (ELCB).

Reveal A surface that surrounds a door or window recess, at right angles to the face of the wall.

Ridge board A board that runs along the ridge of a roof, joining the tops of the rafters.

Ridge hook A fitting for attaching to a standard ladder so that it can be hooked over the ridge of a roof to provide access.

Rip saw A hand saw designed for cutting along the grain.

Riser The vertical portion between treads of stairs.

Saddle piece A section of flashing that fits over the ridge tiles where a chimney breaks through the roof.

Sarking felt Waterproofing felt laid under the tiles or slates of a roof.

Sash cramp A clamping device for holding together large frames.

Scarf joint An overlapping bevelled joint used for joining two boards end to end.

Screed A layer of mortar spread on a concrete slab to provide a surface for flooring materials.

Screeding rails Timber depth guides used when laying a screed.

Scrim tape A special open-weave material for reinforcing the filler concealing joints between plasterboard panels.

Shingles Wooden (usually cedar) tiles for roofing or wall cladding.

Sight rails Horizontal sections of wood fixed at a uniform height to posts along a pipe run, allowing the fall of the pipe to be checked.

Sill A large section of timber or masonry forming the foot of a door or window frame.

Single-leaf wall A narrow wall built a single skin of bricks.

Skew nailing Driving nails diagonally through one section of timber into another to join them at right angles to each other.

Slater's rip A special tool for cutting through nails holding tiles or slates in place.

Sleeper wall A low honeycomb brick wall for supporting floor joists above ground level.

Slip A narrow slice of brick, used for facing purposes.

Soakaway A rubble-filled pit for rainwater disposal.

Soakers Sections of lead sheet fitted beneath tiles as part of the flashing.

Soffit A horizontal board used in conjunction with a fascia board to close off the ends of rafters.

Spalling Crumbling brickwork as a result of weather damage.

Spouting Wooden guttering.

Staging A prefabricated access platform for carrying out repair work on a chimney.

Stiles The vertical frame members of a door or window.

Strings The stout boards that run up each side of a flight of stairs to support the treads.

Stud walls Internal partitions, based on timber or metal frameworks.

Swan neck An offset section of downpipe needed to span the eaves or a section of cladding.

Tamping board A long section of timber used for levelling concrete.

Tenon saw A small hand saw for cutting small sections of timber and making joints.

Tingle A strip of lead or copper used to support a replacement slate or tile.

Tongued-and-grooved Modern floor boards and panels have a tongue on one edge and a groove in the other. When pushed together, the tongue of one board locks into the groove of its neighbour.

Treads The horizontal portions of a staircase on which you walk.

Trimmer A section of timber that supports the ends of joists where they are cut to form a stair well.

Valley gutter Formed at the intersection of two adjacent pitched roofs - may be lead lined.

Vapour control layer Prevents water vapour passing through a ceiling into the roof void above.

Verge The edge of a gable-ended roof, finished with mortar or a special moulding.

Wall plate A section of timber attached to a wall to support the ends of joists or rafters.

Weather bar A strip of metal fixed to a door sill to prevent water flowing under the door.

Weatherboard A timber moulding attached to the foot of a door to throw rainwater clear.

Weep hole An open joint between bricks to allow moisture to drain from the cavity inside.

Useful addresses

Brick Development Association
Woodside House,
Winkfield, Windsor,
Berkshire,
SL4 2DX.

British Board of Agrément
PO Box 195,
Bucknalls Lane,
Garston, Watford,
Hertfordshire,
WD2 7NG.

British Cement Association
Century House,
Telford Avenue,
Crowthorne,
Berkshire,
RG11 6YS.

British Flat Roofing Council
38 Bridlesmith Gate,
Nottingham,
NG1 2GQ.

British Flue and Chimney Manufacturers' Association
6 Furlong Road,
Bourne End,
Buckinghamshire,
SL8 5DG.

The Building Centre
26 Store Street,
London,
WC1E 7BT.

Building Research Establishment
Garston,
Watford,
WD2 7JR.

Department of the Environment
PO Box 151,
London,
E15 2HF.

Energy Efficiency Office
Department of the Environment,
2 Marsham Street,
London,
SW1P 3EB.

Glass and Glazing Federation
44-48 Borough High Street,
London,
SE1 1XB.

HMSO
PO Box 276,
London,
SW8 5DT

Lead Development Association
42-46 Weymouth Street,
London,
W1N 3LQ.

National Cavity Insulation Association
PO Box 12,
Haslemere,
Surrey,
GU27 3AH.

National Federation of Roofing Contractors
24 Weymouth Street,
London,
W1N 3FA.

National Fireplace Association
8th Floor,
Bridge House,
Smallbrook,
Queensway,
Birmingham,
B5 4JP.

Royal Institute of British Architects
66, Portland Place,
London,
W1N 4AD.

Steel Window Association
26 Store Street,
London,
WC1E 7JR.

Timber Research and Development Association
Stocking Lane,
Hughenden Valley,
High Wycombe,
Buckinghamshire,
HP14 4ND.

The Welsh Office
Cathays Park,
Cardiff,
CF1 3NQ.

Acknowledgements

The author and publishers would like to thank the following companies for supplying information and photographs:
British Cement Association
British Gypsum Ltd
Crescent of Cambridge Ltd
Dow Corning Hansil Ltd
Lafarge Plasterboard Ltd
Marley Roof Tiles Ltd
Marshalls Flooring Ltd
Modus Design Ltd
Protimeter plc
Redland Roof Tiles Ltd
Rytons Roofing Products Ltd
Sealocrete PLA Ltd
Swish Home Improvements
TDI (UK) Ltd
The Velux Company Ltd
Wickes Building Supplies Limited

In addition, several photographs were supplied by the Building Research Establishment:
74 Bottom left: BRE Crown copyright photograph, used with permission from the Energy Efficiency Office's Good Practice Guide, *Windows and External Doors*; Bottom centre: BRE Crown copyright photograph, used with permission from the Energy Efficiency Office's Good Practice Guide, *Key Detailing Principles*.
75 Top left: BRE Crown copyright photograph, used with permission from the Energy Efficiency Office's Good Practice Guide, *External Cavity Walls*; Top centre and right: BRE Crown copyright photographs, used with permission from the Energy Efficiency Office's Good Practice Guide, *Windows and External Doors*.
94 Bottom left, centre and right: BRE Crown copyright photographs, used with permission from the Energy Efficiency Office's Good Practice Guide, *Ground Floors*.
99 Bottom left, centre and right: BRE Crown copyright photographs, used with permission from the Energy Efficiency Office's Good Practice Guide, *Ground Floors*.

Index